CRITICAL AUTOETHNOGRAPHY

WRITING LIVES
Ethnographic Narratives
Series Editors:
Arthur P. Bochner & Carolyn Ellis
University of South Florida

Writing Lives: Ethnographic Narratives publishes narrative representations of qualitative research projects. The series editors seek manuscripts that blur the boundaries between humanities and social sciences. We encourage novel and evocative forms of expressing concrete lived experience, including autoethnographic, literary, poetic, artistic, visual, performative, critical, multivoiced, conversational, and co-constructed representations. We are interested in ethnographic narratives that depict local stories; employ literary modes of scene setting, dialogue, character development, and unfolding action; and include the author's critical reflections on the research and writing process, such as research ethics, alternative modes of inquiry and representation, reflexivity, and evocative storytelling. Proposals and manuscripts should be directed to abochner@cas.usf.edu

Volumes in this series:

Erotic Mentoring: Women's Transformations in the University, Janice Hocker Rushing

Intimate Colonialism: Head, Heart, and Body in West African Development Work, Laurie L. Charlés

Last Writes: A Daybook for a Dying Friend, Laurel Richardson

A Trickster in Tweed: The Quest for Quality in a Faculty Life, Thomas F. Frentz

Guyana Diaries: Women's Lives across Difference, Kimberly D. Nettles

Writing Qualitative Inquiry: Selves, Stories and the New Politics of Academic Success, H. L. Goodall Jr.

Accidental Ethnography: An Inquiry into Family Secrecy, Christopher N. Poulos

Revision: Autoethnographic Reflections on Life and Work, Carolyn Ellis

Leaning: A Poetics of Personal Relations, Ronald J. Pelias

Narrating the Closet: An Autoethnography of Same-Sex Attraction, Tony E. Adams

Life after Leaving: The Remains of Spousal Abuse, Sophie Tamas

Playing with Purpose: Adventures in Performative Social Science, Mary M. Gergen and Kenneth J. Gergen

Critical Autoethnography: Intersecting Cultural Identities in Everyday Life, Robin M. Boylorn and Mark P. Orbe, editors

CRITICAL
AUTOETHNOGRAPHY

INTERSECTING CULTURAL IDENTITIES IN
EVERYDAY LIFE

EDITED BY

Robin M. Boylorn

AND

Mark P. Orbe

Walnut Creek, CA

Left Coast Press, Inc.
1630 North Main Street, #400
Walnut Creek, CA 94596
www.LCoastPress.com

ISBN 978-1-61132-313-9   hardcover
ISBN 978-1-61132-314-6   paperback
ISBN 978-1-61132-315-3   institutional eBook
ISBN 978-1-61132-705-2   consumer eBook

Library of Congress Cataloging-in-Publication Data

Critical autoethnography : intersecting cultural identities in everyday life / [edited by] Robin M. Boylorn, Mark P. Orbe ; [foreword by] Carolyn Ellis ; [foreword by] Arthur P. Bochner.
    pages cm. — (Writing lives ; 13)
    Summary: "This volume uses autoethnography—cultural analysis through personal narrative—to explore the tangled relationships between culture and communication. Using an intersectional approach to the many aspects of identity at play in everyday life, a diverse group of authors reveals the complex nature of lived experiences. They situate interpersonal experiences of gender, race, ethnicity, ability, and orientation within larger systems of power, oppression, and social privilege. An excellent resource for undergraduates, graduate students, educators, and scholars in the fields of intercultural and interpersonal communication, and qualitative methodology"—Provided by publisher.
    Includes bibliographical references and index.
    ISBN 978-1-61132-313-9 (hardback)
    ISBN 978-1-61132-314-6 (paperback)
    ISBN 978-1-61132-315-3 (institutional ebook)
    ISBN 978-1-61132-705-2 (consumer ebook)
    1. Group identity. 2. Multiculturalism. 3. Communication and culture. I. Boylorn, Robin M., 1978– II. Orbe, Mark P.
    HM753.C745 2013
    305—dc23
                                                                          2013029131

Printed in the United States of America

∞ ™ The paper used in this publication meets the minimum requirements of American National Standard for Information Sciences—Permanence of Paper for Printed Library Materials, ANSI/NISO Z39.48–1992.

For those whose lives are lived on the margins and experienced at the intersections

Contents

Series Editors' Foreword

Merging Culture and Personal Experience in Critical Autoethnography

Carolyn Ellis and Arthur P. Bochner

*W*E HAD THE GOOD FORTUNE OF BEING MENTORS TO ROBIN Boylorn when she was a PhD student in the Department of Communication at University of South Florida. From the first moment we read her work, we knew she had a gift for writing personal narrative. Her stories literally made us stop to catch our breath. We have been her cheerleaders ever since. Her book, *Sweetwater: Black Women and Narratives of Resilience,* is a tour de force about the lives of Black women in the South. It focuses on her relationships with women in her hometown rural community and how they respond to and survive everyday life together. Now, she has turned her attention more specifically to connecting evocative personal narrative to cultural criticism, an effort we applaud.

We also are pleased to have Mark Orbe as an author in our series. We have long been fans of his work, including his coauthored autoethnography, "The Complexity of Our Tears: Dis/enchantment and (In)Difference in the Academy," which vulnerably and emotionally discusses some of the challenges of being cultural outsiders in the university. As well, his most recent book, *Communication Realities in a "Post-Racial" Society: What the U.S. Public Really Thinks of President Barack Obama,* uses voices of everyday people to examine how identity politics influence public perceptions. Mark writes insightfully about communication, culture, and diversity, and is a caring and supportive colleague who is devoted to providing opportunities for diverse scholars to voice their experiences and create a scholarly community in which they feel at home.

Critical Autoethnography: Intersecting Cultural Identities in Everyday Life is an exemplar of what we had in mind when we began the series, *Writing Lives: Ethnographic Narratives.* These stories blur the boundaries between humanities and social sciences, expressing concrete lived experience in novel and literary forms, depicting local stories and including authors' critical reflections on their lives and writing process.

In this groundbreaking volume, Robin and Mark bring together auto-ethnographic and critical standpoints to examine everyday interpersonal and cultural experiences of identity from the inside out. The authors gently, lovingly, vulnerably, and incisively extend the work of autoethnography and invite us—all of us—to appreciate the ways in which an intersectional approach reveals the relationships among culture, communication, identity, emotions, and everyday lived experience. Through a multiplicity of evocative narratives and theoretical lenses, readers are engaged by the lived experience of similarity and difference at the intersections of diverse racial, class, ethnic, gender, spirituality, age, sexuality, and able-bodied identities. The stories welcome readers into these experiences, encourage us to compare and interrogate our own perceptions, and reveal the challenges and opportunities we face in negotiating our worldviews with the understandings of others in our communities. These stories compel us as readers and participants in the diverse world in which we live to think with open hearts and open minds about discrimination and difference as well as about our commonality within the human experience.

Acknowledgments

*T*HIS BOOK BENEFITS FROM THE FOUNDATIONS OF AUTOETHNOG-raphy and intersectionality, which have been discussed and debated for decades in academia, making the link between our heads and hearts possible. For that reason we thank our forebearers and colleagues for establishing the groundwork from which *Critical Autoethnography* stands. We thank Mitch Allen, our publisher, and Carolyn Ellis and Arthur Bochner, our series editors, for their useful feedback and generous support from the vision to fruition of this project. We also thank the intercultural and interpersonal scholars in this collection whose interest and investment made such a rich and thoughtful collection possible. Thank you for sharing parts of yourselves and your lives to help situate the many ways our cultural identities merge with our interpersonal lives.

We acknowledge Ravin Lawson of RL Customz for the beautiful art he designed for the cover and our (biological and chosen) families for their continuous and generous support while we completed the manuscript.

We also thank our Creator for the opportunity to magnify the voices and experiences of marginalized folk. We don't take for granted the responsibility or the platform.

*

In addition, I, Robin M. Boylorn, thank my academic parents, Art Bochner and Carolyn Ellis, for everything they have taught me and continue to teach me through scholarship and relationship. I owe my critical and editorial eye to their teaching and love. I also acknowledge H. L. "Bud" Goodall Jr., whose legacy I will honor in all that I do, always. I thank my colleagues and mentors who supply me with endless affirmation and support, who are too numerous to name. In particular I thank: Tony Adams, Elizabeth Bell, Keith Berry, Durell Callier, Marcy Chvasta, Ken Cissna, Brittney Cooper, Rex Crawley, Cynthia Dillard, Eric Eisenberg, Sandra Goodall, Ron Jackson, Navita Cummings James, Pete Kellett, Andrew Herrmann, Stacy Holman Jones, Dominique Hill, Mark Hopson, Amber Johnson, Wren Levitt, Michael LeVan, Irma McClaurin, Terrence Merkerson, Jeanine Mingé, Anita Mixon, Susana Morris, Michael Parker, Chris Poulos, Cheryl Rodriguez, Jillian Tullis, Eric Watts, and Mary Weems.

I also thank my former and future students for the ways they continually inspire and challenge me to embrace difference, change, and possibility. To the Crunk Feminist Collective and The Fire This Time Writing Group, thank you for instigating and supporting my words. I am a better writer, activist, and citizen because I am in community with you.

To all of the contributors, thank you for saying yes and for putting up with my Virgoan editing style.

Finally, I want to especially thank my mentor and friend Dr. Mark P. Orbe. I could not be more proud of what we have accomplished together. You are one of my academic heroes, and I am honored to have had this opportunity to work with you. I am humbled at the gift of your friendship, wisdom, and love. You are a touchstone in my life, and your mentorship makes me feel capable and cared for. Thank you for being my coeditor, cowriter, and coconspirator. I look forward to future collaborations.

*

Lastly, I, Mark P. Orbe, acknowledge all of my professional-personal-social-cultural colleagues who offer support for my scholarly work in numerous ways. Traditionally, I use these types of opportunities to highlight family and friends who serve as my core support, however, this time I want to focus on one particular group: Academic peers I had the distinct pleasure of working with over the years on various research projects. Early on in my academic career—following the values of my graduate school socialization—I prioritized single-authored publications; however, over time, I have come to truly value research collaborations as important endeavors where I can embrace opportunities to teach ↔ learn about scholarly inquiry in meaningful ways. Over the years, I've benefitted immensely from my collaborations, including those with Leda Cooks, Carol Bruess, Karen Strother-Jordan, Sakile Camara, Darlene Drummond, Granville King III, Katrina Bell-Jordan, Kiesha Warren-Gordon, Brenda J. Allen, Nancy Cornwell, Eric King Watts, Etsuko Kinefuchi, Ewa Urban, Mark Hopson, Tina Harris, Maria Lapinski, Chris Groscurth, Debra Smith, Wilfredo Alvarez, Joe Ciccarelli, Melodi Everett, Regina Spellers, Nilanjana Bardhan, Angela Cooke-Jackson, Amber Johnson, Tabatha Roberts, Lydia Kauffman, and Nate Swords. These are individuals who have made, and continue to make, my research endeavors so meaningful.

In particular, I want to articulate my heartfelt gratitude to Dr. Robin M. Boylorn. I have been so blessed to add her to my list of collaboration partners. While she often times refers to *me* as *her* mentor, this project has illustrated the transactional relationship between mentors ↔ mentee … in other words, we mentored each other through the process of uniting autoethnography, intersectionality, and cultural communication. The synergy was fantastic! I'm appreciative of the opportunity to learn from such a tremendously talented scholar-activist-teacher-sista-docta-friend. Onward and upward…

Introduction

Critical Autoethnography as Method of Choice

*W*E (ROBIN AND MARK) CAME TO AUTOETHNOGRAPHY FOR SIMI-lar reasons; however, our journeys were distinctly different. Robin's introduction to autoethnography was unexpected. As an undergraduate student at The University of North Carolina at Greens-boro she studied English (Creative Writing) and Communication Studies and never imagined the two would coalesce. During the first semester of her master's program, starstruck and in awe, she listened to her soon-to-be mentor, Bud Goodall, share a story he had written about his mentor. He referred to his "storied scholarship" as autoethnography, or narrative ethnography, a bridge between his cultural curiosities and personal lived experience. The work was beautiful and accessible, and Robin fell in love with the possibilities that existed after that moment, of marrying her love and obsession with storytelling with cultural and social phenomena.

Hers was a gradual process. Before Robin was an autoethnographer, Goodall taught her about ethnography. She read Pacanowsky's (1988) *Slouch-ing Towards Chicago,* and Geertz's (1973) *Deep Play: Notes on the Balinese Cockfight.* She learned, through reading their descriptions, what it meant to capture the essence of an experience and invite the reader into your thoughts (which inevitably include your history and standpoints). She was intrigued by ethnography but still felt lost in what felt like exclusive white male gazes and interpretations. With Goodall's leading she began to write her own narratives, from her particular raced, classed, gendered, sexed positionality, identifying the distinctions between how and why she viewed the world through her lens and what made it different from others. Later she became (one of) the main character(s) of her research stories. Her first autoethnography, "Working Class Black Girl," was presented at the Carolinas Communication Association convention in Greensboro, North Carolina, in 2002, and demonstrated her investment in understanding and representing various and simultaneous identity positions in her writing (something she would later understand to be intersectionality). Later, as a PhD student at University of South Florida, she was educated by Carolyn Ellis and Art Bochner on the art of narrative and autoethnography. Under their tutelage and guidance she began perfecting her craft and merging her creative and scholarly voices.

Compared to Robin's, Mark's journey to autoethnography began much later in his academic career. As an undergraduate and graduate student, he took several methodological courses—each of which focused solely on empirical quantitative analysis. It was not until the first year in his doctoral program that he has any memory of being exposed to qualitative-based scholarly articles. A salient memory remains vivid today: Reading Gerry Philipsen's (1975) *Speaking "Like a Man" in Teamsterville*, being completely engaged and enlightened, and immediately thinking, "I could do research like that." Prior to this experience, he found much of the research in his concentrated area of choice—intercultural communication—to be problematic. What he couldn't articulate then, but can now, is that the objective of most of the traditional intercultural research is to use quantitative methods to discover correlations between specific communication concepts (e.g., self-disclosure, eye contact, tone) and particular cultural groups. The goal is to produce statistically significant differences among random samples that can be generalizable to the larger population. While this is solid scientific practice, in Mark's mind, it is a scholarly process that simply (re)produces cultural stereotypes.

Throughout his educational journey, Mark has had only one course on qualitative research methods. It occurred in his final semester of doctoral study and focused primarily on phenomenology. This one course directly informed his phenomenologically based dissertation and served as the methodological foundation for an ongoing series of projects related to co-cultural theory and other culturally focused topics. Mark's journey to autoethnography came at a time in his academic career when he was an established qualitative researcher with no exposure to autoethnography. He read pieces that used ethnography in different contexts, but the idea that one could shift the ethnographic gaze from others and unto self was a methodological move that remained unacknowledged. Unlike Robin, Mark has received no formal training in autoethnography and has literally learned by reading and writing/doing. His first autoethnographic piece was a collective project focusing on dis/illusionment in the academy from the standpoints of people of color. To this day, the personal/social/cultural transparency and investment—blood, sweat and *tears* (Allen, Orbe, & Olivas, 1999)—that went into this piece marks it as one that he is most proud to have published. The collective power of the self-generated narratives featured in that piece remains a testament to the power of autoethnography.

Even though our relationships to autoethnography are distinct, we both recognize that autoethnography is a powerful method for working with topics of diversity and identity. Autoethnography is predicated on the ability to invite readers into the lived experience of a presumed "Other" and to experience it viscerally. Accordingly, we envisioned a project that would "give voice" to previously silenced and marginalized experiences, answer unexamined questions about the multiplicity of social identities, instigate discussions about and across difference, and explain the contradictory intersections of personal and cultural standpoints. We also aspired to combine narratives that encourage us to better understand and learn from each other while showing the interconnectedness of the human experience. Like Muncey (2010) we do not distinguish doing research from living life.

Culture is a historically situated, socially constructed, and complex term with more than 300 published definitions (Kroeber & Kluckhohn, 1952; Baldwin, Faulkner, Hecht, & Lindsley, 2006). This book, then, approaches culture as pluralistic, subjective, personal, and potentially inclusive. We see cultural autoethnography as similarly positioned. Autoethnography is a research method that connects "the autobiographical and personal to the cultural, social, and political," (Ellis, 2004, p. xix), but its myriad forms and creative representations make it difficult to precisely define (Adams & Holman Jones, 2008; Bochner, 2012; Ellis & Bochner, 2000; Ellis, 2004).

Our goal with this project was to produce a book that offered a range of personal/cultural experiences and perspectives, paying particular attention to the various intersections of identity that influence our daily lives. We also wanted to show readers how to appreciate cultural similarity and difference and to understand how a cultural perspective enhances interpersonal communication skills. By applying self-reflexivity to interpersonal/intercultural inquiry, *Critical Autoethnography: Intersecting Cultural Identities in Everyday Life* contributes to a decades-long conversation about the possibilities of qualitative inquiry and autoethnography (Holman Jones, Adams, & Ellis, 2013; Denzin & Lincoln, 2000).

The unique components of this book are the blending of cultural and interpersonal experience of everyday interactions with others, intersectional components of identity, and the critical treatment of autoethnography as a method. Critical autoethnography shares similarities with Madison's (2012) conception of critical ethnography, which "begins with an ethical responsibility to address processes of unfairness or injustice within a particular lived domain" (p. 5). Critical autoethnographers are invested in the "politics of positionality" (Madison, 2012) that require researchers to acknowledge the inevitable privileges we experience alongside marginalization and to take responsibility for our subjective lenses through reflexivity. We write as an Other, and for an Other. Our diverse contributors include both established and emerging scholars in the field whose work combines exemplary writing skill, a critical lens, and a unique cultural standpoint.

Cultural experiences are oftentimes taken for granted because of the seemingly interconnected and multicultural society we live in. While we acknowledge and appreciate the global significance and relevance of intercultural study, this book focuses on the interpersonal and relational components of intercultural communication within the US context. Further by looking at co-cultures (members of the larger culture who differentiate themselves) and the ways in which their existence and experience/s challenge hegemonic norms (Orbe, 1998), we privilege individual experiences and corporate realities in order to theorize about what we can learn relationally, personally, and culturally through personal narratives.

While each chapter approaches interpersonal/intercultural identity negotiations and the intersections between them, they uniquely use the singular method of autoethnography. This is particularly significant and useful when approaching issues of identity and personal experience with the explicit objective to resist unidimensional treatments of complex phenomenon. Each author engages the complex ways in which their own identities are best understood through explorations of intersectionality—the cultural synergy that is created through interactions of race/ethnicity, gender/sex, socioeconomic status, sexuality, nationality, age, spirituality, and/or abilities. Individually, each chapter provides powerfully thick descriptions of everyday negotiations of culture that promise to increase understanding of diverse perspectives. Read together, the chapters collectively present a set of communicative realities that warrant the necessity of methodological approaches that reflect the inextricable relationship among culture, identity, and communication.

Society shapes our narratives, identities, and lives (Kehly, 1995). Within this introductory chapter we will briefly describe how autoethnographic inquiry developed into our methodology of choice for exploring issues of culture, power, and communication in society. We will introduce the main ideas the book addresses, such as intersectionality, identity, and autoethnography. We also will discuss the role of social and cultural identity in everyday interactions to discuss interpersonal and intercultural communication as lenses for personal reflection and relationships. In addition, we will offer a brief overview of each chapter, and the conceptual/theoretical frameworks that will inform the chapters within each particular section. By explaining the thematic organization of the book, providing succinct chapter summaries, and contextualizing and tying the chapters together through a conceptual/theoretical framework we create a productive roadmap for readers to follow.

Autoethnography and Intersectionality

The term *autoethnography* has multiple meanings (Reed-Danahay, 1997) but largely refers to both the method and product of researching and writing about personal lived experiences and their relationship to culture (Ellis, 2004; Ellis, Adams & Bochner, 2011). Autoethnography involves the "turning of the ethnographic gaze inward on the self (auto), while maintaining the outward gaze of ethnography, looking at the larger context wherein self experiences occur" (Denzin, 1997, p. 227). Autoethnographers research themselves in relation to others.

For the purposes of this book we define autoethnography as cultural analysis through personal narrative. We encourage a critical lens, alongside an introspective and outward one, to make sense of who we are in the context of our cultural communities. Similar to Chang (2008) we "expect the stories of autoethnographers to be reflected upon, analyzed, and interpreted within their broader sociocultural context" (p. 46).

Reed-Danahay (1997) explained autoethnography as an intersection of three writing genres:

> 1) "native anthropology," in which people who were formerly the subjects of ethnography become the authors of studies of their own group; 2) "ethnic autobiography," personal narratives written by members of ethnic minority groups; and 3) "autobiographical ethnography," in which anthropologists interject personal experience into ethnographic writing. (p. 2)

While autoethnography has traditionally been tied to either autobiography or ethnography (Reed-Danahay, 1997; Ellis, 2004), Chang (2008) argues that autoethnography "should be ethnographic in its methodological orientation, cultural in its interpretive orientation, and autobiographical in its content orientation" (p. 48). She further explains three descriptors that distinguish autoethnography from ethnography as a method, while acknowledging that autoethnography is ethnographic:

> First, like ethnographers, autoethnographers follow a similar ethnographic research process by systematically collecting data … analyzing and interpreting them, and producing scholarly reports, also called autoethnography. In this sense, the term "autoethnography" refers to the process and the product, just as "ethnography" does. Second, like ethnographers, autoethnographers attempt to achieve cultural understanding through analysis and interpretation. In other words, autoethnography is not about focusing on self alone, but about searching for understanding of others (culture/society) through self.... The last aspect of autoethnography sets it apart from other ethnographic inquiries. Autoethnographers use their personal experiences as primary data (pp. 48–49).

Autoethnography is a method that allows for both personal and cultural critique. Because people's lives and ideologies are influenced by multiple cultural dimensions and relationships, our book features varied points of view and intersectional experiences of difference. The chapters interrogate several meanings of autoethnography but focus on connecting the autobiographical with the ethnographic to tell stories that are informed by and help make sense of lives in a cultural context, making these stories commentaries on culture and self-reflexive accounts. As Ellis and Bochner (2000) contend, "reflexive ethnographies primarily focus on a culture or subculture, [and] authors use their own experiences in the culture reflexively to bend back on self and look more deeply at self-other interactions" (p. 740).

Reed-Danahay (1997) argues that "the postmodern/postcolonial conception of self and society is one of a multiplicity of identities [and] of cultural displacement" (p. 2). This positioning of the personal and culture at the periphery makes space for autoethnographic engagement to acknowledge the various standpoints that exist within one person and to situate them culturally. By acknowledging difference, which influences how we see and experience the world, autoethnography has the capacity to resist mythical normative perspectives that don't account for the diversity of race, age, class, gender/sex, sexuality, ability status, education, religion, and region, which also represent a distinction in experiences (Allen, 2010; Ellis, Adams & Bochner, 2011). Autoethnography is oftentimes serendipitous, occurring when we are going about our everyday lives. Autoethnography is also therapeutic, embodied (Berry, 2012), performative (Spry, 2001), and queer (Adams & Holman Jones, 2008), speaking from, for, and to the margins.

The concept of intersectionality—exploring how multiple aspects of identities simultaneously are manifested within interactions with others—has steadily emerged as important in the study of culture over the last two decades (e.g., Crenshaw, 1991). For example, Kimberlé Crenshaw, a critical race scholar, coined the term *intersectionality* when discussing the legal implications that potentially work against black women because of racism and sexism. However, she was not the first person to interrogate the implications of layered identity positions. The Combahee River Collective Statement (1982), written by a group of black lesbian feminist organizers, introduced the concept of interlocking oppressions from which Crenshaw's work is based. Audre Lorde (1984) also wrote about intersecting identity standpoints that further marginalize the marginalized. Other identity factors, such as gender, sexual orientation, social class, ethnicity, religion, age, ability status, and education also come into play through relational and casual interactions. However, only recently have communication scholars embraced intersectionality within their research with any regularity (e.g., Carrillo Rowe, 2008; Chávez & Griffin, 2012). Autoethnographic scholars, however, have routinely identified and used their multiple standpoints to situate their stories and lives to call out positions of privilege and expose moments of vulnerability (see Adams, 2011; Berry, 2012; Boylorn, 2012; Calafell, 2012; Durham, 2004; Griffin, 2012).

Within this edited volume, our intention is to produce a cutting-edge resource that highlights the ways in which an intersectional approach to exploring the inextricable relationship between culture and communication

(Orbe, 1998) and the influence of preexisting and potential relationships provides insight beyond that which is possible through frameworks. More specifically, we highlight the productivity inherent within autoethnography as a means to enhance existing understandings of lived experiences enacted within social locations situated within larger systems of power, oppression, and social privilege.

Interpersonal and Intercultural Communication as Lenses for Personal Reflection & Relationships

Historically, cultural forms of communication were studied through traditional social scientific approaches that focused on generalized cultural norms defined through how different they were from Western standards (Houston, 2002). Over time, several trajectories of intercultural communication research from critical, interpretive, postmodern, postcolonial, and performative perspectives emerged within the field. These research studies helped to theorize the complexities, intersections, politics, and nuances of identities as they play out in communicative contexts where culture played a salient role. Such research has established how culture and communication are inextricably linked (Brislin, 1993; Orbe, 1998) and generated pedagogical and scholarly approaches that regard all human communication as a point on an interpersonal ↔ intercultural continuum (Orbe & Harris, 2007; Samovar & Porter, 2001). Our book is grounded in the epistemological assumption that interpersonal and intercultural communication are "two sides of the same coin," (Orbe & Bruess, 2005, p. 14) and are best understood as such. Consistent with this approach, we will offer theories including cultural contracts theory, co-cultural theory, dialectical theory, complicity theory, self-presentation theory, communication theory of identity, coordinated management of meaning theory, sensemaking, cultural dialectics, narratology, relational dialectics, symbolic interactionism, and standpoint theory to discuss how and why identity is considered a personal, social, and cultural construct.

A consistent theme of this book is the use of cultural-critical autoethnography and interpersonal/cultural communication practices to provide insight into the messy, complex nature of diverse sets of lived experiences. While some individual research projects have taken a similar approach, this is the first collaborative collection that features how autoethnography can provide rich descriptions to highlight the similarities and differences across diverse cultural standpoints. In this regard, we will explore how the saliency of similarities (interpersonal) and differences (intercultural) permeate everyday life in complex ways. Further, because our book uses an intersectional approach, every chapter incorporates multiple aspects of identity.

There are varied and myriad definitions of intercultural communication. A widespread understanding of intercultural communication is the communication between people from different cultures. Karlfried Knapp defines intercultural communication as the interpersonal interaction between members of different groups (Knapp, 1987; Knapp & Knapp-Potthoff, 1987). Following Knapp's definition, we offer an academic framing for the book that connects intercultural communication and interpersonal communication to simultaneously investigate the personal influences of culture on relationships and relationships on culture. We talk about autoethnography as a critical method by using three central features of critical theory, which include: to understand the lived experience of real people in context, to examine social conditions and uncover oppressive power arrangements, and to fuse theory and action to challenge processes of domination. We also elaborate on the ways in which individual autoethnographies are in conversation with one another and offer a commentary on the intersection of identity, culture, and relationships.

A primary goal of interpersonal communication is to learn how to better relate and communicate with others. By exploring the dynamics of inter-personal/intercultural communication we will increase cultural awareness by understanding how they influence each other. For example, how does one's membership in a particular co-culture influence their sense of self and their interactions with other members both inside and outside of their group? We will interrogate the ways that difference influences our lives and how our relationships with intimate and unknown others serve as opportunities for communicative enlightenment. We make connections between different types of similarities and difference and offer readers personal/cultural insight through the lenses and lives of our contributors.

Autoethnography as Method of Choice

Culture is made possible through lived experience (Berry, 2012), and auto-ethnography is inherently a cultural practice. Our stories are instrumental in constructing our identities and they help inform our interpersonal relation-ships (Bochner, 2012). The chapters in this book approach autoethnography from multiple perspectives and genres, sometimes incorporating traditional scholarship with experimental writing techniques. While contributors were urged to write their personal narratives, we also encouraged them to reflect on the interpersonal, intercultural, and intersectional aspects of their stories, folding in theoretical frameworks to their experiences. However, depending on the theme and scope of individual chapters some incorporate citations while others rely on the verisimilitude of the experience for confirmation.

Chapter Overview

As editors we organized the chapters thematically, focusing on categorical similarities that link the experiences and/or social issues represented in each essay. However, we understand that the themes we developed overlap and that many of the chapters could successfully be included in multiple sections. Our organizational choices are intended to guide readers through the stories with theoretical connections that link and intersect across thematic difference.

Section I: Complicating Mundane Everyday Life Encounters

In the first section the authors use autoethnographic reflexivity to discuss issues that are simultaneously (inter)personal and (inter)cultural (Berry & Clair, 2011). They reflect on seemingly mundane moments that become life changing. By engaging the retrospective lens of autoethnography, they use their stories to engage their identities as evolving and vulnerable.

In the opening chapter, Jeanine Mingé and John Sterner reflect on how their lives and romantic relationship was changed by a cancer diagnosis. Focusing on the intricate and particular moments in their lives and relationship, they invite the reader into the intersections of identity, sexuality, and geography while reflecting on issues of illness, medicine, and spirituality. They share their journey through vignettes and excerpts, negotiating the interpersonal and intercultural reality that "cancer changes everything."

Tabatha Roberts's essay engages her experience as a first-generation college student and the complexities of her identity due to her socioeconomic status, lifestyle, gender, and ethnicity. She reflects on childhood experiences and her relationship with her parents to explain her goal of challenging supposed inevitable educational outcomes for marginalized and unprivileged individuals. She highlights the ways that social stigmas and traumas can be overcome through retrospective sensemaking.

Tony Adams examines post–coming out complications in his essay that chronicles how coming out as a gay man has negatively impacted his familial relationships. By focusing on the complications that happen after one is already "out," he uses everyday experiences to illustrate the struggles he experiences to maintain interpersonal relationships with people who do not fully acknowledge his sexuality and long-term relationship. By critically engaging what he refers to as "queer melancholy," he makes sense, through retroactive analysis, of the sadness that results from his fractured relationships.

Section II: Embracing Ambiguous and Nonbinary Identities

The next section of the book centers on narratives that resist normative and binary identity constructions. The three chapters in this section challenge cultural constraints and representations by simply being themselves, incorporating the interpersonal challenges that occur within families and communities when we fail to perform expected cultural identities. Amber Johnson negotiates the labels and restrictions of her race, class, and sexuality in her performative autoethnography that includes excerpts from an interview with her father. In Negotiating *More:* (Mis)labeling the Body, she discusses the complications of being labeled (different and "normal") and situates herself as a "cultural hybrid."

Richie Hao writes about his in-flux intercultural identities in what he refers to as "diasporic hybridity," challenging what it means to be authentically Chinese. He compares his ethnic (in)authenticity to fortune cookies, a product that he feels, like himself, is "an American construction of Chineseness."

Finally, Bryant Alexander uses his positionality as a gay black man to interrogate his presence-absence in family photographs (borderless frames) and invites the voices of marginalized students to join his voice in negotiating what he calls "bleeding borders of identity." He uses autoethnography and pedagogy to introduce student performance work as exemplars of critical intercultural autoethnography and to extend the possibilities of what collaborative, intersectional, and intercultural autoethnography might look like.

Section III: Negotiating Socially Stigmatized Identities

We often present ourselves based on how we see ourselves and how we see other people seeing us. The fourth section includes four chapters that reflect on the challenges of living with and responding to socially stigmatized identities. Collectively, the authors interrogate their privileged and disadvantaged positionalities as they relate to race, class, gender/sex, sexuality, and ability. They challenge assumptions of social identity (linked to privilege) by revealing their double lives (the ways in which their intersectional identities oftentimes require social and cultural adjustments and performances).

In A Story & A Stereotype, Robin Boylorn discusses the problematic myths that surround black female identity and how those stereotypes are influenced by social class. She challenges the notion that black women's assumed anger and inherent strength are insignificant signifiers of self-perception. By offering a historical narrative of the two most common stereotypes of black women (one allegedly positive and one negative) she uses her personal experiences/stories to think through the cultural myths and their class-based interpretations by juxtaposing stereotypes and storytelling.

Desiree Yomtoob reflects on conflicts she experiences based on people's perceptions of her. As an Arab-American, Jewish, nonheterosexual-middle-aged woman, she uses her lived experiences and witnessing of discrimination to interrogate orientalization, racialization, sexism and heteronormativity.

Patrick Santoro offers an embodied autoethnographic performance script that chronicles his journey to self-acceptance of his body type through a discussion of the white gay gaze and aesthetic. His piece offers a responsive narrative to representations in media and culture that attempt to dictate hegemonic norms of sexuality and attractiveness. He uses a burgeoning online relationship and his responses to stock images of desirable masculinity to offer an intersectional take on self-actualization and acceptance.

Finally, Dana Morella-Pozzi writes about her privileged/disadvantaged experiences as a student and faculty member with a nonvisible disability. In what she terms *the terrible dichotomy*, she discusses the idea of being simultaneously il/legitimate and the conflicts she experiences. She discusses intersectionality from multiple positions of privilege and marginalization to encourage disability awareness.

Section IV: Creating Pathways to Authentic Selves

In the final three chapters the authors offer autoethnographies of "becoming" that are demonstrated through their intersectional selves. Mark Orbe's chapter, for example, reflects on class performances and identity negotiations in terms of his working-class poor upbringing and current upper-middle-class realities. Sarah Amira de la Garza chronicles her spiritual and personal journey, citing the intersections and assumptions that are often connected to ethnic and religious identity performance. Rex Crawley (re)tells an illness narrative that was originally shared through a public blog he wrote to document his experience. His story is told through the lens of Christian faith and modern medicine to discuss black masculinity, spirituality, and health.

*

All the chapters in *Critical Autoethnography* work together to make sense of how identity, culture, and relationships are interconnected. The essays are in conversation and response to each other as they relate to various themes of experience and universality. For example, Roberts's essay on discrimination focuses primarily on socioeconomic status but is linked to Morella-Pozzi's chapter on her experiences of discrimination and il/legitimacy. Both chapters challenge hegemonic presumptions about difference in the academy from different perspectives (one linked to disability and the other to social background). Boylorn and Orbe write about their classed and raced experiences as frameworks for resisting negative categorizations. Both chapters offer a class critique to better understand their intercultural positionalites. Crawley's chapter, like Boylorn's, considers how race stereotypes sometimes complicate the experience and analysis of marginalized folk by linking black masculinity to faith, but can also be examined alongside Mingé and Sterner to look at how unexpected illness influences romantic relationships, personal identity, and gender performance. The latter chapters consider illness from the role of both the person who is diagnosed and their caregiver/s.

Santoro and Adams's chapters are written from the perspective of white gay men and consider the cultural consequences of difference through a lens of nonheterosexuality. Santoro, however, focuses on intercultural and social challenges, while Adams concentrates on his interpersonal and familial relationships. Yomtoob, Hao, de la Garza, Johnson, and Alexander's pieces all challenge what it means to be authentically oneself when you are perceived differently by the public. Hao and Johnson look specifically at issues of hybridity, while Yomtoob, de la Garza and Alexander offer reflexive accounts of their personal experiences being "othered." Alexander extends his personal musings to include performative pieces from former students as a way of inviting the reader to consider the pedagogical possibilities of critical cultural autoethnography.

The stories presented in this volume uncover personal and cultural realities that can be best understood through narrative interrogation. The chapters combine to offer a diverse and complex collection of autoethnographies that are critical, vulnerable, situational, personal, eye-opening, and relevant, and they serve as exemplars for understanding how cultural identities intersect in our everyday lives.

References

Adams, T. E. (2011). *Narrating the closet: An autoethnography of same-sex attraction.* Walnut Creek, CA: Left Coast Press, Inc.

Adams, T. E., & Holman Jones, S. (2008). Autoethnography is queer. In N. K. Denzin, Y. S. Lincoln, & L. T. Smith (Eds.), *Handbook of critical and indigenous methodologies* (pp. 373–390). Thousand Oaks, CA: Sage.

Allen, B. J. (2010). *Difference matters: Communicating social identity.* (2nd ed.). Long Grove, IL: Waveland Press.

Allen, B. J., Orbe, M., & Olivas, M. R. (1999). The complexity of our tears: Dis/enchantment and (in)difference in the academy. *Communication Theory, 9*(4), 402–429.

Baldwin, J. R., Faulkner, S. L., Hecht, M. L., & Lindsley, S. L. (Eds.) (2006). *Redefining culture: Perspectives across the disciplines.* Mahwah, NJ: Lawrence Erlbaum Associates.

Berry, K. (2012). (Un)covering the gay interculturalist. In N. Bardhan & M. P. Orbe (Eds.), *Identity research and communication: Intercultural reflections and future directions* (pp. 223–237). Lanham, MD: Lexington.

Berry, K., & Clair, R. P. (2011). *Contestation and Opportunity in Reflexivity [Special issue]. Cultural Studies ⱷ Critical Methodologies, 11*(2).

Bochner, A. P. (2012). On first-person narrative scholarship: Autoethnography as acts of meaning. *Narrative Inquiry, 22*(1), 155–164.

Boylorn, R. M. (2012). Dark-skinned love stories. *International Review of Qualitative Research, 5*(3), 299–309.

Brislin, R. (1993). *Understanding cultures influence on behavior.* Orlando, FL: Harcourt Brace & Co.

Calafell, B. M. (2012). Monstrous femininity constructions of women of color in the academy. *Journal of Communication Inquiry, 36*(2), 111–130.

Carrillo Rowe, A. (2008). *Power lines: On the subject of feminist alliances.* Durham, NC: Duke University Press.

Chang, H. (2008). *Autoethnography as method.* Walnut Creek, CA: Left Coast Press, Inc.

Chávez, K. R., & Griffin, C. L. (2012). *Standing in the intersection: Feminist voices, feminist practices in communication studies.* Albany: SUNY Press.

Crenshaw, K. (1991). Mapping the margins: Intersectionality, identity politics, and violence against women of color. *Stanford Law Review,* 1241–1299.

The Combahee River Collective (1982). A black feminist statement. In G. T. Hull, P. B. Scott, & B. Smith (Eds.), *All the women are white, all the blacks are men, but some of us are brave: Black women's studies* (pp. 13–22). Old Westbury, NY: Feminist Press.

Denzin, N. K. (1997). *Interpretive ethnography: Ethnographic practices for the 21st century.* Thousand Oaks, CA: Sage.

Denzin, N. K., & Lincoln, Y. S. (Eds.) (2000). *Handbook of qualitative research.* (2nd ed.). Thousand Oaks, CA: Sage.

Durham, A. (2004). Verbal exchange, *Qualitative Inquiry, 10*(4), 493–494.

Ellis, C. (2004). *The ethnographic I: A methodological novel about autoethnography.* Walnut Creek, CA: AltaMira Press.

Ellis, C., & Bochner, A. P. (2000). Autoethnography, personal narrative, reflexivity. In N. K. Denzin & Y. S. Lincoln (Eds.), *Handbook of qualitative research* (2nd ed., pp.733–768). Thousand Oaks, CA: Sage.

Ellis, C., Adams, T. E., & Bochner, A. P. (2011). Autoethnography: An Overview [40 paragraphs]. *Forum Qualitative Sozialforschung / Forum: Qualitative Social Research, 12*(1), http://nbn-resolving.de/urn:nbn:de:0114-fqs1101108.

Geertz, C. (1973). *The interpretation of cultures: Selected Essays.* New York: Basic Books.

Griffin, R. A. (2012). "I am an angry black woman: Black feminist autoethnography, voice, and resistance." *Women's Studies in Communication, 35*(2), 138–157.

Holman Jones, S., Adams, T. E., & Ellis, C. (2013). (Eds.), *Handbook of autoethnography.* Walnut Creek, CA: Left Coast Press, Inc.

Houston, M. (2002). Seeking difference: African Americans in interpersonal communication research, 1975–2000. *Howard Journal of Communications, 13,* 25–31.

Kehly, M. J. (1995). Self-narration, autobiography and identity construction, *Gender & Education, 7*(1), 23–31.

Knapp, K. (1987). English as an international lingua franca and the teaching of intercultural communication. *Perspectives on Language in Performance, 2,* 1022–1039.

Knapp, K., & Knapp-Potthoff, A. (1987). Instead of an introduction: Conceptual issues in analyzing intercultural communication. In K. Knapp, W. Enninger & A. Knapp-Potthoff (Eds.), *Analyzing intercultural communication* (pp. 1-13). Amsterdam, Mouton de Gruyter.

Kroeber, A. L., & Kluckhohn, C. (1952). *Culture: A critical review of concepts and definitions.* Cambridge, MA: Harvard University Press.

Lorde, A. (2007). *Sister outsider.* Berkeley, CA: Crossing. (Original work published 1984).

Madison, D. S. (2012). *Critical ethnography: Method, ethics, and performance* (2nd ed.). Los Angeles, CA: Sage.

Muncey, T. (2010). *Creating autoethnographies.* Los Angeles, CA: Sage.

Orbe, M. P. (1998). *Constructing co-cultural theory: An explication of culture, power, and communication.* Thousand Oaks, CA: Sage.

Orbe, M. P., & Bruess, C. J. (2005). *Contemporary issues in interpersonal communication.* Los Angeles, CA: Roxbury.

Orbe, M. P., & Harris, T. M. (2007). *Interracial communication: Theory into practice* (2nd ed.). Thousand Oaks, CA: Sage.

Pacanowsky, M. (1988). Slouching towards Chicago, *Quarterly Journal of Speech,* 74 (4), 453–467.

Philipsen, G. (1975). Speaking "like a man" in Teamsterville: Culture patterns of role enactment in an urban neighborhood. *Quarterly Journal of Speech, 61,* 13–22.

Reed-Danahay, D. E. (Ed.). (1997). *Auto/ethnography: Rewriting the self and the social.* New York: Berg.

Samovar, L. A., & Porter, R. E. (Eds.). (2001). *Communication between cultures* (4th ed.). Belmont, CA: Wadsworth.

Spry, T. (2001). Performing autoethnography: An embodied methodological praxis, *Qualitative Inquiry, 7* (6), 706–732.

SECTION I

Complicating Mundane Everyday Life Encounters

LIKE GRIFFIN (2012), WE ARGUE THAT THEORIES ARE LENSES THROUGH which we can view communication with greater clarity. Before each section, we highlight several theories that can help frame your reading of the different chapters. The first section of the book will set the stage for readers by featuring three chapters that highlight the inherent value of studying everyday life events through autoethnography. Individually each chapter demonstrates how routine life interactions are packed with meaning in terms of how self is experienced within larger cultural and social frames. Collectively, this section features intersections of cultural identities informed by gender, sexuality, socioeconomic status, age, and lifestyle. In this section, *narratology, symbolic interactionism,* and *relational dialectics theory* are offered as organizing frameworks to unite these chapters and serve as a bridge for subsequent sections.

Narratology

Narratology is the "study and theory of narratives, or complex stories—what they are made of, how they are structured, and what we gain from using them as a vehicle for communication" (Browning, 2009, p. 673). Within this approach, *narrative* represents an umbrella term for forms of communication that have: (a) a sequence of events (beginning, middle, and end), (b) some form of casual development between sequences that produces a conclusion; and (c) memorable descriptions of events. The field of communication has long established itself as a discipline interested in studying the meaning in narratives, and autoethnography is a primary means through which human stories are explored (Bochner, 1994; Fisher, 1987).

Narratology is a scholarly strategy to assist in a sensemaking process that counters a rational-scientific model (Fisher, 1987). Narrators make sense of everyday and significant life events through powerful descriptions that include similes, metaphors, phrases, terms, and other codes. Narratives can be told through various points of view—they can be local or distant, universal or idiosyncratic, or reflective of a character's view or the view of the narrator (Browning, 2009). The most powerful narratives are written in styles that draw the reader into the story in meaningful ways.

Walter Fisher's work on narrative theory represents a key example of the productive nature of narratology. According to Fisher (1987), human beings are storytellers, and all forms of communication are best understood as stories. Narrative theory is grounded in three key ideas. First, humans experience and understand life as a series of ongoing narratives—a casual development of connected sequences that produce meaningful conclusions. Second, individuals make life decisions based on good reasons that emerge from life stories. Because of this, a powerful story serves as an effective means of persuasion. Third, and finally, evaluation of stories is less about the evidence or strength of logical arguments and more about how compelling the story is to the receiver. To demonstrate this third idea, Fisher developed a means to evaluate the work of stories based on specific criterion: *narrative rationality.* Narrative rationality is composed of judgments based on two twin standards. The first is *narrative coherence.* This standard judges the internal consistency of an individual's thoughts, behaviors, and actions and relates to how well the story hangs together. *Narrative fidelity,* the second standard that comprises narrative rationality, involves judgments regarding the believability of the story. It is a standard that speaks to the quality of a story in terms of striking a responsive chord with the reader. While some criticize narrative theory as just another story (Warnick, 1987), narratology remains a powerfully insightful lens through which to understand human communication.

Symbolic Interactionism

In *Mind, Self, and Society,* Mead (1934) describes the concept of self in terms of its direct relationship to various segments of social life. His work marks a shift from a focus on the self to one on the communication (symbolic interaction) between self and others. Although some communication scholars have identified problems associated with Mead's work (e.g., Tanno & Gonzalez, 1998), his attention to the important relationship between self-identity and social life highlights the central role that communication plays in identity formulation. In this regard, Mead's contributions inform the current perspectives of identity development and negotiation, especially those that appear in the literature associated with the field of communication.

Simply put, identities are co-created and re-created in everyday interactions (Yep, 2002). This general idea is grounded in Mead's work and subsequently strengthened by the advances of his students. For instance,

Blumer (1969) has championed the idea that the sense of self emerges from a process of definition/redefinition that occurs through social interaction. In other words, identity is negotiated—formed, maintained, and modified—through our interactions with others. Identity also simultaneously influences these very interactions through our expectations and perceptions of others' behaviors (Hecht et al., 1993). In essence, a person's sense of self can be seen as an integral part of that person's social behavior (and vice versa). Part of a person's social behavior includes finding appropriate names and labels that locate the self in socially recognizable categories. Most often, we gain our self-identities through a process of contrasting in-group and out-group characteristics (J. C. Turner, 1987). In short, we come to understand who we are as we compare and contrast ourselves with others.

One of the central aspects of Mead's (1934) symbolic interactionism framework is the idea of a *generalized other*, a concept he uses to refer to the collective body from which the individual sees the self. Throughout your life, you have learned these perceptions from years of socialization and interaction with others. Sometimes self-perceptions can be grounded through critical life incidents, events, or interactions that carry significant weight in terms of how we see ourselves. Other times, self-perceptions can be tied to specific individuals with whom we spend large amounts of time. In this regard, each person has a number of *significant others* who have been particularly influential in her or his identity development; these individuals can include family members, friends, teachers, and others.

Symbolic interactionists argue that the images others communicate to a person are a central aspect of identity formation. Mead (1934) used the concept of *looking glass self* to describe the mental self-image that people develop as they see themselves through others' eyes. Yet, another central element is the reaction to one's looking glass self. While the power of these messages is especially great during early socialization, individuals gain agency as they become more aware of their ability to negotiate (accept, reject, ignore, navigate, etc.) the looking glass selves that exist. Gradually, some of these meanings generated through this interaction are generalized over time and become established as core elements of your identity.

Relational Dialectics Theory

As an application of twentieth century Russian theorist Mikhail Bakhtin, relational dialectics theory represents an interpretive lens through which we can understand how communication constitutes personal, social, and familial relationships (Baxter, 2007, 2009). Within this theoretical framework, the term *dialectics* emphasizes Bakhtin's conception of meaning construction as a struggle between competing or opposing discourses. Simply put, *dialectics* are a "dynamic knot of contradictions in personal relationships" (Griffin,

2012, p. 155) that result in tensions that are negotiated through various means of communication.

The main idea of relational dialectics theory is that human relationships involve the negotiation of similar sets of dialectical tensions. Situated within different contexts (individual, relational, and societal), these tensions exist between opposing forces that are important, desirable, and necessary for human existence. Several key ideas form the foundation of the theory. First, different types of relationships experience different clusters of core tensions. While much of the early research was focused on romantic relationships (Baxter & Montgomery, 1996), the theory has been applied to a variety of interpersonal, organizational, and intercultural relational contexts (e.g., Bochner & Eisenberg, 1987; Rawlins, 1992; see description of cultural dialectics in Section IV). Second, relationships are defined over time by the ways in which partners manage tensions. Communication plays a definitive role in how individuals negotiate the dialectical tensions that they experience in various relationships (Hoppe-Nagao & Ting-Toomey, 2002). This leads directly into the third key idea: Negotiating relational tensions is an ongoing communicative process. Given the ever-changing nature of human relational experiences, one can never fully create a permanent resolution to the tensions that are experienced.

The vast majority of work on relational dialectics theory has been on the development of primary tensions within romantic relationships (Baxter & Montgomery, 1996). In particular, three core tensions have been identified. *Autonomy ↔ connection* is the first primary tension and focuses on the simultaneous need for individuals' independence and intimacy within romantic relationships. This tension speaks to the relational contradiction between a desire for connection and a desire for separation. The second tension is *stability ↔ change*. This dialectic speaks to the opposing needs for certainty and uncertainty (or predictability and novelty)—both of which are important for relationships. The third dialectical tension for romantic relationships, *openness ↔ closedness,* is explicitly a communicative phenomenon. It speaks to the need to be expressive, open, and transparent in one's communication while simultaneously honoring the importance of selective self-disclosure and concealing certain things from one's partner. In short, human existence—and by extension, social life—represents a dynamic knot of contradictions that require constant negotiation through communication.

Theories as Lenses

We have described three theoretical frameworks to help structure your reading of each chapter in this section. While any number of theories highlighted throughout the book can provide a productive lens through which to understand the communicative experiences as described by each author featured in this section, these three seem especially relevant. As you read through each chapter, think critically about the following questions:

- How might you describe the power of each autoethnography featured in this section? What specific features (metaphors, phrases, terms, language) of each chapter were the most moving for you?
- What particular conclusion do you think that author intended for their chapter? What casual development of sequenced events was described to lead you to that conclusion?
- Can you identify the generalized and significant others that play an important role in each of the authors' identities? What critical incidents are described within each chapter?
- Thinking about your own looking glass selves, what critical incidents play an important function in your own self-concept?
- What specific dialectical tensions are described by each author in their respective chapter? How do these reflect opposing contradictions in their social lives?
- What tensions do you think are present in autoethnography as a methodological framework? Can you see these tensions (i.e., revealment ↔ concealment) at work in each chapter as it is written, or are they more implicit in the end product?

References

Baxter, L. (2007). Mikhail Bakhtin and the philosophy of dialogism. In P. Arneson (Ed.), *Perspectives on philosophy of communication* (pp. 247–268). West Lafayette, IN: Purdue University Press.

Baxter, L. (2009). Relational dialectics theory. In S. W. Littlejohn & K. A. Foss (Eds.), *Encyclopedia of communication theory* (pp. 837–840). Thousand Oaks, CA: Sage.

Baxter, L., & Montgomery, B. M. (1996). *Relating: Dialogues and dialectics.* New York: Guilford.

Blumer, H. (1969). *Symbolic interactionism: Perspective and method.* Englewood Cliffs, NJ: Prentice-Hall.

Bochner, A. (1994). Perspectives on inquiry II: Theories and stories. In M. Knapp & G. R. Miller (Eds.), *Handbook of interpersonal communication* (2d ed., pp. 21–41). Thousand Oaks, CA: Sage.

Bochner, A., & Eisenberg, E. (1987). Family process: System perspectives. In C. R. Berger & S. Chaffee (Eds.), *Handbook of communication science* (pp. 540–563). Beverly Hills, CA: Sage.

Browning, L. (2009). Narrative and narratology. In S. W. Littlejohn & K. A. Foss (Eds.), *Encyclopedia of communication theory* (pp. 673–677). Thousand Oaks, CA: Sage.

Fisher, W. R. (1987). *Human communication as narration: Toward a philosophy of reason, value, and action.* Columbia: University of South Carolina Press.

Griffin, E. (2012). *A first look at communication theory* (8th ed.). New York: McGraw-Hill.

Hecht, M. L., Collier, M. J., & Ribeau, S. A. (1993). *African American communication: Ethnic identity and cultural interpretation.* Newbury Park, CA: Sage.

Hoppe-Nagao, A., & Ting-Toomey, S. (2002). Relational dialectics and management strategies in marital couples. *Southern Communication Journal, 67,* 142–159.

Mead, G. H. (1934). *Mind, self, and society.* Chicago, IL: University of Chicago Press.

Rawlins, W. (1992). *Friendship matters: Communication, dialectics, and the life course.* New York: Aldine de Gruyter.

Tanno, D. V., & Gonzalez, A. (1998). Sites of identity of communication and culture. In D. V. Tanno & A. Gonzalez (Eds.), *Communication and identity across cultures* (pp. 3–10). Thousand Oaks, CA: Sage.

Turner, J. C. (1987). *Rediscovering the social group.* London: Basil Blackwell.

Yep, G. A. (2002). Navigating the multicultural identity landscape. In J. N. Martin, T. K. Nakayama, & L. A. Flores (Eds.), *Readings in cultural contexts* (pp. 60–66). Mountain View, CA: Mayfield.

Warnick, B. (1987). The narrative paradigm: Another story. *Quarterly Journal of Speech, 73,* 172–182.

CHAPTER ONE

∞

The Transitory Radical
Making Place with Cancer
Jeanine M. Mingé and John Burton Sterner

THIS WAS A SIMPLE STORY OF PLACE, LOVE, AND FAMILY THAT MARKS the way place seeps into a body, demands of it differently than the town and geography before. The intersections of identity, sexuality, and geography influence how I make place with sex, love, and home. Within the place of Topanga Canyon, California, we, John and I, create a newfound partnership built on love and trust. And this love demands of it differently than the relationship before.

But cancer changes everything.

MEET-CUTE.
I watch as two prospective lovers graze arms in a "meet-cute moment" over the coffee creamers and additions. This stranger laughs and says to her, "That was almost a romance movie moment right there." And watching them, I slide into a wave of silent tears, here in this on-campus coffee shop. I am catapulted back into our, John and my, moment. Our first meeting was a meet-cute, an accident. The graze of his hand on my shoulder as he noticed my tattoo turned into conversation and formed into this love. I knew I tattooed her on my skin for a reason. He is the reason.

DISCOVERY.
I reach up to the stubble on his cheek. I draw myself closer to his lips. I pull my body close to his. We kiss; hold lips together with a soft force. I hum breath into his mouth. I break away and look deeply into his eyes. He smiles and hums. I move my fingers on his neck, up to his ear. I feel his

neck protruding with heat where there shouldn't be heat. I stop. He looks at my worried face. And he says, "Feel this. I found it a while ago." I draw my fingers where his rest between the lip of his jawbone and his neck. He moves his fingers away so I can apply pressure. I feel a small hard mass. It feels dense, hot. I feel pain in my stomach. I can tell—it's bad. I pull away again and look at him with wide eyes.

My tone is serious, "You need to get that checked out. It isn't normal. Soon, ok? Promise?" He nods, and I wrap my arms around him. He folds over me and pulls his body on top of mine. We fall into the bed—enraptured.

SIMPLE STORY.

I found love, real love, in the mountains of Topanga. This is a simple story of love and place. I've discovered the way place can seep into the body, become at once home and peace, chaos and calm. It is a simple story of love unfolding in the mountains on the dusty ground across the ocean. A simple story of love complicated by my desire to have children, one child with him, and his resistance. Our conflict magnified in daily desire, when he pulls out. When I ache for his completion inside me. Our complication erupts when I can't sleep, worried that we might not survive because our futures look so different. He already has children. He is 48, and I am 33. Our 15-year age difference might get the better of us. But I love him. I toss and turn in and out of sleep and daily dreaming, "He is it. I know it."

BODY SILENCES.

"But it is not only in endings, in collapse and death, that the body imposes silence upon our efforts at narration. Illness narratives point to an even more disconcerting narratological truth: all bodies, even those that show no signs of disintegration or disease, challenge narration" (Belling, 2010, p. 229).

Johnny's body never told the story of a possible cancer. He is not one to risk his health. He preserves it. Johnny has always been healthy, an avid surfer, a runner. Once I met him, I quit smoking cigarettes, because I knew I wanted to be with him forever. I couldn't let that unkempt habit get in the way of our love. After smoking cigarettes for 16 years, I quit cold turkey. I sweat and shook in his arms for one night of toxic release, and I will never pick up a cigarette again. I am the one who is cancer-free. Seems impossibly unfair.

The doctors say to him, "We just have to chalk it up to bad luck, there is no reason why you should have this cancer."

BEING HERE.

He grabs a log, a trunk of a tree. He walks outside to split it, to add it to our wood-burning stove. I hear the cracking bark, the thud of prospective warmth. I am home.

We are home, together.

FINALLY.

He comes to me a month later and points to his lump in his throat. He says with a tremble in his voice, "I need to get this checked out."

"Ok. I will call them today, ok?"

I dial the VA hospital. He becomes his last name and a number, the last four digits of his Social Security number. I speak with the receptionist. "Can I set an appointment for Sterner, ####? We discovered a lump in his neck that seems really out of place. I am pretty worried."

"A lump in his neck? That sounds serious. I would get him here as soon as you can. Don't even worry about an appointment. Just come straight into the ER tomorrow morning." I set the phone down and take an intense inhale and exhale.

We do.

"THEY ARE BAD CELLS, THE MEAN CELLS."

"We were told to come into the ER by someone on the phone. I'm not sure if it's the right place to be, but I have a lump on my neck. It doesn't hurt or anything."

I interrupt, "Don't downplay it, ok?"

She laughs out loud, "She knows what is what. She will take care of you. Alright baby, go on in."

A nurse asks him, "Can you step on the scale for me?"

They shuffle us into the waiting room, and we are scheduled to meet with his RN. She doesn't seem to take him seriously. But she sends him to get blood tests and reluctantly schedules a same-day biopsy in ENT (Ear, Nose, and Throat).

We move from waiting room to waiting room, from test to test, from nurse to nurse. Up and down elevators. We do not speak about the possibility of a cancer diagnosis, as if saying it out loud would make cancer appear.

Dr. L, a tall man in a white coat with blue embroidered letters, saunters to the front. He pushes his thin-framed glasses up the bridge of his nose. He calls, "Mr. Sterner?" He laughs an awkward bubbled laugh. "Hey, man. I'm Dr. L. I come in here every once in a while. Do a little work. Help you guys out. Follow me." He walks us around a corner. He looks back over his shoulder as he walks. "Ya know, after all the government has put you through, I am happy to help." He brings us to a back room, sits us down on two chairs propped against a wall. The room is crowded, awkward, set up in a makeshift fashion, test tubes on rolling carts, slides and a microscope.

"So what I am going to do here is to take a sample of the lump in your neck, rather than having to wait for the results, ya know like the typical long process that makes you wait, we are, my team and I, going to get the results right here. We'll treat it a bit, put it on the slide and take a quick look. Sound good?"

I don't think it sounds good, but it sounds efficient, a bit urgent, and I am happy that Dr. L is a go-getter, a let's get things done right here, right now kinda guy. I look at John sitting to my left. His jaw seems tight, but in typical John fashion, he connects with the doctors, he smiles, he laughs, he is loving and kind. His eyes shine, but I feel the thin veil of fear covering his body.

Dr. L introduces us to his team. "This here is Betsy, the best at her job, and Mimult, my trusty sidekick. They are here to help you, we do this once a month, roll our stuff down here from UCLA and help you guys out, ya know? You served us, now let us serve you."

It's a bit like shock and awe—in shock that the biopsy is going to happen right here, right now, and in awe that the results are also going to be in, right here, right now.

He puts on blue rubber gloves. He grabs a needle out of a package. "Now, you aren't afraid of needles are you?"

John shakes his head. "Nope. I have a high tolerance for pain."

"I am going to numb it with this swab. Now, I am not going to lie, this is going to hurt a bit." The needle sticks deep into his neck. He moves it around like he is swirling a cauldron. John's eyes shut tight, tighter; he gulps and winces. He takes a deep breath. He exhales slowly as the needle is taken out.

Dr. L takes the needle and hands it to his assistants. They put some of the cells on the slide, some in the test tube. He claps his hands awkwardly together and says jovially,

"Ok, let's see what we have here." They treat the slides. Push the slide underneath the microscope. The woman with dark skin and a grandmotherly face, soft and kind brown eyes, swallows hard. She moves away from the slide and locks eyes with the younger man with olive skin and thin bones. He moves to take a look. He clears his throat. Dr. L moves to take a look.

"Hum. Ok. Let me see here. Ok." He moves away from the microscope and back to in front of us. He sits in a strange position with his legs in a wide V.

He claps his hands together and says, "Ok let me just come right out and say it, I see some bad cells in there. So I am so sorry but it looks like they are malignant."

I wonder why he won't use the word *cancer*.

Johnny swallows hard, and his face goes pale.

"What we can't tell right now is what kind of bad cells they are. Can we take a few more vials? Are you ok for me to take another sample? I know it hurts, but rather than wait to go under to test it, we can just grab what we need right here to make the assessment. Can you stand another needle?"

"Yea, I mean it hurts but do what you need to."

36

"Great, let me see, if I can just grab the lump maybe that will help alleviate the pain." He runs his thumb and forefinger over John's skin in a grotesque fashion. He pulls out the lump and sticks the needle in. Johnny flinches but not too much. He presses his lips together. Once the needle is out of his neck for the fourth and last time, he says, "That didn't hurt as much, when he pulled it out."

They take the sample and look at it again under the microscope. "What we are doing right now is looking for any cell that will give us a clue as to what type of cancer this is. Most cells tell us, but some don't tell us right away. Betsy, any clues yet?" Dr. L turns to Betsy, who is glued to the microscope.

"Nothing yet."

John takes a breath and asks to use the bathroom. I sit there with them. In Silence. Dr. L tries to speak to me, but the words move over my body like rum. Numb and breathing slowly, I take in the words, "bad cells, malignant."

Cancer.

"Let me go check on him. It has been a while." I find the closest men's room and knock on the door.

"You ok?" I know that question can't be answered lightly, or sanely, or with any form of consciousness. That the answer to that question is most likely, "Absolutely not, you crazy bitch." But he, in his wisdom and kindness answers, "Yea, I'm ok. I just don't know how I am going to tell my son, Wil." We walk back to the room and sit down on the hard plastic chairs for the next round of news.

"We don't know what kind of cancer it is. But we are going to take it to the lab, do all of the funky tests we do, and we are going to let you know as soon as possible. If you want, you can even give me a call. I know it isn't protocol but I will call you as soon as I know. What is your cell phone number? Rather than having you wait, I want you to feel taken care of, after all you have done for us, it is the least I can do for you. And I know how the government has treated its soldiers, and believe you me, it isn't well."

He walks us, the numb, the forever changed, to the front office. He shakes John's hand and tells him, "We will take care of you. I promise."

What he didn't tell us, what we discovered over the course of these two months, is that cancer changes everything.

AHHHHH.
And now, as I type, in this fucking Thai restaurant, in the middle of Tarzana, waiting for my car to be finished with detailing, I want to throw my water glass across the table, shatter it, my thoughts, my angst, this pain, against the pink and purple-hued wall. I want to throw such a fit that I might be arrested, or contained, or held by someone, tight and close to the chest. So that I may sob uncontrollably, but still feel in control, to be

told that it will all be all right. Anyone, please, lock me up, straightjacket and all. Please.

HE

holds me against his chest, my legs and his curl. He repositions so I can see the laptop on his lap. Our ankles curl against each other. My toes scrape his skin. He laughs and returns the gesture. I pull back and howl, and laugh and hit him lightly on the shoulder. "Stop it," I whine and snuggle closer into his armpit. He chuckles, giggles softly and lets me sink further into him, into this moment.

VISITOR PASS.

We arrive at ENT, the head and neck clinic on the basement floor of the hospital. In the waiting room, we wait. I take my small black field note journal out. We wait.

We meet Dr. K, a young head resident here at the VA. I stare at this badge and wonder about the relationships, the hours, the time spent in these hospitals. I hope he is one of the good ones. I hope he will speak to us clearly, like humans, like we have beating and fear-filled hearts.

He explains, "We found a cancer in your neck, we aren't quite sure of the primary source, about 10 percent of carcinomas have an unknown primary. Knowing the primary changes the way we treat the cancer. So let's find it ok? I'm just gonna take a look here. Open." John opens his mouth, and the doctor sticks his fingers down his throat. John gags hard. He kicks his legs up as his whole body convulses. He laughs and says, "I have a crazy gag reflex. So don't be mad if I throw up on you."

I giggle. "Don't turn this way, ok?"

Next steps—a tonsillectomy and biopsy surgery to find the primary source, he has to have a PET scan and a CT scan to make sure the cancer isn't anywhere else in his body. The surgery will be scheduled in two weeks. It feels like too long of a wait. We want it out right now. But he reminds us—we have to get blood tests done, go to the pre-op clinic, take these precautionary steps to "measure ten times and cut once."

WELLNESS TRAIL.

On the basement floor of the hospital, we walk with our heads held high and our hands intertwined. He points to a sign that hangs from the ceiling. "You see that?"

I look up and read it, "Wellness Trail."

"Yep, we are on the Wellness Trail."

QUESTIONS.

He dictates, and I write questions, for the next doctor, for the next time.

"I want to talk to the person who reads the actual scan. Is that a possibility?"

"I want to ask my friend Dr. W about options, get my second and third opinions."

"I want to bring up my headaches. What's going on there?"

"I want to know the duration of the actual surgery. How long will I be under?"

"Are they just going to keep digging around in there?"

"I also want a clearer picture of the recovery time."

"I want to know their thoughts about integrative oncology. Do they even care about nutrition?"

I look at him and ask, "Will it affect your fertility?"

DEAD OWL.

The owl died, the great horned owl that has been following us, lingering on the fence post, screeching all morning, all night. Blinking yellowed eyes that followed us on our morning walk. Steven found it on the side of the road, near the oak tree.

CROSSWALK.

He walks faster than I do. I whine, "Babe, can you wait up?" His long legs slow their stride. He turns to his left and reaches his hand back for me to grab it.

"Watch out," he warns as we cross the street, to reach the entrance into the hospital. A car, silver Honda Civic pulls to the side. And Dr. L jumps out.

"Hey, Mr. Sterner, so good to see you," he says jovially and extends his hand for him to shake it. "So, good news in there. They discovered it's local. The CT scan didn't show cancer anywhere else in your body! Good news. I am glad they found out that it isn't anywhere else and that they have a plan." John and I look at each other. My heart races with joy.

I pull him closer to me as we walk now, across the next crosswalk, with pep in our steps. He warns, "Don't get too overzealous. We still have a long way to go."

"Yep," I say warmly, "On our wellness trail." I hug the side of my face into his chest. He smiles and turns to speak to the security guard at the entrance of the hospital.

"You know what, Babe?"

"What, Love?" I ask and squeeze his hand.

"I've been treated like gold here."

"Good, we need to feel protected, taken care of, on this journey."

PRE-OP.

The nurse reads off of the screen as I look over her shoulder. "You will have a bilateral tonsillectomy and panendoscopy with biopsy."

He looks at her and straightens out his long legs, "What does that mean?"

She moves her wire rim glasses down her nose. She looks at him squarely. "They are going to remove both of your tonsils, look around and biopsy different parts of your throat, tongue, and mouth to find the primary cancer source. Ok?" He nods. "Now, let's go over your history and your health regimen." She begins to ask him questions, about his workout schedule, his daily routines. I see him puff out his chest a bit, the looming fear of surgery embedded in his answers. He wants to let us know he is strong, to feel strong, to be well. She asks, "Do you work out?

"I surf every day." He smiles, shifts in his chair, and says confidently, "I am probably the most fit person in this building."

"Ok, then. What about when you bleed, does it take a while to heal?"

"I heal in five minutes."

"Do you ever feel numb in your appendages, like your feet, fingers, toes?"

He scoffs at the question, laughs, and boasts, "Only when I cut off my own circulation."

She then asks, "What about your teeth? Do you have dentures?"

He looks at me and responds with a glimmer in his eyes, "Only as a model."

I laugh and remember the folding brochure for dentures and dental treatment with Johnny's smiling face right on the cover. His only modeling job for this denture company tried to convince the masses that they too could have teeth like him. His smile now, wide and mischievous, masks a great, haunting fear.

ORDINARY AFFECT.
He is asked to fill out living directives, to be carried out by his son and myself, if by chance the surgery goes awry. We go over each question about life support, about life-sustaining treatments, end-of-life care. This isn't an ordinary effect, but a heightened awareness, a shift of focus, a wake-up call. I hold his hand. I kiss his face. I speak softer, kinder. I say, every hour, "I love you—with all of me."

HE
turns to me and says, "You have no idea what it's like to be here, living with this fear, that I might die, that I won't be here for you."

TONSILLECTOMY.
I wait in the hospital room. After he was wheeled away to the surgery, I pace, I sit, I scratch notes, I half watch the television, I wait. I pace, I sit, I scratch notes, I half watch the television. I pray.

Then, I call my mother.

EAT.

After the surgery, he won't eat. The food scratches his raw and ravaged throat. I see pain in his eyes, desperation, exhaustion. I blend vegetables and protein powders, fruits, and organic coconut ice cream. He takes sips and sleeps. I wait until he has the energy to hold me close.

COMMUNITY.

Women bring food. Friends call and stop by. I write a letter to his ex-girlfriend. I say, "Things have changed. I am here if you have any questions or want to know what's going on in this process. I am here with an open heart. Light, love, Jeanine." She calls. She calls every day. She brings food, medicine, water. She wants to organize a fund-raiser. I cry for her generosity, her kindness, her open heart.

Cancer changes everything.

TREATMENT PLAN.

We are told the treatment plan by several different doctors at several different times, in what seems like several different languages, slowed tongues dripping out tales of caution for the caregiver. He will need radiation, five times a week, every day, for seven to nine weeks. During this process, he will need chemo, once every two weeks.

Watch for fever, for nutrition. Keep him eating. Watch for nausea, constipation, fever. Make sure he does not miss an appointment, skipping a treatment changes everything. If he becomes too weak, too tired, sick in any form, bring him to the hospital. If his fever reaches 100.5, bring him immediately to the emergency room. Do not wait. He won't have an immune system to fight off any infection. The infection is what kills most people being treated with chemotherapy for cancer. I watch, diligently, for any sign of fever, any sign of infection.

RADIATION ONCOLOGY.

I wonder about this nurse, the way she is looking at me, at him, mostly at him. I think she finds him attractive. And, she doesn't know what to make of us, me, the younger one. Him, the handsome man, with stage-four cancer. I wonder if she thinks I am his daughter, or his mistress, his sister maybe? But, she won't bring herself to call me his girlfriend, his wife, his partner.

We keep hearing the same instructions. This nurse says to him without making eye contact with me, "Force yourself to eat. It's going to be rough, but you can't afford to lose weight. You are skinny. You have to eat, even when food tastes awful, even when it burns, eat as much as you can."

Then, she turns on a video, a strange instruction video on the radiation process. A computer simulation of a person, without genitals, lies in the computer modulation of the radiation machine, then a red beam of light comes out of the machine, like a ray gun and penetrates the computer model. I giggle to myself, I want to turn to him and make light of the scenario. I want to make him laugh, but perhaps this isn't funny. The man next to us is in a walker, I wonder if he thinks it's funny. He isn't laughing, but holds his eyes open slightly. I wonder about them, both of them, watching this. I wonder how it might feel to know this radiation—that causes cancer—is the same thing that may cure them.

He is moved to the dentist's office. The dentist, oral surgeon, and gum specialist, all look at his teeth for possible cavities, teeth that could be a problem after the radiation, during the chemo, after the chemo when he won't have the immune system to keep his teeth to survive a possible infection. They decide not to pull teeth, but to keep them in. In the 20 years that he hasn't gone to the dentist, he only has two small cavities. I marvel at the strength of his teeth. When I was just ten, I had to have all of my teeth filled. I guess I was born with weak teeth, and he was born with the genetic possibility of cancer.

I walk back to the radiation office, to ask for a sooner appointment, to schedule our lives for the next three months. She calls me by the wrong name and then says on the phone to someone else, "Mr. Sterner's ... um, whatever she is to him, is here." I should offer my name again to her, our relationship, our love. I'm too tired and stressed to say anything. I smile and nod my head. She dismisses me easily and shuffles me out the door without further changes or instructions, except to come back once the dental work is done.

COMMUNION.

It's one of those perfect Topanga days, on the edge of the ocean, high in the mountains, the lush green mountains. As a typical Californian mountain girl, I float out of yoga class to get a carrot orange juice from the local café. Johnny is surfing at Topanga beach, and for now, I wait for him to come pick me up. It's almost surreal, the life we lead together. It's so new, only one year and six months into this relationship, and we have faced some difficult trials—the end of his past relationship, the opening into this one; the fact that women in this town love him, want him, want to be a part of him, his body; me asking for boundaries and wanting so much to trust him.

And as we fold together, in a strong communion, I still desire a child with him. Life has been throwing difficult curveballs our way, mostly now, it is the cancer that pushes at us, but ironically, it is the cancer that may strengthen our union.

This tepid September day beckons softness, a disposition of stillness and calm. The wind shifts the unfolding sweat from silk skin. I'm tired today, lulled into folding yawns and soft sips of breath. I don't really want to connect with anyone, but hide in the shades of an oak tree. With him. On the edge of the pond, at the top of a mountain, on the edge of the ocean. I want to feel him close, as close as bodies can get.

My friend passes me and waves, perhaps knowing I don't want to connect, she moves along. A crow caws, from across the pavement, and I realize, perhaps I am not supposed to push people away right now, but ask them to care for him, for me, for us—to tap into the strength of community and spirit I have desired for years. I have to remind myself to still extend myself in this time of difficulty. I need to give just a bit more. This giving is love.

He isn't back yet, but I can't blame him, he's in the water, with the wave and sun. An Avett Brothers song loops in my head—the one specific line, "If I live the life I am given, then I won't be scared to die."

A woman in an orange print skirt and tall boots struts out of the coffee shop. She sips her coffee, and I am aware of the way she throws her shoulders back with confidence.

An orange butterfly pulses through the air, full wing strut. I want to strut like that through this pain, through this fucking cancer. He will be ok. I will be ok. I don't know our future, not after my best friend, Caroline, an oncology RN, got on the phone with me and cried when I told her the prognosis. She gave his life a number of years, and I cried with her, for the first time, I cried with my entire belly.

Perhaps, this release shows me I don't feel safe enough with my friends here to really cry, to let it out, to find my voice in sadness and grief, as if showing this grief might offer up a death sentence. I have to stay strong, for them, for him. Perhaps, I have to stay strong for me. The crow caws again and flies across the parking lot. Another message, perhaps, or perhaps a song.

I can't lose myself in this cancer.

MARRY ME.
On the ride home, I see his reflection in the rearview mirror—his gray and black stubble frames his strong chin. My eyes move to his eyes, dark honey brown, with that perfect spark of kindness. He sees me looking at him. He sharply inhales, as if his breath was taken from him, then he smiles. "Oh wow," he says with soft joy and admiration. "I am going to marry you one day. I know it."

"Ah!" I laugh out, "That is the sweetest thing you have ever said to me, ever. I will remember this day, this rearview mirror forever." He laughs and says, "Me, too." Then his eyes move back to the road.

WAITING ROOM.
The front desk at Dental Service Reception bustles with phone calls and patients; nurses and doctors move in and out. There is always the veteran left in a wheelchair, sleeping, who waits to move to his next destination. I wonder about their caregivers, those that love them. Where are they? Why do they

wait here alone? How long will they wait? I wonder about those that served our country, how they are served, and treated, and honored on their return.

I wonder about the care in health care, the numbers, swarms, and volumes of people that need health care, to be cared for, to feel loved and honored, safe, and at home in their lives, in sickness and in health. And, I can't help but realize, without family, community, and friends that will care for you, the world, the earth, the local actions of the day-to-day mean very little.

HE

looks up from the small kitchen table. His long, toned six foot one inch-tall body fits cozily on the country kitsch green table that hugs the kitchen walls. He says, "Little by little, your brain numbs your knowing." I smile. I fumble for menial tasks to complete. "Are you listening?" he asks, as I walk towards the sliding glass door to pick up a stranded sock.

"Yes, I'm here," I assert as I move back into the kitchen to focus all my attention only on him, on his words. "Oh, I thought you were gone. Ok, the more I meditate on it—everyday, something happens, and I get a little more confidence. I'm making choices to get help. And, it lightens the load—a lot. Seeing Dr. H yesterday was a big one."

I smile and nod. He continues, "I'm super grateful."

Coyotes, a wild pack of them, howling and screeching as if they are tearing apart a poodle interrupt our conversation. Miles howls and barks loudly. I jump to close the door because I don't want him, my 13-year-old dog, to follow them into the night. Johnny looks at me wide-eyed, "That makes me want to run over there."

"Where?" I ask.

"Over there," and he is gone. Barefoot, running full speed up the hill of the lawn, into the woods, past the property line, chasing the howl of the coyote.

EPILOGUE

This story is not my story. It is his story, and subsequently as his primary caretaker, our story. This cancer narrative began only three months ago, and it is, for both of us, only beginning. This story will end before his treatments begin but will most likely be read in this edited volume, months after his treatments have stopped. By the time you read this, we will know if the cancer has been killed and he has been cured. By the time you read this, I may have (heaven forbid, and all angels and goddesses and gods, spirits here and otherwise, please keep him here with me) lost him.

This story isn't a simple story of place making, but making place with illness. Making place with illness is finding peace in the chaos, in the unease of liminality. We exist in what I call the *transitory radical*, a liminal space that moves us violently and locally from one "place" to another. The transitory radical is a liminal space that has no beginning, no clear ending, and yet is marked by the radical shift in perspective of place and desire. We stand on the jagged threshold, at the mercy of healing toxins and doctors, to move us from this place into another safely, soundly, and without permanent injury.

In the transitory radical, my focus shifted from the meta-level inter-sectional elements of identity to the sharply focused, day-to-day action of sustaining life. To survive the transitory radical, I mark the celebratory, everyday of interpersonal relationships (Pelias, 2011), the mundane (Holman Jones, 2005), and ordinary affects (Stewart, 2007) in autoethnographic research. The lived experience of illness happens in the place where bodies collide, learn, and relearn, try and try again. The transitory radical contorts our understanding of home. I order the house in waves of cleanliness. It needs to be clean to prevent infection, to keep the germs at bay. He orders his life in waves of nausea, pills, and visits from friends and loved ones. We aren't focused on place making, home building, or family making. We aren't focused on past subjectivities or identity politics outside or inside of the home. Our place is health-focused, conscious and insecure, painful and inflammatory, loving and fearful—for both of us. Even in this remaking of expectations within our home, it is still—albeit embedded with tension, stress, renegotiation of roles, and expectations—a place of love, of communion, of community.

This is in no way a simple negotiation of our embodied experience. The transitory radical creates rifts and mends seemingly gruesome relationship tears. Seemingly battered and strained relationships take different shape in our lives. Pains are forgiven, and unexpected relationships form—all in the effort of keeping him alive, and happy. Citing Kenneth Burke, Lynn Harter (2009) states, "Health care would be impossible if not for our human capacity to order and embody lived experience in narrative form.... Narratives, thus, represent 'equipment for living' sense making resources that allow individuals to size up circumstances and craft livable truths" (141). Perhaps then, even in its disorder, this piece will offer a new understanding of the transitory radical place of illness. Perhaps it will offer, "images of how to live well in the midst of inescapable suffering, trauma, and disability associated with the lived experience of illness" (Harter & Bochner, 2009, p. 114). As we move forward on our wellness trail, exist still in the transitory radical, we look both outward and inward, ethnographically and autoethnographically, to investigate communication between cancer patients, family members, and health care providers (National Institutes of Health, 2007; Schonwetter et. al, 2006; Tullis, 2010).

The local, in the minutiae, the seemingly ordinary moment is part of the construction and creation of our knowledges (Adams & Holman Jones, 2011; Noy, 2009). And yet, the local moments of the illness narrative within the transitory radical do not make sense. Illness incoherently reorders the sensible into nonsensical place making and marking in transition. The stories shift and move with the numb, the haze, and uncontrollable movements towards chaos into the terror of the possibility of losing the love of your life, of possibly losing your life. I write this story and the stories to follow with "concrete action, dialogue, emotion, embodiment, spirituality and self-consciousness" (Ellis, 2004, p. 38), to make it past and through the transitory radical, in order to narratively and emotionally stay alive.

References

Adams, T., & Holman Jones, S. (2011). Telling stories: Reflexivity, queer theory, and autoethnography. *Cultural Studies ↔ Critical Methodologies, 11,* 108–116.

Belling, C. (2010). Narrating oncogenesis: The problem of telling when cancer begins. *Narrative, 18*(2), 229–247.

Ellis, C. (2004). *The ethnographic I: A methodological novel about autoethnography.* Walnut Creek, CA: AltaMira Press.

Harter, L. (2009). Narratives as dialogic, contested, and aesthetic performances. *Journal of Applied Communication Research, 37*(2), 140–150.

Harter, L. M., & Bochner, A. P. (2009). Healing through stories: A special issue on narrative medicine. *Journal of Applied Communication, 37*(2), 113–117.

Holman Jones, S. (2005). Autoethnography: Making the personal political. In N. K. Denzin & Y. S. Lincoln (Eds.), *Handbook of qualitative research* 3d ed. (pp. 763–791). Thousand Oaks, CA: Sage.

National Institutes of Health (2007). *Patient-centered communication in cancer care: Promoting healing and reducing suffering.* U.S. Department of Health and Human Services.

Noy, C. (2009). On driving a car and being a family. In P. Vaninni (Ed.), *Material culture and technology in everyday life: Ethnographic approaches* (pp. 101–113). New York: Peter Lang.

Pelias, R. (2011). *Leaning: A poetics of personal relations.* Walnut Creek, CA: Left Coast Press, Inc.

Schonwetter, R. S., Roscoe, L. A., Nwosu, M., Zilka, B., & Kim, S. (2006). Quality-of-life and symptom control in hospice cancer patients receiving chemotherapy. *Journal of Palliative Medicine, 9,* 638–645.

Stewart, K. (2007). *Ordinary affects.* Durham, NC: Duke University Press.

Tullis, J. A. (2010). Bring about benefit, forestall harm: What communication studies says about spirituality and cancer care. *Asian Pacific Journal of Cancer Prevention, 11* (Middle East Cancer Consortium Supplement), 67–73.

CHAPTER TWO

Negating the Inevitable
An Autoethnographic Analysis of First-Generation College Student Status

Tabatha L. Roberts

*A*S A CHILD, I WAS RAISED IN SEVERAL APARTMENT COMPLEXES located in the southwest suburbs of Chicago. The suburbs are less "diverse" than the city. Many Chicagoans feel like suburban kids have it easy because we didn't grow up around gangs or in heavily populated areas. We are also assumed to be one of two evils, either we are more naive than our inner city counterparts, or we are financially privileged and take advantage of our parents' hard work. I hate those assumptions. I grew up in four apartment complexes surrounded by families that had been kicked out of the housing projects in the south and west sides of Chicago. Although these apartment complexes are located in one of the richest counties in the United States, they house poor, single mothers of several racial and ethnic backgrounds and their latchkey kids. These apartments also house gangbangers, drug dealers, sexual predators, and families trying to work their way up from lower-to-middle socioeconomic classes. I lived among these people. I am one of these people. I share some of the same stories as these people.

***

This essay is about my lived experiences as a first-generation college (FGC) student from a working-class background. I combine autoethnography and Weick, Sutcliffe, and Obstfeld's (2005) theory of organizational sensemaking to reflect on my diverse experiences and how they informed my development as an FGC graduate/student in the process of attaining a master's degree. By combining autoethnography with organizational sensemaking theory, I invite the reader to make sense of my personal development as I simultaneously make sense of my lived experiences. I offer a layered account autoethnography (Ronai, 1995), which interweaves my memories and reflections to exemplify the complex and evolutionary ways that my experiences with culture, social class, and power have impacted my positionality, development, identity negotiations, and status as a first-generation college student/graduate. As I examine these sociocultural topics, I am referring to intersectionality (Crenshaw, 1991), specifically how the intersections of my cultural identities have informed my understandings of power and my experiences with oppression within higher education institutions. Through the stages of the sensemaking framework, I revisit the unconventional path I took to higher education—from undergraduate to master's level—and reflect on particular moments and relational dilemmas that informed my choices.

"Negating the inevitable" means fighting against labels, stereotypes, and judgments. This chapter is not just about my path *in* higher education as a first-generation college student—it is about my path leading *to* higher education and the stages of sensemaking I have experienced *because* of it. This chapter is also about the things life taught me before I went back to school. It is about who I was, who I am becoming, and who I will be. It is about negations and possibilities. Most importantly, this chapter is in response to those researchers and teachers who are convinced that first-generation college students won't make it (at worst) or will only make it against seemingly insurmountable odds (at best) (Terenzini, Springer, Yaeger, Pascarella, & Nora, 1996).

I wrote the following poem as an undergraduate student to demonstrate the powerful affects that culture and interpersonal relationships have on the development of a first-generation college (FGC) student.

***

I am

*A daughter, born to a single mother, who is the youngest of 7; the strongest
person I know
I am the "only child" to everyone else, but a sister to someone I've never met
I am spoiled even though my mother struggled for most of my young years
I am unable to explain it, but I am aware of what drugs are, what they
look like, and how they affect my father, at age 4
I am, at age 5, also aware of what a crack house looks like, how "hypes" react over the pipe,
and I am a new friend to a boy who is also stuck in the bedroom coloring on the wall
I am unable to tell my mother the events of my weekends with "daddy"
I am still in awe of him
I am older and no longer feel like it's okay to be absent in your daughter's life
I am bitter, mean, and absent in his
I am accepting of the drug world and most of my friends do them in high school*

48

I am a raver, a pot-head, a mixture of Pink Floyd and Rhythm and Blues
I am confused when pot turns into heroin and my friends are no longer experimenting
but are addicted
I am exposed to an "epidemic" of bratty suburban drug users and I am thankful my
conscience is too strong to participate
I am a 17-year-old drop out with a G.E.D.
I am no longer accepting the darkness that is my past
I am, instead, aware that it is up to me to make decisions, and I am confident that I am
capable of success
I am one of five national 1st place award winners in Philadelphia for comedic public
speaking
I am proud, blown away, and more confident than I have ever been in my entire life
I am, again, reminded of my past
I am a god mother to a boy whose mother, my cousin, has forgotten him for the "snake bite"
of the needle
I am hiding my purse at Christmas
I am angry that at 25 this is happening to her, when it should've been in high school
when it was normal to be a moron!
I am pissed as hell at her absence in his life
I am aware that I hate her for her actions, love her for the person she is deep down
inside, but I will never respect her for allowing the venom to turn her into a devil
I am at a wake for her sponsor
I am at a wake for grandma
I am at a wake for my best friend whose heart stopped working at 24 because the
venom that used to run through his veins stopped the blood flow to his heart
I am a woman with no faith
I am aware that I have no answers to the scariest questions in the world
I am trying to be strong with my soul feeling empty
I am loved by the people who help me get through it
I am a daughter to a single mother who's the most amazing woman I know
I am a daughter to a father who has been clean now for over 10 years
I am still spoiled even though I try not to be
I am grateful for the opportunities I have had, the privileges I have been exposed to, the
stages in my life that I have learned from, and the people in my life that have guided
me through it all
I am a strong woman with a strong belief in herself
I am eventually going to have faith
I am eventually going to answer some questions
I am aware that because I am who I am …

I am going to be anything I want to be.

***

I wrote this poem while I was a student at a private college in Illinois. The class was Intercultural Communication, and it was one of the first classes I enrolled in after my transfer from a local community college. At the time of my transfer, I was a 25-year-old, full-time bartender and part-time undergraduate student. I had spent the previous five years figuring out my place in higher education and the world.

The poem was written for an assignment titled "I am." The premise of the assignment was to tell a story about yourself that described different aspects of your identity. I was excited about the assignment, but I worried about being judged by my professor for sharing personal information. I had always been open about my life with my friends, but what would a stranger think of me? I struggled with how I was going to explain myself without telling my story. The parts of the poem that spoke of sadness, confusion, disappointment, and heartache were temporary. Even as an undergraduate I knew that one day I would "find the answers" to the scary questions. Looking back, I realize that the scary questions were related to my path in higher education. I didn't fit in. *What was I doing there? Why didn't my professors appreciate my point of view? How was I going to get through it? How was I going to make change?*

***

I was poor growing up. My father was a drug addict. My mother raised me by herself. Neither of my parents graduated high school. I was a high school dropout. These lived experiences paint a grim picture for a young woman who is the first in her family to enter college. If I had asked a student affairs expert or a scholar publishing in higher education journals about my future in college, they would have warned me of the difficulties ahead. They would say that because I am a first-generation college student I am at a higher risk of dropping out my first year (Ishitani, 2003). They would tell me that because I am Hispanic and born to a low-income family, I have a higher likelihood of dropping out of college altogether (Braxton, Duster, & Pascarella, 1988). They would remind me that because my parents never attended college, I have a lack of cultural capital or low SES (socioeconomic status), so I am "at risk in nearly every step on the path to college, including completing high school, expecting a college degree, acquiring college qualifications, receiving parental encouragement, and understanding the college application and financial aid process" (Wells & Lynch, 2012, pp. 674–675). Accordingly, they would take two factors of my SES—parental education and parental occupation—and pair them with my other cultural identity markers, such as my race, ethnicity, and gender, and tell me that others like me have a lower college attrition rate than traditional students (Ishitani, 2006; Pascarella & Chapman, 1983; Pascarella & Terenzini, 1978, 1980). But what they wouldn't be able to explain about my future or educational path is that statistics do not define me. My parents did not graduate high school or attend college, but their lived experiences have influenced my life choices and my decision to continue my formal education. No one could have predicted that my father's drug addiction and experiences with depression would focus me. There are no quantitative methodologies that could explain how my mother's struggles with single-motherhood would motivate me. *I will not recycle my parents' mistakes or misfortunes. I will not add to these statistics. I will represent first-generation college students in a new light. I will write a new story.*

***

My mother gave birth to my sister when she was 15 and had me when she was 19. My mother raised me but gave my sister up for adoption at the insistence of her parents. My grandparents set up a private adoption when they realized my mother was pregnant, forcing her to give her child away. I was nine when I found out I had an older sister somewhere. Discovering this news made me think of my mother in new ways. As a child, I thought that my mother was the strongest person in the world, but as I got older, I started to understand that my mother was human.

***

My mother has two innate characteristics—patience and forgiveness. These qualities have enabled her to keep people in her life that are toxic—especially men. All of the men my mother married or dated were addicts. My father, who for the majority of my life was addicted to crack cocaine, was no different. It is because of him that my mother raised me by herself. After my father, she dated several men with addiction problems—including a recovering alcoholic, who she married and now shares her life with. For years, my mother dealt with my stepfather's addiction. We would find liquor bottles hidden in our kitchen cabinets. My stepfather would fall down the stairs in his underwear. He got in a car accident with my friends and me in the car when he was drunk. She never left.

***

It has always been difficult to talk to my mother about the details of her life. The facts of my sister's adoption, for example, have always been unclear. I was also never allowed to ask my grandparents about the adoption process. My family treated the situation as if it never happened. But I couldn't accept that fate for my sister, my mother, or myself. As young as I can remember, I was always open about my life and my family's struggles. And although my transparency negatively affected my reputation in particular social circles (especially high school), I never allowed myself to keep things hidden. My openness enabled me and my mother to build a strong relationship and has inspired her to gain independence from her parents. I began a search for my sister when I was 15. Last year my mother gathered the courage to join me in the search. We are now reunited with my sister, and for the first time in her life, my mother is free from my grandparents' constraints.

***

One of the major lessons I learned from my mother's lived experiences is to never allow anyone to dictate my life. Whether it is a man, a teacher, or a parent, I make my own decisions. I choose my path in life. But watching my mother work as hard as she did to raise me by herself is what inspired me to *stay* in college. I made the decision to continue my education because I didn't want to be a single mother. I didn't want to make the same choices in men. Education gave me the tool to become a better person and motivated me to change the direction of my life. I am the first person in my family to attend college, and my mother is my biggest supporter. She and I have grown up together.

***

My father is one of five. In 1997 his sister was murdered. Her body was found tied up in a suitcase in the Chicago River. Both of my uncles have been to prison. My father's childhood reminds me that prejudice and racism still exist. His story shows me what my life might have looked like if I traveled down the same broken road.

***

My father dropped out of high school in the ninth grade. He joined a gang and became a crack cocaine addict in his later teens. I believe some of his childhood experiences contributed to his poor choices. When he was young, he was locked inside his bedroom by his brother's father and was forced to watch him beat my grandmother until she was unconscious. He uses this story as a justification for being absent in my life. He tells me about his childhood experiences to remind me how lucky I am.

***

My father lived in Skokie, Illinois, during his elementary school years. The population in Skokie was mainly Jewish, and my father experienced a lot of discrimination from his teachers and friends because he was Puerto Rican. He felt pushed out of the school system because of his ethnicity.

After my father dropped out of high school, he found haven in the streets on the west side of Chicago. However, after several stints in jail he felt that there was more to life than gangbanging and drug use, so he decided to give high school a second chance. In an oral communication class he was assigned to give a speech about his life. He chose to talk about his experiences in jail and the meaning of his tattoos. He received a bad grade. His teacher claimed that the topics he discussed were inappropriate, and she belittled his confidence. He felt judged because of his life path. He dropped out of high school again and never went back.

***

I wonder what my father's life would have looked like if his teacher recognized he was trying to turn his life around. I wonder what kind of grade she would have given him if she knew about his family life growing up and privileged his experience. I wonder if my earliest memories of spending time with my father would have been different if he would have been treated differently. I was five.

***

Strolling down the dark hallway I'm holding my father's hand tightly. I am in an unfamiliar place. The ceilings are high and a dark wood color. As we enter the room a woman is violently shaking back and forth in an old rocking chair. Her head is slightly bent toward her breasts. Her skin is dark mahogany, and her eyes are yellow and hollow. I notice that her hand has been amputated.

I look up, "Daddy, why is that lady missing her hand?"

"Because, Tabby, she fell asleep on it and lost all the blood circulation to her hand."

***

When I asked him about that woman later in my life, he told me she shot heroin in her veins for so long that a doctor had to amputate her hand. He also told me that when he returned to the crack house later that week, he found her shot to death.[1]

***

As we pass the unfortunate woman, there are dozens of men fighting in the kitchen. The lights are faded to a dim yellow, and I can't make out what the conflict is about. Daddy pushes my butt and tells me to go to the bedroom; he will come get me when he is done. On my way to the room I watch to see what is going on. I realize that the men are fighting over a crack pipe. My dad joins them in the kitchen and makes his way into the crowd. There is a little boy with a curly afro in the bedroom. He is standing on the bed, coloring on the wall. I stand on the bed next to him, and we begin jumping up and down, drawing circles of blue and purple on the dingy walls. I had fun that weekend with Daddy.

***

My cousin is a heroin addict. Her story is intertwined with mine. She was like my sister growing up. She was older than me, but I felt sorry for her because her father didn't show her love and her mother was/is an epileptic who had to financially depend on men. My cousin got lost in the mix.

When we were kids, she was teased a lot. She had buckteeth and cross–eyes, and I spent many summers in my dress shoes, beating up the kids in our apartment complex for calling her names. We lost our innocence together as children, and then in high school, we experimented with drugs, partied our asses off, and dropped out of school. After she had a baby, something changed. She began using heroin, and I saw—for the first time as an adult—my childhood being replayed through her son's life. She was everything I hated about my father.

***

I think my innocence was stolen from me. Even today it is hard for me to admit the things I have done. I was young, and I saw a lot, but it wasn't even half of what other people I knew were experiencing. I lost my innocence through their lives. Through their pain, I connected with a world I didn't understand, and to this day, do not understand. I was nine when I drank my first beer, smoked my first cigarette, kissed my first boy, and lied about my age. The constant moving from apartment complex to apartment complex made it impossible to keep any friends. Looking back, however, those apartment complexes were all located in the same town, but my nine-year-old mind imagined them being long distances away. Each new complex added a new layer to my identity. Each new complex made it possible to be another person. I met more and more impoverished, damaged young bodies. These people helped define who I was. Their stories are enmeshed in my childhood. As I reflect on those years, the more entangled the stories become. When you're young, nothing matters but the people you see every day. Every time Sonja's mom smacked her upside the head, I felt it. Every time Courtney's mom drank herself into oblivion and called her a piece of shit, I cried with her. Every time Casey shoved a needle in her arm to hide the pain of her father's drug addiction, I was there to hold her. But I was also engrossed in it all. I provided the vein when hers stopped working. I got high to keep from wasting the poison. I lost my innocence living their lives.

***

I made different choices when I decided to be my own person. Once I started college, I began to find my own power, but I quickly realized that I was not like other students. As an FGC student from a working-class background, I was different. I was an outsider. I didn't understand hierarchy or why professors had the title of Dr. in front of their name. At the community college I attended, I befriended most of my teachers. When I transferred to the private college, I assumed I would build similar relationships. However, I discovered in a meeting with one of my professors that the title of Dr. separated me from my teachers. When I sat down in one of my professor's offices, she told me that my voice should always be lower than a professor's. She told me that I should research my professors because most of them are experts in their field. She also told me that I should be careful of how I was building my reputation in the communication department. It was obvious that she had heard about me from other professors. From that day on I learned how to play the game in academia. I started to understand why my father dropped out of school. I began to understand the power of labels.

***

Researchers have used a variety of labels to describe first-generation college students since the 1980s. For instance, researchers use descriptors such as *at-risk* (Educational Resources Information Center, 1987), *underprepared* (Bartholomae, 1985; Rose, 1989), *nontraditional* (Query, Parry, & Flint, 1992), and/or *socially or economically disadvantaged* (Lippert, Titsworth, & Hunt, 2005). Johnson (1994) contends that "*high risk students* first appeared in the Educational Resources Information Center's (ERIC) (1987) *Thesaurus of ERIC descriptors* in 1980 ... as 'students, with normal intelligence, whose academic background or prior performance may cause them to be perceived as candidates for future academic failure or early withdrawal'" (p. 35). Further, the U.S. Department of Education's National Longitudinal Study (as cited in Engle, Bermeo, & O'Brien, 2003) describes first-generation college students as "more likely to be female, older, African American or Hispanic, have dependent children, and come from lower-income families" (p. 14). First-generation college students are presumed to be less prepared than their "traditional" counterparts (Chen, 2005). Research (e.g., Berkner & Chavez, 1997; Engle, et al. 2003; Vargas, 2004) indicates that such students are less prepared because they have lower aspirations for college, they lack the social support to plan for college, and they cannot afford the cost of college.

***

I am a half-Hispanic, half-white *graduate* student who dropped out of high school. When I dropped out of high school I joined the National Guard. Before going to boot camp, I tested and passed the G.E.D. and began studying at a local community college. It was there that I began to see the value of education. It was there that I gained confidence in myself. I was 17 when I walked into my first communication class. My professor was funny, young, vibrant, and full of life. He saw potential in me and asked me to join the speech team. I began performing poetry, drama, and comedy. At a forensics competition in Philadelphia, I performed a comedic public speech about the lack of Latino leaders. Suddenly, I was one of five first-place award winners in the country. I was on top of the world.

***

After five years at the community college, I transferred to a private college and was assigned a temporary transfer advisor in administration. Her role was to map out my educational career and introduce me to my departmental advisor. Instead of placing me in a sophomore-level class, my transfer advisor placed me in a 400 (upper) level class in media criticism during my first semester. The professor, "Dr. Milihan" was the director of the department. Interestingly, he had also been a judge at several of my speech competitions while I was in community college.

Dr. Milihan had a reputation. According to other students and faculty, he was very traditional and strict. As the semester began, I noticed that he did not seem to like me. I assumed he was frustrated because I was overwhelmed with the upper-level class and was experiencing difficulty learning rhetorical concepts. In an attempt to ease the tension, I used information I gathered about him to reach him on a more personal level. For instance, I had to write an abstract on an article for one of the first assignments in class. In an effort to build solidarity I decided to write a feminist criticism on the content. My attempts to impress him failed. In fact, my assignment was graded less than average.

Dr. Milihan advised me to sign up for his office hours to discuss my future in his class. When I entered his office, he immediately began questioning my educational background. He started by asking "*what is your grade point average?*" When I explained that my grade point average was 3.9, he responded with "*no, I'm not asking what your GPA was at the community college—what is your grade point average here?*" I was stunned! I didn't understand why he was questioning my answer, nor did I understand why I had to convince him I was telling the truth. He then proceeded to look at my personal information and ask me about my goals. When I told him I was interested in teaching communication courses at a community college, he snarled and rolled his eyes. When I asked him why he responded that way he said: "*I always have problems with transfer students from community colleges. Their education is inadequate, and instructors from community colleges do not prepare their students to transfer to esteemed colleges like this one. We have to work harder for students like you. And frankly, I don't get paid enough to deal with this. In my opinion, students who start off as freshmen in a four-year school are more successful and prepared for difficult classes.*"

***

For the first time in my life, I felt class. I didn't know what it was called at the time, or what it meant, but what I was experiencing was class discrimination. I came from a working-class background. Not only was I the only one in my family to attend college, but I was unable to afford the tuition for a university. After I paid for community college, the only option I had to afford my bachelor's degree was relying on grants and transfer scholarships awarded based on my grades. I knew I could succeed in his class, but I had no idea how to convince him that I was a good student.

***

It wasn't just my working-class roots that produced this discrimination. Dr. Milihan is a white male scholar. I was a young Hispanic undergraduate student. His discriminatory comments did not stem solely from my choice in schools or his acknowledgment that I was in a low-income tax bracket. Although I am not sure which of my identities troubled him (i.e., my age, sex, or ethnicity), it was at that moment that the intersections of my identity were working against me. However, if he would have asked me about my story, I could have given him some insight into the hard work that it took me to get to a private college. I could have told him that I had struggled with my father's drug addiction and my mother's choices in men. If he would have listened to where I came from, he would have realized that I needed to go to a community college because I couldn't afford expensive tuition. He would have known that my grade point average enabled me to get the scholarships I got—and he would have appreciated my accomplishments at the community college. But instead, he relied on stereotypes. He compared my working-class background and my prior education to those of students who were succeeding in his classes.

***

Studies have shown that first-generation college students are not the only students unprepared for college level courses (Murphy & Hicks, 2006; Orbe, 2004; Putman & Thompson, 2006). Accordingly, many students find that their FGC status gives them a sense of pride and motivates them to act as role models for their siblings and fellow students (Orbe & Groscurth, 2004). Attaining a college degree for many first-generation college students means taking "the first step toward a better future" (Putman & Thompson, 2006, p. 134) and involves making a choice for a better life. Those who come from working-class backgrounds/neighborhoods also find haven in motivating their community by sharing their collegiate experiences (Orbe, 2004; Orbe & Groscurth, 2004). When compared with non-first-generation college students, studies have shown that FGC students had the same expectations to obtain higher level degrees (Murphy & Hicks, 2006; Somers, Woodhouse, & Cofer, 2004). Students who do find it difficult to transition into college often comment on the low quality of high schools they attended prior to their college experience, while others reported having inadequate guidance from teachers and advisors in college (Engle et al., 2003).

***

I left Dr. Milihan's office and convinced myself that higher education wasn't for me. Having a highly esteemed professor tell you that you are not worth his time is disconcerting, to say the least. College should have been the place that helped me develop, but at the time it was darker than the crack houses I visited with my father. When I called my mother and told her what happened she encouraged me to stay in school. "Forget about him. He won't matter after you graduate."

***

After I completed Dr. Milihan's class, much of the confidence that I had gained in my academic abilities vanished. However, during my second semester I took two classes—a women's studies course and a communication theory course. Each class was taught by a feminist professor, and the curriculum and readings they chose to use for these classes enabled me to slowly rebuild my tarnished self. For example, muted group theory (Ardener, 1975) and co-cultural theory (Orbe, 1998) led me to a path of healing by lending me theoretical language to explain my experiences. I realized that in order to graduate, I had to strategically communicate with my professors to appease the power dynamics at play.

***

Writing the "I Am" poem was the first time I enacted (i.e., labeled with meaning) who I was within the context of the academy (Weick, 1995; Weick et al., 2005). It was the first time that I was honest about my past. Accordingly, the poem presents the first stage of *enactment* in Weick et al.'s (2005) notion of sensemaking as an intraorganizational evolution that begins with the process of categorizing discrepancies in normal everyday life circumstances. For me, these *discrepancies* (addiction, loss of hope, discrimination, and other barriers) were there all along, but I didn't understand how they affected my position within the academy or my status as a first-generation college student. I also did not understand how to emancipate myself from them. The second stage of Weick et al. (2005) is the evolutionary process of *selection* (writing about my experiences in college). By writing about these experiences, I am partaking in a "combination of retrospective attention, mental models, and articulation [by] perform[ing] a narrative reduction of the bracketed material [I discussed in the enactment stage] to generate a locally plausible story" (p. 414). In other words, as I write about my experiences through autoethnography, I am creating a new story; one that provides the framework for my commitment to help other FGC students and also for the third stage of the evolutionary process—*retention*. According to Weick et al. (2005), "when a plausible story is retained, it tends to become more substantial because it is related to past experience, connected to significant identities, and used as a source of guidance for further action and interpretation" (p. 414). Hopefully this chapter will be a source of guidance for other students—FGC or not—to work against the labels others impose on their identities.

58

***

For me, and many others, college offered a way to rethink my "identities and reconfigure them in new ways" (Azmitia, Syed, & Radmacher, 2008, p. 11) and the "I Am" poem was the first time I began to see myself within the context of an organizational structure. However, the part of my identity that is a first-generation college student did not become salient until I entered my master's program (Azmitia et al., 2008; Orbe, 2004; 2008). Being a first-generation *graduate* student has helped me realize that my story reflects the experiences of other first-generation college students. I was born to a lower-income family (Engle et al., 2003), I dropped out of high school (Bartholomae, 1985), my parents never went to college or didn't finish high school (Chen, 2005), and I relied on governmental funding to pay for college (Berkner & Chavez, 1997; Engle, et al. 2003; Vargas, 2004). But having the unique positionality as both a teacher and FGC graduate student has focused my attention to a more engaged pedagogy (Pensoneau-Conway, 2009), and my experiences during undergrad have helped me understand the type of teacher I *don't* want to be. I want students to have a safe space to learn without constraint. Additionally, I want teachers and students to theorize difference (Warren, 2008) instead of relying on stereotypes. I want the classroom to be the site where teacher and student simultaneously learn and grow together (Fassett & Warren, 2007).

***

Reflecting on my diverse lived experiences has been an empowering process, allowing me the opportunity to give "power to" (Bate & Bowker, 1997) myself and others. Personally, this process of sensemaking and autoethnography means taking a critical step toward forging a new identity; an identity that involves giving agency to other FGC students so they might come to understand their own positionalities and identities in the academy.

Note

1. On a return visit to the crack house days later the author's father discovered the dead bodies of the woman with the amputated hand and other addicts he used drugs with. They had all been murdered. Though at the time she did not distinguish the crack house from any other place she visited with her father, she recognizes in retrospect that her father's addiction put both of their lives at risk.

References

Ardener, S. (1975). *Perceiving women.* New York: John Wiley & Sons, Inc.

Azmitia, M., Syed, M., & Radmacher, K. (2008). On the intersection of personal and social identities: Introduction and evidence from a longitudinal study of emerging adults. *The Intersections of Personal and Social Identities. New Directions for Child and Adolescent Development, 120,* 1–16.

Bartholomae, D. (1985). Inventing the university. In M. Rose (Ed.), *When a writer can't write* (pp. 134–165). New York: Guilford.

Bate, B., & Bowker, J. (1997). *Communication and the sexes* (2d ed.). Prospect Heights, IL: Waveland Press, Inc.

Berkner, L., & Chavez, L. (1997). *Descriptive summary of 1995–96 beginning postsecondary students: Six years later.* Washington, DC: National Center for Education Statistics.

Braxton, J. M., Duster, M., & Pascarella, E. T. (1988). Causal modeling and path analysis: An introduction and an illustration in student attrition research. *Journal of College Student Development, 29,* 263–272.

Chen, X. (2005). *First-generation students in postsecondary education: A look at their college transcripts.* Washington, DC: National Center for Educational Statistics.

Crenshaw, K. (1991). Mapping the margins: Intersectionality, identity politics, and violence against women of color. *Stanford Law Review, 43,* 1241–1299.

Educational Resources Information Center (ERIC). (1987). *Thesaurus of ERIC descriptors.* Phoenix, AZ: Oryz.

Engle, J., Bermeo, A., & O'Brien, C. (2003). *Straight from the source: What works for first-generation college students.* Washington, DC: The Pell Institute for the Study of Opportunity in Higher Education.

Fassett, D. L., & Warren, J. T. (2007). *Critical communication pedagogy.* Thousand Oaks, CA: Sage.

Ishitani, T. T. (2003). A longitudinal approach to assessing attrition behavior among first-generation college students: Time-varying effects of pre-college characteristics. *Research in Higher Education, 44,* 433–449.

Ishitani, T. T. (2006). Studying attrition and degree completion behavior among first-generation college students in the United States. *Journal of Higher Education, 77,* 861–885.

Johnson, G. M. (1994). An ecological framework for conceptualizing educational risk. *Urban Education, 29,* 34–49. doi: 10.1177/0042085994029001004

Lippert, L. R., Titsworth, B. S., & Hunt, S. K. (2005). The ecology of academic risk: Relationships between communication apprehension, verbal aggression, supportive communication, and students' academic risk statuses. *Communication Studies, 56,* 1–21.

Murphy, C. G., & Hicks, T. (2006). Academic characteristics among first-generation and non-first-generation college students. *Faculty Working Papers from the School of Education, Paper 8.* http://digitalcommons.uncfsu.edu/soe_faculty_wp/8

Orbe, M. P. (1998). From the standpoint(s) of traditionally muted groups: Explicating a co-cultural communication theoretical model. *Communication Theory, 8,* 1–26.

Orbe, M. P. (2004). Negotiating multiple identities within multiple frames: An analysis of first-generation college students. *Communication Education, 53,* 131–149. doi: 0363452010001682401

Orbe, M. P. (2008). Theorizing multidimensional identity negotiation: Reflections on the lived experiences of first-generation college students. *New Directions for Child and Adolescent Development, 120,* 81–95.

Orbe, M. P., & Groscurth, C. R. (2004). A co-cultural theoretical analysis of communicating on campus and at home: Exploring the negotiation strategies of first generation college (FGC) students. *Qualitative Research Reports in Communication, V,* 41–47.

Pascarella, E. T., Chapman, D. (1983). A multi-institutional path analytical validation of Tinto's model of college withdrawal. *American Educational Research Journal, 20,* 87–102.

Pascarella, E. T., & Terenzini, P. (1978). The relation of students' precollege characteristics and freshman year experience to voluntary attrition. *Research in Higher Education, 9,* 347–366.

Pascarella, E. T., & Terenzini, P. (1980). Predicting freshman persistence and voluntary dropout decisions from a theoretical model. *Journal of Higher Education, 51*, 60–75.

Pensoneau-Conway, S. (2009). Desire and passion as foundations for teaching and learning: A pedagogy of the erotic. *Basic Communication Course Annual, 21*, 173–206.

Putman, A., & Thompson, S. (2006). Paving the way: First-generation Mexican American community college students in a border community speaking out. *International and Intercultural Communication Annual, 29*, 121–142.

Query, J. M., Parry, D., & Flint, L. J. (1992). The relationship among social support, communication competence, and cognitive depression for nontraditional students. *Journal of Applied Communication, 20*, 78–94.

Ronai, C. R. (1995). Multiple reflections of child sex abuse: An argument for a layered account. *Journal of contemporary ethnography, 23*, 395–426.

Rose, M. (1989). *Lives on the boundary: The struggles and achievements of America's underprepared.* New York: The Free Press.

Somers, P., Woodhouse, S., & Cofer, J. (2004). Pushing the boulder uphill: The persistence of first-generation college students. *NASPA Journal, 41*, 418–435.

Terenzini, P., Springer, L., Yaeger, P., Pascarella, E., & Nora, A. (1996). First-generation college students: Characteristics, experiences, and cognitive development. *Research in Higher Education, 37*, 1–22.

Vargas, J. H. (2004). *College knowledge: Addressing information barriers to college.* Boston, MA: The Education Resources Institute (TERI).

Warren, J. T. (2008). Performing difference: Repetition in context. *Journal of International and Intercultural Communication, 1*, 290–308.

Weick, K. E. (1995). *Sensemaking in organizations.* Thousand Oaks, CA: Sage.

Weick, K. E., Sutcliffe, K. M., & Obstfeld, D. (2005). Organizing and the process of sensemaking. *Organizational Science, 16*, 409–421.

Wells, R. S., & Lynch, C. M. (2012). Delayed college entry and the socioeconomic gap: Examining the roles of student plans, family income, parental education, and parental occupation. *Journal of Higher Education, 83*, 671–697.

CHAPTER THREE

Post–Coming Out Complications

Tony E. Adams

C OMING OUT—THE ACT OF DISCLOSING AN OFTEN-INVISIBLE AND stigmatized identity—can be a turbulent interactional event (Defenbaugh, 2011; Myers, 2012). There are complications in deciding how and when to disclose, and there may be a variety of dilemmas tied to the disclosure process (Adams, 2011; Barton, 2012; Gray, 2009). Out-ness is not a one-time affair but is instead contingent upon relationship: I may be out as gay with my mother but not with the cashier at the grocery store; I may be out to some of my students but not all of them; and I may be out to my neighbor but not out to my neighbor's cousin (see Halley, 1989; Sedgwick, 1990). While coming out is often a canonical and sometimes scarring event for persons with same-sex attraction, the turbulence and uncertainty within relationships tied to this attraction does not end with the initial disclosure; as Burgess (2005) observes, just because a person comes out about her or his same-sex attraction does not mean that the attraction will no longer be an issue.

For instance, in *Narrating the Closet: An Autoethnography of Same-Sex Attraction* (Adams, 2011), I describe the family situation of James, an interviewee from an earlier project who stopped visiting his parents' home after telling them that he identified as gay (1988). During the times when he did visit, they heavily monitored his activities: They prohibited him from using regular dinnerware, instead requiring that he use "paper cups and paper plates and plastic silverware" (p. 23), and when he would use the bathroom, his mom would make sure to spray Lysol disinfectant on everything that he touched. Initially, James tolerated their ignorant reactions because he had come out to his parents at a time when HIV/AIDS was misunderstood and at a time when being gay was synonymous with having the disease. However, such monitoring practices continued, and James stopped going home; he was tired of tolerating his parents' ignorance and dismissive treatment.

I also described the experience of Dave, another interviewee, who had to tell his mother numerous times that he identified as gay (Adams, 2011, pp. 125–126). Dave initially came out to her in 1996, but in 2000 she asked him if he had a girlfriend; he reminded her that he identified as gay. In 2003, she asked him if he was dating any women; he told her again that he found men attractive. In 2007 and in 2008, she asked about Dave's attraction to women and, each time, Dave reminded her about his same-sex attraction. Even though Dave came out to his mother in 1996, her repeated questioning indicates denial about or dismissal of his stated sexuality. As of this writing, Dave continues to find innovative ways of telling his mom about his attraction and about his past relationships with men with the hope of not being surprised by her heteronormative questions and erroneous assumptions.

Others have described life after coming out as well. Wright (2011) notes how his sexuality, post–coming out, "continues to obstruct" the relationship he has with his parents (p. 78); Fox (2010) describes processes of having to repeatedly come out to his father who, suffering from Alzheimer's disease, continues to ask Fox if he has met "any nice, Jewish girls" (p. 8); and Waugh (2009) tells about his mother who, also suffering from Alzheimer's, continues to ask him about finding a wife. Cooper (2010) writes about how some mothers, post–coming out, may now have to worry about their kids being harassed about their mothers' same-sex attraction, and Glave (2005) writes about post–coming out situations with once-close heterosexual friends, situations such as the tensing up by these friends when same-sex attraction is mentioned (especially around children!), the cringe on these friends' faces when he calls his (same-sex) partner "Honey" or "Sweetie," and how, after disclosing his same-sex attraction, they would then rarely ask about his dating experiences or his meaningful and intimate relationships with men.

In this project, I further investigate the characteristics of relationships *after* the disclosure of same-sex attraction, what I term *post–coming out complications*—those moments of distress and the unexpected disdain that can emerge in a relationship *after* the initial coming out act. For instance, I am interested in the complications that emerge in the relationship I have with my mother and father *after* telling them that I am gay, the complications that emerge with other family members *after* they learn about my sexuality, and the possible moments of tension and conflict that occur with others *after* they learn about my intimate and meaningful relationships with men. I tell four stories that illustrate post–coming out complications among my family members, and I analyze each story in terms of the relational impact it has on myself and on the particular other(s). I conclude with suggestions about maneuvering post–coming out complications as well as describe how these complications have thrust me into a kind of queer melancholy, especially in relationship to my family.

63

Before continuing, I must make two qualifications. First, I do not want to suggest that coming out about same-sex attraction is no longer important, but rather that the struggles tied to this attraction, at least for some relationships, do not end once coming out happens; the struggles of same-sex attraction may continue to perpetually complicate the lesbian, gay, bisexual, or queer person's relations with certain others. Second, I focus on the relational *complications* post–coming out rather than the calm and happy moments in a relationship after such a disclosure. This focus is intentional: With most of my writing, I try to make sense of difficult relational experiences—experiences that I do not understand and experiences that need to be changed. While I have experienced many good times post–coming out, and while there may be some satisfying moments in the relationships I describe, the critical thrust in my writing directs me toward experiences of harm and concern; I write to help make difficult relationships better.

Complicating Family I

December 2006. I travel from Tampa, Florida, to Danville, Illinois (my hometown), with Terry, my then-boyfriend, who members of my family had not yet met.

Jane, my aunt and my father's sister, was one of my favorite relatives. She always supported me through difficult adolescent times, and, when I came out to Jane in 2002, she provided me with much-needed affirmation and support. She encouraged me to tell other family members about my sexuality, and she phoned often, usually once every two weeks. I remember us talking about the irrationality of homophobia. I never thought that her once-supportive stance would change.

"Hi, Jane!" I say on the phone. "Terry and I are driving through Atlanta. We should be in Danville tomorrow. We can't wait to see you and your new house!"

"Hi, Tony," she responds, unenthusiastically. "Have you told your dad where you are?"

"Yes," I answer. "He knows that we'll arrive tomorrow. I can't wait to see you and your new house—and I can't wait for you to meet Terry!"

Silence.

"Drive safely," she says. "I'm sure your dad will be glad to see you."

"Umm … thanks," I reply. "I'm sure he will be glad to see us, too. Good-bye."

"Good-bye," she mumbles.

I thought nothing of the awkward interaction until I arrived at Danville and talked with my father. He told me that Jane and Mike, her husband, did not want Terry and me to visit them; they didn't approve of the "gay lifestyle" and did not want gay men in their house.

Post–coming out complications: While I perceived Jane as once accepting of me when I came out, my perception changed a few years later. Jane and I still talk occasionally, about once every other month, but we have never been as close as we once were; our relationship has changed in new and painful ways, and my sexuality has fractured our relationship. As of this writing (2013), she still has never met Jerry, my partner of more than five years.

Complicating Family II

May 2010. While attending a conference near Danville, my father picked me up at my hotel so that we could have dinner. Since I had eaten a large lunch and probably would not have much to eat, I told him that he could choose the restaurant. He chose Hooters—a restaurant that features scantily clad female servers and a large male clientele, and a restaurant that celebrates objectification, sexual desire, and heterosexuality.

Once seated, the server comes to our table, rubs my back, and sits on my lap, all the while talking with my dad. I become uncomfortable, not because of the abrupt intimacy and invasion of my personal space by a stranger, but because the hypersexualized context and my complicity in the server's intimate actions might mark me as heterosexual. The server asks how I am doing, and I nervously reply, "fine." I stare at my dad, who smiles at me, and I hope that he senses my discomfort.

I have been to Hooters before, and I know that such intimacy is sometimes a part of the experience. However, I am worried about the assumptions of sexuality that may be thrust on my body, not just the server erroneously reading me as heterosexual, but also my dad reading me as questioning or as ashamed of my sexuality, and/or reading me as a liar if I do not come out to her.

My sexuality strains the relationship I have with my father (see Adams, 2006, 2012). He rarely asks about my partner, and, when I was single, he never asked if I was dating anyone (a common practice for him when I was not yet out). Further, while I sent him a copy of my book about same-sex attraction and coming out (Adams, 2011), he has never asked about any of the content. Given this information, my father's presence and our relational history complicated my response to the server at Hooter's. Had I been alone or with my lesbian and gay friends, I would not have had any reservations about telling the server that I identified as gay (and, consequently, that her overly sexual flirtations were unnecessary). But I was with my father, and I did not want to make the situation awkward by telling the server, upon meeting, that I was gay, not because I feared her reaction, but because I did not know how my father would react to such an abrupt disclosure. A post–coming out complication: I did not just inform my father of my same-sex attraction—I came out to him seven years prior (2003)—but my same-sex attraction continued to thwart my experience with him.

65

Complicating Family III

December 2010. My mother tells me that she wants a holiday photograph of our family to send in the mail, to (her) friends and (our) family.

"That's a great idea," I say. "I'm sure Jerry [my partner] will agree to it."

"Oh," she replies. "I thought it could be just you, me, and Michael [her husband]."

A picture together, a family picture of the three of us, absent my partner of more than two years. In this moment, I do not believe that she was being malicious or unloving—I believe that she likes and loves Jerry. However, in this moment she did not define him as "family."

"Why can't Jerry be included in the photo?" I ask.

"Because he's not family," she says. "The two of you aren't married."

"We can't get married," I respond, angrily. "Same-sex marriage is not legal in Illinois."

"Then he's not allowed in our family photograph," she replies.

A scarring moment in our mother-son relationship—I left this conversation feeling invalidated and angry, particularly because Jerry and I didn't matter to her and that, in order to matter, we must get married, a legal impossibility in our state/nation.

Marriage isn't that important to me. I do not need any legal body telling me who I can or should love, and I do not need any legal contract to legitimate my love for a person. However, my mother's comments were larger than marriage—they illustrated ignorance and a lack of acceptance with which I had to confront. Further, this interaction had nothing to do with coming out; I had come out to my mother eight years prior (2002). This interaction indicated a need for me to validate the legitimacy of my same-sex relationship for her, in the name of family.

Post–coming out complications: If my mom does not consider Jerry family and I do, and if she only wants a picture of her, me, and her husband absent my partner, and I refuse, then our family history, as documented in photos, will no longer exist. If she is ashamed of my partner or does not consider us family, and we do, the larger family unit is affected. Our conflict is not tied to coming out to her, but rather from her inability to recognize us—two men—as family. Memories fade; relationships strain.

Complicating Family IV

November 2012. My mom tells me how Jane, her neighbor, spends a lot of time with her son's wife, Jane's daughter-in-law. My mom then says that she wishes that she had a daughter-in-law with whom to spend time. I mention that she could spend time with Jerry, my partner. She says that he cannot be like a daughter-in-law because he is a man and because he isn't as sociable as Jane's daughter-in-law.

I leave this conversation sensing that my mom is upset because she cannot spend more time with my partner. I do not take her comments as a critique against my same-sex attraction, only that she wishes that my partner might socialize with her more.

A few hours later my mom mentions again that she wishes that she had a daughter-in-law and that Jerry, because he is a man, could never be as sociable as a woman. She then says that she wishes she had (biological) grandchildren, something that Jerry and I could never have together. I tell her that she has never mentioned grandchildren before and that if we wanted children we could adopt.

I leave this conversation feeling sad and angry—sad if my mom mourns that I do not have a relationship with a woman or if she misses having a daughter-in-law or if she desires biological grandchildren; and angry because I am tired of justifying my (same-sexed) partner, tired of thinking that I must again say that I will probably date men for the rest of my life, tired of thinking and talking about my (lack of hetero) sexuality with her. What made her comments even more difficult is that I fear further talking about her desire for a daughter-in-law or her desire for grandchildren because of what she might say—I do not want to hear "I wish that you were not gay" or "I wish that you were married to a woman," particularly since I no longer have much tolerance for this kind of heteronormative discourse, especially from my family. If I heard my mom say these hurtful things, I might have to eliminate contact with her, an act that, out of care for myself, I hope to not have to do.

The post–coming out complications: Even though I came out to my mother in 2002, I continue to negotiate my same-sex attraction with her. And this negotiation continues to trouble my relationship with her, manifest by my desire to not want to talk and visit with her much out of a fear of hearing harmful or neglectful discourse about my sexual orientation and about my meaningful and intimate relationships with men. While I understand the sadness my mom might have if Jerry and I do not have children, I am tired of explaining to the same person, again and again, that I am proudly—not apologetically—attracted to men. Further, I would never say to my mom, repeatedly, "I wish you were a man," or "I wish you were not White," or "I wish you were not older than 50." These comments would not make much sense, especially since they would isolate a characteristic that she could not (easily) change—a feeling that I also have about my same-sex attraction.

Navigating Post–Coming Out Complications

Relationship talk is a significant part of everyday life. In many contexts, I hear people asking about boyfriends, girlfriends, engagements, and marriages, and I am exposed to conversations about the size of rings and the complexities of weddings, the desire to exchange vows, the pros and cons of (monogamous) commitment, the dilemmas of being single, and the importance of family. Pre–coming out, I even remember friends and some members of my family wanting to buy me a celebratory cake once I lost my virginity by having sex with a woman.

Post–coming out, relationship talk among my family has nearly ceased; I came out and into silence (Adams, 2011). There is the aunt who has never asked about Jerry; my father who, while nice and welcoming when Jerry is present, rarely asks about our relationship; the cousin who slowly ended contact with me after I came out to her; my mother who sometimes does not treat my relationship as legitimate or secure because I am not legally "married" (even though marriage is a legal impossibility for me/us); and the numerous other family members who never ask about my dating experiences or my intimate and meaningful relationships with men. And let me emphasize: Before coming out—before I told these people that I found men attractive—*all* of these people *regularly* asked if I was dating anyone, and, if I was dating (a woman), how the relationship was doing; after coming out, I rarely receive either of these questions.

I understand these neglectful and silencing experiences with the perspective of dialectical tensions—competing pressures within relationships that can motivate dis-ease and conflict (Baxter & Montgomery, 1996). For instance, I struggle with the openness-closedness dialectic, with wanting to be honest about my feelings with my family while recognizing that, in so doing, I risk vulnerability and protection. I want to be open about my meaningful and intimate relationships with men and call attention to the silences I feel that family members have cast against my sexuality, but I fear saying something because I do not want to hear more disparaging comments about or disaffirming silences toward my relationship, comments and silences that have already characterized these relationships for more than a decade.

I also struggle with the connectedness-separateness dialectic, with wanting to spend time with my family but also wanting, or needing, to stay separate from them (Baxter & Montgomery, 1996). Refusing contact has become more necessary for my self-care: I am exhausted from having to tolerate homophobic statements, ignorant and disparaging commentary about my sexuality, and cold silences. When my partner is with me, I am tired of worrying about how to explain to others who he is and why we, as a couple, matter. I also do not want to put my partner in any situation in which his safety may be compromised.

And so I find myself living increasingly separate from family members. I do not attend family events such as birthday parties, retirement celebrations, and funerals, and I do not want or encourage family members to visit me. During the few times that I do visit, I rarely bring Jerry.

I assume that my/our avoidance may contribute to my mother's desire to have a close daughter-in-law, but I am exhausted from having to justify my sexuality and the realness of my relationship with Jerry. However, by living increasingly separate from my mom, she further loses the possibility to better connect with Jerry, which may then motivate her to be open with me about a desire for a daughter-in-law, an openness that may motivate me to question her acceptance of my sexuality and that, again, may encourage me to stay away. We both/all lose.

Navigating post–coming out silences can be difficult as well. It is easy to criticize a member of my family for disparaging me upon coming out—that is, for reacting negatively, for saying mean things, for being physically or verbally abusive upon initial disclosure of my same-sex attraction. However, life after coming out is quite silent: I have less and less explicit content to use as evidence of prejudice and nonacceptance. For instance, in all of the everyday complications I have described, there has never been any overt disdain for my sexuality. Rather, I experience a kind of implicit negligence in my everyday affairs, negligence that I must first address explicitly and then explain why such negligence is unacceptable or how/why it hurts.

I do try to make my same-sex attraction and my relationship a prominent part of my (remaining) conversations with my family—not in a "Hi, I'm Tony, and I'm gay" sort of way, but instead by using phrases like, "Jerry, my partner," or by saying, "Jerry and I" in reference to topics like living together, sharing bank accounts, and making significant purchases (e.g., buying a car, going on vacation). But I recognize that in being subtly open, in reminding others of my attraction and my relationships in seemingly mundane ways, I expose myself to additional post–coming out complications. For instance, if I mention Jerry and the other person abruptly tries to change the topic of conversation, then I may unexpectedly have a post–coming out issue—an issue that may then encourage me to refuse further contact with the person.

While dialectical tensions never fully disappear from relationships, flaring up in uncertain ways and at unknown times, I find myself tolerating acts of prejudice and ignorance much less, especially when these acts come from a family member I once thought loved and accepted me unconditionally. I want to be acknowledged, and I want the relationship I have with my partner to be acknowledged; for me, silence has become an unacceptable act of disconfirmation (Hyde, 2006). My health, happiness, and safety now come first, and sometimes this means refusing contact with homophobic others, and sometimes this means refusing to visit to the place that I once called home.

I do not want to suggest that I do not miss my family—I miss them greatly. But my attempts at self-care and my attempts to integrate my intimate, meaningful relationships with men into my everyday life have strained our relationships to each other. And so, when I think of missing them and when I think about what I need, when I think of how our relationships are, have been, and could be, I am thrust into a prolonged sadness, a kind of queer melancholy.

(Queer) Melancholy

> "Is it painful? Their avoidance, awkwardness, and downright
> rejection of you and those for whom you care?
> Well yes, of course. Of course it hurts, deeply. Severely."
> —Thomas Glave, Words to Our Now (2005, p. 120).

The accumulation of sad experiences and the rejection by once-close family members has been difficult. It has been difficult to recognize that some of the people whom I love (and once loved) avoid acknowledging my same-sex attraction or the relationship that I have with my partner, especially since I have been out to these people for more than ten years and since my partner and I have been together for more than five years. I also feel the cumulative impact of these experiences—with the exception of three supportive and loving cousins, one of whom identifies as bisexual, *every* relationship I have with family members has been damaged by my disclosure of same-sex attraction. I have had one aunt, two uncles, and one close family friend die and I have not attended their funerals; I thought that if I did go, I would have to go alone, as my partner would not be welcome (even if he was welcome, I would worry about his/our safety or that we, as a couple, would be disregarded). I rarely visit my hometown, and, when I do, I feel weird about going out in public with family members and having interactions similar to the one at Hooters—that is, of being asked, perpetually, if I have a girlfriend or if I am married, questions that require complicated answers, especially if I am around family members who already rarely acknowledge my same-sex attraction.

My avoidance—an avoidance that I now find necessary for *my* well-being—propels me into a kind of queer melancholy, a prolonged sadness heavily informed by my same-sex attraction and others' reaction to/lack of acknowledgment of this attraction. While I miss the familial relationships I once had—relationships that felt different before I came out—and while I sometimes feel guilty for not tolerating the silence and disdain that my family project towards my nonheterosexual body, I also feel as though I can no longer tolerate silence about my attraction, my dating experiences and past relationships, or my long-term meaningful and intimate relationship with a man I love.

What makes such melancholy even more difficult is that I am not sure that it can be remedied easily or any time soon. I could force a discussion about the narrow and exclusive definitions of family, manifest by decisions about who to (not) include in a photograph and who may serve well as an in-law, but I fear hearing more negligent and hurtful discourse. If melancholy functions as a by-product of self-care and safety, then I guess melancholy is my/our lot in life—I would rather stay silent and protected and live with perpetual sadness than hear honest but negligent or hurtful discourse.

Conclusion

The experiences I have described illustrate some of the relational dilemmas that can happen post–coming out. While I feel as though coming out continues to be an issue for many persons with same-sex attraction, there are also issues that emerge after disclosure; same-sex attraction can continue to influence a relationship.

Before I conclude, I want to acknowledge the ways in which my physical location and social identities such as sex, race, and age complicate my experiences with sexuality.

Much of my once-close family still live in Danville, Illinois, a rural town of about 30,000 people. Because of this, any ignorance or prejudice that they might have towards same-sex attraction may stem from not having much exposure to or experience with persons who identify as lesbian, gay, bisexual, or queer (Barton, 2012; Gray, 2009). I had never met an LGBQ person until 2000, when I was 21 and after I had moved away from Danville; before then I was, unfortunately, ignorantly homophobic.

Familial experiences of sexuality may also be different from familial experiences of sex and race. For instance, given that families often consist of men and women, being female or male is not necessarily deviant. The expectation that men and women compose families is not a novel or unfathomable expectation either. Many families also have race (or a few races) in common; I have never heard a story about parents *not* liking their child *solely* because of the child's race. However, a LGBQ child might be the *only* LGBQ person in a family; as Weston (1991) remarks, "those who come out find themselves called upon to explain how it is that a duck could have come from a family of swans" (p. 75). Because of this, the LGBQ child may bear the lone task, and burden, of explaining her/his same-sex attraction to (ignorant) heterosexual others, and of combating malicious discourse by family members who do not accept same-sex attraction or who believe that it is the child's fault for choosing to be LGBQ (Barton, 2012).

Further, I feel that my queer melancholy increases as I age—increasingly, I find myself less tolerant of neglectful discourse about my meaningful and intimate same-sex relationships. In an effort of self-care, I am less able to associate with prejudiced, hateful, and possibly unsafe others. Being older, I also have the privilege of relying less on my family for once-necessary financial and social support.

71

While I have described post–coming complications that have occurred in some of my relationships, I do have many joyful relationships made possible by my same-sex attraction: the students who tell me that I gave them courage to tell others about same-sex attraction; the gratification that comes with fewer everyday struggles with coming out; the close friendships I have with many LGBQ others; and the meaningful, intimate, and loving relationships that I have had with men. However, with my family, I do not have many joyful experiences since coming out.

Even though I consider myself very out, my sexuality still influences, even tarnishes, my relationships with others. I continue to create a family of choice, of best friends and close colleagues, especially since the rifts within my family seem to be difficult to mend, at least at the time of this writing. I miss my past relationships, but I also can no longer tolerate prejudice and ignorance. I miss others, and I do believe that they may miss me, and I am saddened that my same-sex attraction continues to complicate our remaining time together.

References

Adams, T. E. (2006). Seeking father: Relationally reframing a troubled love story. *Qualitative Inquiry, 12,* 704–723.

Adams, T. E. (2011). *Narrating the closet: An autoethnography of same-sex attraction.* Walnut Creek, CA: Left Coast Press, Inc.

Adams, T. E. (2012). Missing each other. *Qualitative Inquiry, 18,* 193–196.

Barton, B. (2012). *Pray the gay away: The extraordinary lives of Bible Belt gays.* New York: New York University Press.

Baxter, L. A., & Montgomery, B. M. (1996). *Relating.* New York: Guilford Press.

Burgess, S. (2005). Did the Supreme Court out in *Bush v. Gore?* Queer theory on the performance of the politics of shame. *differences, 16,* 126–146.

Cooper, M. (2010). Lesbians who are married to men. In C. Pullen & M. Cooper (Eds.), *LGBT identity and online new media* (pp. 75–86). New York: Routledge.

Defenbaugh, N. L. (2011). *Dirty tale: A narrative journey of the IBD body.* Cresskill, NJ: Hampton Press.

Fox, R. (2010). Re-membering daddy: Autoethnographic reflections of my father and Alzheimer's disease. *Text and Performance Quarterly, 30,* 3–20.

Glave, T. (2005). *Words to our now: Imagination and dissent.* Minneapolis: University of Minnesota Press.

Gray, M. (2009). *Out in the country: Youth, media, and queer visibility in rural America.* New York: New York University Press.

Halley, J. E. (1989). The politics of the closet: Towards equal protection for gay, lesbian, and bisexual identity. *UCLA Law Review, 36,* 915–976.

Hyde, M. J. (2006). *The life-giving gift of acknowledgment.* West Lafayette, IN: Purdue University Press.

Myers, W. B. (2012). Joyful moments of sorrow: Autoethnography and atheistic joy. *Qualitative Communication Research, 1,* 195–208.

Sedgwick, E. K. (1990). *Epistemology of the closet.* Berkeley: University of California Press.

Waugh, T. (2009). [Untitled interview]. In R. R. Rao & D. Sarma (Eds.), *Whistling in the dark: Twenty-one queer interviews* (pp. 85–96). Thousand Oaks, CA: Sage.

Weston, K. (1991). *Families we choose: Lesbians, gays, kinship.* New York: Columbia University Press.

Wright, N. (2011). Realizations about connections: A literacy/teaching narrative. In J. Battis (Ed.), *Homofiles: Theory, sexuality, and graduate studies* (pp. 77–81). Lanham, MD: Lexington Books.

SECTION II

✧

Embracing Ambiguous and Nonbinary Identities

THE SECOND SECTION COMPRISES THREE CHAPTERS THAT EXPLORE the tensions that exist between ascribed (self-defined) and avowed (other-defined) cultural identities. Embracing autoethnography through intersectionality, these chapters highlight the messiness inherent within multidimensional identities that resist simplistic, binary categories. As the authors engage issues of race, ethnicity, sexuality, class, and nationality, they demonstrate the value of identities that embrace ambiguous understandings of self that replace either/or distinctions with both/and conceptualizations. *Self-presentation theory, communication theory of identity,* and *complicity theory* will be introduced as organizing structures for these chapters.

Self-Presentation Theory

Goffman's (1959) self-presentation theory is a classic framework used to describe how individuals use verbal and nonverbal communication to communicate positive images (i.e., *face*) of themselves in public spaces. It is a theory that provides insight into how individuals communicate to create and maintain an image for public consumption. The theory is based on several assumptions related to image management (Burgoon, Guerrero, & Floyd, 2010). First, individuals manage multiple images across different contexts. Second, image management focuses on behaviors that are associated with maximized outcomes. Third, individuals use different image management techniques (e.g., assertive or defensive) directed to a generalized audience.

Fourth, and finally, image management concentrates specifically on how a single person encodes certain verbal and nonverbal behaviors (as opposed to the process of impression formation—how others decode that information).

Self-presentation theory draws on a theater analogy to describe how people present themselves in everyday life through the different roles that they embrace and perform in public. According to Goffman (1959), people engage in preparation *back stage* (out of the audience's view) and then perform their roles *front stage*. Performance involves wearing specific costumes, manipulating various props, closely following different stage directions, and reciting one's lines. Performances, however, are not enacted in isolation; they are contingent on the audience and others in crucial supporting roles. Metts (2009) explains how Goffman's metaphor is most obvious in different scripted roles such as teachers, lawyers, nurses, and doctors, however, she also argues that ordinary, everyday interactions are performed in similar ways. Our back stages may take the form of our bedrooms, apartments, or private offices; these are the spaces where we prepare and practice for our public performances. The different roles that we play come with their own sets of artifacts (props), dress (costumes), and communication expectations (scripts). Various situations and audiences call for different performances, and individuals make verbal and nonverbal choices as they take various stages.

Self-presentation is strategic, and Jones and Pittman (1982) identify five different types of strategies that individuals use to produce different attributions (see Metts, 2009). First, individuals use *ingratiation* (e.g., doing favors, giving compliments, being positive) when they want to be perceived as friendly or likeable. Second, the strategy of *self-promotion* (e.g., telling others about one's accomplishments, displays of awards) is used when people want to be perceived as competent. Third, individuals who desire to be seen as worthy will use different strategies that subtly demonstrate their abilities, competence, or integrity. These strategies are known as *exemplification*. Fourth, *supplication* is the strategy used when people seek to be perceived as helpless. Tactics associated with this strategy involve claims of ignorance or inaptitude in order to elicit nurturance from others. The fifth, and final, strategy is used when individuals desire to be perceived as powerful or in control. When *intimidation* is the goal, self-presentation focuses on displays of anger or control and a willingness to use coercion or punishments.

Communication Theory of Identity

According to the communication theory of identity (CTI), identity is a naturally communicative and relational phenomenon (Hecht et al., 2003). Communication builds, sustains, and transforms identity. At the same time, identity is expressed through communication (Jung & Hecht, 2004). Identity is best understood as multidimensional and holistic in nature. As such, a major assumption of CTI is that identity is located in four interconnected layers: personal, enacted, relational, and communal (Hecht et al., 2003).

The theory originators assert that the *personal frame* of identity encompasses an individual's self-concept or self-definition. The personal level of identity is partially constructed from the messages received from relational others; however, the location is within the individual. The second frame of identity is the *enacted frame*; it is based on the idea that identities are communicatively manifested during social interactions. According to CTI, identities emerge through our interactions with others and are communicated either directly or indirectly through social roles, behaviors, and symbols (Hecht et al., 2003). This frame treats self as a performance and makes communication the location of identity (Hecht, Warren, Jung, & Krieger, 2005).

The *relational frame* captures how identities emerge in reference to others, specifically significant relationships like friendships, romantic partners, and family members. In this regard, relationships themselves constitute units of identity (Hecht et al., 2005). Finally, the *communal frame* points to a group of people or a particular community bonded by a collective memory as the locus of identity (Hecht et al., 2003). The community has its own identity and illustrates the joint identities of the individuals who associate with it (Golden, Niles, & Hecht, 2002; Witteborn, 2004). Thus, identities arise from group associations and social networks (Hecht et al., 2005).

Although we have discussed each of these four frames separately, CTI explains that the frames are always interrelated and never separate. The ways in which the different frames influence, confirm, and contradict one another help to capture the ongoing process of identity negotiation. Within the CTI framework, it is known as *interpenetration* (Jung & Hecht, 2004). One's personal identity, for example, cannot be considered without the context of the relational, enacted, and communal layers (Hecht et al., 2005). Although the frames coexist and cooperate in the composition of a person's identity, they do not always work in accord; instead, they may contradict or compete with one another, revealing inevitable *identity gaps* (Faulkner, 2006; Jung & Hecht, 2004). By definition, identity gaps reflect contradictions between the different frames and oftentimes stimulate active forms of identity negotiation.

Complicity Theory

According to McPhail (1994, 2002), complicity theory extends some of the ideas central to Afrocentricity by challenging the underlying assumptions that see African Americans and European Americans as naturally different. Complicity theory represents a framework that was created specifically to study issues of race, language, and communication. While McPhail's work has focused on issues of race and racism, it provides great insight into all forms of cultural difference and oppression.

Complicity theory is grounded in two key ideas. First, at the core of racism is a language system that divides and ranks human beings in black-and-white terms (McPhail, 1994). According to McPhail (1991), what has been created is a "language of negative difference" (p. 2) that affects social reality. In order to challenge racism, you must challenge the language that we use regarding race. This is important because race designations are made and maintained with no recognition of commonality and interdependence. In other words, racism is not merely a problem of "Blacks" and "Whites," it is a consequence of understanding the world through black-and-white terms (McPhail, 2002). A second key idea central to complicity theory is that dominance and marginality are not fixed states (McPhail, 1994). The theory challenges the idea that racism is a social practice of domination that can be reduced simply to oppressors and oppressed or victimizers and victims. According to complicity theory, racism reflects the Western tendency to produce essentialist classifications and categories—separate, distinct, general groups. What it fails to take into consideration is how racism exists within a social system that also marginalizes people based on gender, class, age, sexual orientation, and the like (McPhail, 1994).

As a means to advance the ideas central to complicity theory, McPhail introduces three key concepts: complicity, coherence, and implicature. *Complicity* involves using language that highlights differences instead of commonalities and emphasizes division at the expense of unity (McPhail, 1994). Productive race relations can never occur when complicity is the norm. Instead, we must move from complicity to coherence. *Coherence* is a concept that emphasizes interconnectedness and commonalty (McPhail, 2002) in attempts to facilitate harmony in discourse. It avoids a focus on the negative differences and critiques existing frameworks that depict human beings in terms of separate and distinct races. While complicity hinges on the idea of negative difference as oppositional forces, coherence sees difference as complementary (McPhail, 1996). The final key concept, *implicature,* involves a basic acceptance of the belief that we are all implicated in each other's lives (McPhail, 2002). Implicature is grounded in the idea that we are all connected; what affects one of us, affects all of us. In short, complicity theory provides great insight into the role that language structures serve in understanding self and others. While shifts in language alone may not solve complex systems of oppression (McPhail, 2009), they remain an important point of critical analysis.

Theories as Lenses

In this section, we describe three theoretical frameworks that provide insight to the each of the chapters. You can use one of these theoretical lenses to understand all three chapters, each theory to understand each particular chapter, or a combination of both. As you read through each chapter, think critically about the following questions:

- How can you apply the metaphor of theater, or a play, to understand each of the chapters? Can you think of times when your public (front stage) performances of different personal, social, and cultural roles were consciously different than those that you enact privately (back stage)? How might these differences—our use of specific words, displays of artifacts, and dress choices—be related to decisions to conform to or resist images traditionally associated with our different social or cultural groups?
- Both self-presentation theory and the communication theory of identity see communication as a performance of identity. Do you think that "performances" (in this vein) mean that people are communicating inauthentic selves (being fake)? Or does it reflect the complex ways that individuals emphasize certain images in certain contexts?
- What examples of identity gaps exist in the autoethnographic descriptions of each author? How do the four frames of identity reflect contradictory images?
- Given the communicative experiences of the authors featured in this section, how can the basic ideas of complicity theory be applied to sex/sexism, class/classism, nationality/ethnocentrism, and sexuality/heterosexism?
- What examples of languages of negative difference appear in each chapter? Can you understand how some language works against understanding the world in new ways? In terms of race, culture, nationality, class, and sexuality, what are some language choices that we can make to resist the status quo that promotes difference and division?

References

Burgoon, J. K., Guerrero, L. K., & Floyd, K. (2010). *Nonverbal communication*. New York: Allyn & Bacon.

Faulkner, S. L. (2006). Reconstruction: Being LGBTQ and Jewish. In M. Orbe, B. J. Allen, & L. A. Flores (Eds.), *The same and different: Acknowledging the diversity within and between cultural groups* (pp. 95–120). Washington, DC: National Communication Association.

Goffman, E. (1959). *The presentation of self in everyday life*. Garden City, NY: Anchor/Doubleday.

Golden, D. R., Niles, T. A., & Hecht, M. L. (2002). Jewish American identity. In J. N. Martin, T. K. Nakayama, & L. A. Flores (Eds.), *Readings in intercultural communication: Experiences and contexts* (pp. 44–52). New York: McGraw-Hill.

Hecht, M. L., Jackson, R. L., & Ribeau, S. A. (2003). *African American communication: Exploring identity and culture* (2e). Mahwah, NJ: LEA.

Hecht, M. L., Warren, J. R., Jung, E., & Krieger, J. L. (2005). The communication theory of Identity: Development, theoretical perspective, and future directions. In

W. B. Gudykunst (Ed.), *Theorizing about intercultural communication* (pp. 257–278). Thousand Oaks, CA: Sage.

Jones, E. E., & Pittman, T. S. (1982). Toward a general theory of strategic self-presentation. In J. Suls (Ed.), *Psychological perspectives on the self* (pp. 231–263). Hillsdale, NJ: Lawrence Erlbaum.

Jung, E., & Hecht, M. L. (2004). Elaborating the communication theory of identity: Identity gaps and communication outcomes. *Communication Quarterly, 52*(3), 265–283.

McPhail, M. L. (1991). Complicity: The theory of negative difference. *Howard Journal of Communications, 3*(1&2), 1–13.

McPhail, M. L. (1994). *The rhetoric of racism.* Lanham, MD: University Press of America.

McPhail, M. L. (1996). *Zen in the art of rhetoric: An inquiry into coherence.* Albany: State University of New York Press.

McPhail, M. L. (2002). *The rhetoric of racism revisited: Reparations of separation?* Lanham, MD: University Press of America.

McPhail, M. L. (2009). Complicity theory. In K. Foss & S. Littlejohn (Eds.), *The encyclopedia of communication theory* (pp. 160–161). Thousand Oaks, CA: Sage.

Metts, S. (2009). Impression management. In S. W. Littlejohn & K. A. Foss (Eds.), *Encyclopedia of communication theory* (pp. 506–509). Thousand Oaks, CA: Sage.

Witteborn, S. (2004). Of being an Arab woman before and after September 11: The enactment of communal identities in talk. *The Howard Journal of Communications, 15*, 83–98.

CHAPTER FOUR

Negotiating More, (Mis)labeling the Body
A Tale of Intersectionality
Amber L. Johnson

*In some ways I have wanted to live somewhere else, do something else
and be somebody else as I grew up. Not exactly rejecting all that I was
… as it stands I like myself; but I just wanted "more." What that means
is that although I enjoyed my life, I still entertained fantasies of more
… more flavor, more excitement, more experiences, … more, more,
more. This has led to much cognitive dissonance over the years.*
My father, Woody Johnson (personal
communication, December 5, 2011).

GROWING UP BLACK IN LOS ANGELES, AND THE OFFSPRING OF Woody Johnson, my father, meant wanting to be something *more*. My siblings and I created fairy tales. My younger brother would tell people he had an entirely different family somewhere north and that he was mixed with something he didn't know. Perhaps Mexican, Indian, Native American, Middle Eastern, Ethiopian. He could blend. His birth mother was Black. His father, race and origin unknown, got her pregnant and ran. We adopted him when he was two. My little brother, who could blend in with more than 100 different countries, was adopted by a Black family. He is Black now; but he tells people he is White. I correct him from time to time, as if that is my place. Either way, it makes him *more*. He is different, special. My older brother used to tell people he was from Compton. That made him gangsta. Tough. Cool. Hard. *More*. I was Light Skinned. Pretty. Smart. Articulate. Mixed? Exception. *More*. Labels attached to my body. Labels design to characterize something *more*.

Critical Autoethnography: Intersecting Cultural Identities in Everyday Life, edited by Robin M. Boylorn and Mark P. Orbe, 81–95. © 2014 Left Coast Press, Inc. All rights reserved.

These   stories
      live
inside   labels.

Adhesive squares attach to neatly pack-aged envelopes dictating where to go,

signaling where one came from,
   a self-addressed stamped envelope calling the body home.
Stories.
   Stories fester, out, open across lines made to spill. Stories weaken the adhesive, pulling away at edges, creating a roughness I call negotiation.
   No more neat handwriting. Just messy ideas, ideologies. Labels
     always on the borders of the body
       tucking in, holding up, framing, orienting, addressing, negotiating.
Stories. Waiting to pull, discolor, shed, replace, reify, untangle, manipulate, make believe.
What happens when we peel the labels off? Naked,
   the body becomes a series of stories
designed to bend in recognition towards labels calling the body home.
   The body does not always know the language calling it
But the body can feel the spirits that beckon with more labels
Home. Away. negotiate
Foreign. Black. Weird. negotiate
Awkward. Here. Beautiful. negotiate
Come

Come into the labels that call you.

You are what your body answers to.

   As a child, I told people I was a mutt. Much like the labels avowed and assigned to my body, I am a cultural hybrid situated within a strategic rheto-ric (Nakayama & Krizek, 1995) designed to integrate and control (Kraidy, 2005). Bits and pieces of this and that come together on my skin. Society expects the pieces to fit together nicely or risk being discarded.
Labeled puzzle pieces.
     Paint by numbers.
       What happens when the pieces just don't fit?
We negotiate them into their too tight, too round, too square, too large, too rigid spaces, changing both our piece/peace, and the pieces we fit into.
   Using intersectionality as theoretical framework and autoethnographic performance as method, I reflect on my body as a series of stories chosen

to tease out the intersections of my identities and the ways in which their structures massage my understanding of self, others' perceptions of me, and my perceptions of others perceiving me. I share three stories. The first one is of a trip to Ghana, West Africa, where I felt my Whiteness for the first time. The second story shares my childhood growing up a class chameleon, where I experienced lower- , middle- , and upper-class living. A third story shares my sexuality and the implosion that occurs when we don't have access to language that can neatly package our desires.

My goal, then, is to formulate understanding, however temporary, in the reflexive moments of storytelling and/as negotiation. As Alexander (2006) contends, this is a "story of intercultural encounter and countercultural experience. A story of academic reporting as confessional tale and reflexive auto/ethnography as personal sense making on a terrain of cultural experience" (p. 2). This performative autoethnography is about negotiating the labels assigned, rejected, desired, and/or pursued within the contested terrain of interpersonal/intercultural culture. Because of the contested nature of epistemology, I choose to tell stories that interrupt instead of accept, reveal instead of cover, create possibility instead of resolve (Boylorn, 2011).

Method

Performative autoethnography calls for inserting the bodily flesh and its many positions as ways of knowing. Engaging what Alexander and Warren (2002) term *autopoetic* narratives,[1] I summon a creative yet critical articulation of my lived experiences in a textual performance where different perceptions and standpoints of the same experiences enter conversation (Conquergood, 1985, p. 9) and create new memories and new experiences, that, in this case, foster a space for understanding and possibility.

The temporal spaces of possibility and understanding command reflexivity. "The poetic or narrative text is reflexive, not only in its use of language but also in how it positions the writer in the text and uses the writer's experiences as both the topic of inquiry and a resource for uncovering problematic experience" (Denzin, 1996, p. 217). Uncovering problematic experience provokes frustration. As Goltz contends, "writing the 'I' is frustrating," (2011, p. 387) because "I" teases *us* for not knowing *us*, pushing *we* to dialogue with *we* in a "never-finished relational process." We tell our stories as an "I," and retell them through scholarship, only to reveal that with every retelling, we know our "I" less and less. However fickle the process, it is necessary, or crucial as Langellier (1999) proclaims:

> Identity and experience are symbiosis of performed story and the social relations in which they are materially embedded: sex, class, race, ethnicity, sexuality, geography, religion, and so on. This is why personal narrative performance is especially crucial to those communities left out of the privileges of dominant culture, those bodies without voice in the political sense (p. 129).

Performance autoethnography then highlights three concerns: how cultural practices shape identity, how identity shapes cultural performance (Alexander, 2005), and how publicly responsible autoethnography addresses central issues of self, gender, race, society, and democracy (Denzin, as cited in Alexander, 2006, p. 425). The body as a cite of knowing evokes cultural memories tied to broader conversations of class, gender, race, and other markers of identity, as well as the possibility for new identities to develop. My goals here are to use critical reflexivity to engage three stories as a form of resistance and provide a fluid, open text to perform variation, test the limits of certainty, and leave room for interpretation, misunderstanding, and not knowing (Adams & Holman Jones, 2011; Gingrich-Philbrook, 2005; Madison, 2006; Pollock, 2006). Following Boylorn's (2011) successful plan to trouble boundaries of race, marking them as incessant and in constant negotiation, I wish to trouble boundaries of binary labels attached to nation, class, and sexuality in addition to race, and the ways in which markers of authenticity, desire, and positionality influence our perceptions of self. Like Boylorn, my goal is not to resolve my identity issues, but to offer possibility embedded in conversations, experience, reflection, discursive practices, and performativity. I begin with a tale across the Atlantic in Ghana.

On Being Labeled White: Race and Nationality

Race matters differently depending on where you stand physically. Robin Boylorn speaks to race matters in American research, positing that "Black folks self-awareness and self-consciousness is oftentimes based on the powerful influence of how we see ourselves as 'raced' plus other factors instead of just the other factors" (2011, p. 179). Race stands at the foreground of conversation, because that is what people see when they look at us (Boylorn, 2011). Race matters in research. What happens when people see other things? Is it always a product of race first, or can those other things shadow our Americanized versions of race matters? What happens when we remove the body from American race contexts and leave the brain behind? Race mattered in Ghana, but nationality mattered, too, and was far more salient for me than the race matter. I felt multiple parts of myself forming the whole while I stood in that foreign place, with those foreign questions, and foreign spectators who were home. I didn't see myself as the foreigner. In my eyes, they were the foreigners. My American history taught me 'twas truth. Because they weren't a part of my worldview, even though something kept pulling them towards my center, a gravitational force that spoke in collisions, I gazed upon them as the Other.

A Boxing Match with Self

I am in their home
They are foreign
I am in their backyard
They are difference
I stand on their soil
They are not supposed to be here
I am visitor
No, you are owner
Oh beautiful for spacious skies
I want to love you
I am taught to fear you
For amber waves of grain
I want to touch you
I am taught to run from your dis-ease
I want to laugh with you under golden hues lining the sky with purple majesty
Purple mountain majesty
  Oh beautiful,
  America, American
NO!
  I cannot love you and be an American
No, you are visitor.
  I, owner
This America, across the wilderness
This America, til all success be nobleness
  But then you smile
  I am drunk off jollof rice and palm oil
  American girl in a foreign place full of foreigners
    What have They done?

> "I spent the first half of my life learning to rule myself, to grow a
> will, and now at midlife I find autonomy is a boulder on my path
> that I keep crashing into. I can't seem to stay out of my own way.
>   I've always been aware that there is a greater power than the
> conscious I. That power is my inner self, the entity that is thesum
> total of all my reincarnations. The Godwoman in me" (Anzaldúa,
> 1987, p. 50).

They say our super-conscious mind holds ALL information; a collective
memory of our existence as people, not as individuals. What Anzaldúa calls
the "sum total of all my reincarnations." My trip to Ghana speaks to those
reincarnations and the sum total of people I once belonged to, possibly, but
stripped from, however temporarily. My super-conscious mind
remembers.

August 2002. A 22-hour plane ride through Amsterdam and into Ghana.
Plane Ride=Orientation=Fear.
I was prepped to fear you since I learned to read elementary textbooks. I
was coached to fear you when I began taking steps towards this journey. I
was told to fear you during that plane ride. My mind, oriented to fear. My
body, organic, unafraid, anticipating something different.

My feet touch the dusty gold soil. *Home* chanting in my ears somewhere
in the distant horizon. Close enough to hear, too far to pinpoint a location.
I sense nostalgia, even over the warning signs.

"These people are relentless. They will beg you for money. If you give it
to one person, the rest will flock to you and follow. Keep your possessions
close, your money closer."

I walk out of customs and into the warm air. *Home.* I see familiar faces. *Home.*
I am not afraid; my mind tells me I should be. My body is in Ghana. My
mind is in America. I feel like I am home more than any other place I have
ever been, which creates an awkward feeling of (dis)placement and dis-ease
because my conscience is telling me I am not home. I feel a strong desire
to sensationalize, but also to understand at the same time. It is awkward,
but comforting. Hard to explain. Even harder to feel. Over the course of
my visit, I get two reactions from Ghanaians.

Ghanaian: Are you White?

Me: No.

Ghanaian: Is your mother White?

Me: No.

Ghanain: Is your father White?

Me: No.

Ghanaian: So your mother is White.

Me: No.

Ghanaian: So your father is White.

Me: No.

Ghanaian, persistent still: Then what are you mixed with?

My witty comeback: Black and Blacker.

Most of them laugh and look at me sideways. I learn that race is about
skin, not story.

The other reaction is very different. As we travel further from Accra, people
begin to tell me who I am.

Ghanaian: You are Ashanti. Your people are Ashanti. You look just like
them.

We visit an Ashanti village in Kumasi. I am amazed at how many family
members I see in this space. People that look like me, my mother, my siblings, my great grandmother Jessie. I feel at home, while still feeling (dis)
placed and a certain dis-ease. They do not know me, they do not look at
me the way my family looks at me. To feel home and not feel recognized is

a difficult feeling. I want them to call me by name, recognize me the way I recognize them.

Abruni. I am White in their eyes, but also relative. I learn to see myself as White for the first time. I can trace my Whiteness twice. My Great Grandmother Mimi was a French woman who fell in love with a Black man. Her family ostracized her, so she moved with him to Chicago and gave birth to my mother's father. My other Great Great grandmother was raped by her slave master. My grandmother's skin and features remain evident of that lineage. She can pass for White, but she does not. She married a very dark-skinned Black man and birthed five children. My father was born before that marriage, fathered by a lighter-skinned Black man from New York City. I am White, if only in small doses. But my stories paint a different picture. I need you, reader, to hear those stories. I grew up in Inglewood, California, in predominately Black neighborhoods, with Black friends, Black music, Black food, Blackness. I have been called Black my entire life. The few who didn't call me Black asked, "what are you mixed with?" signaling some sort of difference. But never outright asking, "Are you White?" In Ghana, I felt my Whiteness for the first time. A student once said to me in her final performance, "You are what you answer to." I love the quote, but I immediately want to ask, "Does it matter who is doing the calling?"

The clearest part of my journey through Ghana occurs when I visit El Mina Slave Castle. The emotion and spirit I feel as I walk through too tight tunnels into slave quarters overwhelms me. I brush my hands against the concrete slab, once littered with more than 100 beautiful Ghanaian women and their menstrual blood, feces, urine, and sickness. A balcony stretches two stories above, overlooking the concrete. A slave master once stood on that balcony, beckoning his woman for the evening, every evening. He rapes women every night who sleep in their menstrual blood, feces, and urine. My heart is heavy. I walk through the point of no return, a 1.5-foot-wide gate five steps from the ocean, where small boats dock to carry Ghanaians to ships destined to cross the Atlantic Ocean. I rub my fingers along silent walls that carry the heavy whip of beatings, hunger, disease. I hold back my tears. This castle does not need my tears. As we gather our things to leave, we step through a small gift shop.

A gift shop at the entrance to a slave castle.

A gift shop.

I notice a bright yellow T-shirt that reads, "May those who died rest in peace. May those who return find their roots." I lose it. Writing these words, I lose it again.

To return is to come full circle, to meet in the center, and brings together the loose ends of experience. I have the slave master's blood in me. *Abruni.* The Ghanaians and their questions spotted him in my skin. Perhaps the same man who stood hovering over the balcony choosing which woman to rape that evening. I am him; I am her, too. Raped at the tender age of 15, I know how she feels. I am the American who was taught to fear Africa. To be overprotective of my stuff (Shange, 1997/1975). I am the descendent of slaves; my roots connect to a tree branch in Kumasi; *home* chants louder in my ears. I am remembering my roots in the center. I am home. I box with myself. I don't want to be White. I don't want to be American. I don't want to be a slave. I don't want to be raped. But I want to feel whole again. *More.*

The idea of something *more.* "What are you mixed with?" The question signifies Whiteness, goodness, *more.* I felt like the ability to pass as mixed gave me a certain edge over other Black girls. My two female cousins have a Black mother and White father. They were always *more.* We constantly compared our hair, our skin, our homes. They represented *more.* To be asked that question made me *more.* But I never answered *yes* despite knowing I had White lineage in my family history. I didn't desire to be *more;* I wanted to fit in, be another Black girl amongst my Black girlfriends. Being *more* is difficult in elementary and secondary school. Walking through Elmina Slave Castle, being *more* suddenly shifted. White became bad; an identity associated with such heinous acts that I felt repulsed, mortified, angry, hurt. It was no longer *more.* Being a rape survivor, a Black woman who descends from those amazing women that survived meant *more* in that moment. How does one accept the *more* without refusing *more?* We negotiate.

I must learn to embrace what I have learned as a series of ambiguous experiences, as open texts where I can reflect on the self and test knowledge and the limits of certainty. I need to leave room for interpretation, misunderstanding, not knowing (Holman Jones & Adams, 2010, p. 211). If what I once knew stands, I don't like that person. I want to be whole, at the center. I must redefine my orientation so that language lives closer to my experience, but remains open. I don't have to box with myself. I am a foreigner returning to find roots that call my name. *Home. You are what you answer to.* "And suddenly I feel everything rushing into a center, a nucleus. All the lost pieces of myself come flying from the deserts and the mountains and the valleys, magnetized toward that center. *Completa*" (Anzaldúa, 1987, p. 51). Some of those lost pieces cut, slash, prick, indent. Some of those pieces caress, hug, rub, impregnate me with possibility. However they come, they are mine/ours/yours meeting at a center. I answer. *Home.*

On Being Labeled Poor, Rich, Middle: Class Chameleon

Class defines a large part of who we are and how we see our bodies. It moves through our intersections seamlessly, quietly, like an obedient houseguest helping us reorganize our closets. It is always there, dictating what we can and cannot do, but in silent ways. It isn't until we meet someone from a different class that we become cognizant of our ubiquitous houseguest, or the way she has taken up residence in our front room. The way our clothes don't hang right anymore, or are out of place. Perhaps some things got thrown out with the trash. The people who made me aware of my class standing were my parents. I am a class chameleon. I grew up in multiple neighborhoods, with multiple incomes, with multiple parents, doing multiple things.

I remember my mother having 20K in the bank, a three-bedroom, two-bathroom house in a nice neighborhood, walking distance from the best school in Inglewood. I remember the kids from her "inner city" school in Compton, California, coming to *our* house at the end-of-the-year swim party, wading in *our* oversized Jacuzzi, and eating *our* barbeque. We were fortunate enough to share, so we did. But there was always a disconnect. *They* went back *home* at the end of the day. I remember riding in *our* silver corvette with red leather interior to go shopping at Nordstrom's, where a clerk would put shoes on my small feet, humor me with cute jokes, and tell me how beautiful I was. I remember never feeling hungry or wondering what we were having for dinner. I remember *more*.

I also remember less. I remember my mother moving us next door after her divorce, to a smaller house with roaches, no Jacuzzi in the backyard, and less food in the pantry. I remember moving to a condo after that, then an apartment. I remember eating bread and butter sandwiches, lucky if we had sugar to go with it. I remember talking about not being able to afford something.

I also remember mobility. I remember coming out of the space of less, and my mother buying a beautiful house, and cruising around town in her drop-top Lexus. My mother may have had to struggle, but she made survival look good. She was honest about where she was in life. My mother was no chameleon. She was who she was, and she was not apologetic.

And then there is my father, chameleon extraordinaire. He had friends all over town, from Palos Verdes to Northridge, California. When I was a little girl, he would pick me up in his huge, big bucket boat Mercedes. He lived the life of a bachelor, in a nice one-bedroom apartment with three different sparkling pools and matching girlfriends for each one. He had a smile that could dazzle anyone. He would take me to parties in neighborhoods most people only dream of. He talked the talk and walked the walk, like he owned the palace next door.

As a child I distinctly remember feeling a shift in my person when I would ride up to multimillion-dollar homes in that big boat of a Mercedes. They were different from where I lived, but I pretended to belong, just like my daddy. And a chameleon I, too, became. I learned how to pair one expensive item with several cheap ones to look chic. I learned how to shop at thrift stores in Beverly Hills and Hollywood. I learned to speak the language. I learned that even though my father lived in that Mercedes sometimes, and had very little cash flow or assets before I became an adult, he managed to travel all over the world, earn a PhD, become a day trader, and grow his wealth. He went from poor and having good friends, to middle class with the same good friends, to upper class with the same good friends. He made bootstraps look enticing.

Because of these two distinct experiences of shifting between classes, one purposeful and deliberate, the other circumstantial, I learned that class was about navigating intersections, and not a hindrance. Perhaps that is because the foundation for my parents' navigation was middle class. Using what little they did have, my parents chose to move between and beyond class distinctions. My middle-class foundations provided me with a certain degree of class mobility that is not always possible for people in other income levels. Navigating the intersection of class hasn't always been stable, but it is much easier to pretend from a middle-class space because of access to language, transportation, shopping, and education. I recognize the privilege that is middle-class status and the privilege that extends from mobility.

On Being Labeled Heterosexual or "I'm Coming Out"

In my mother's eyes, I am daughter, student, smart, perfect, feisty, fine, fashionable.
In my father's eyes I am princess, intelligent, poised, strong, reflection.
In my colleagues' eyes I am bossy, witty, humorous, loyal, friend.
In my children's eyes I am soft, comforting, lumpy, silly, stern.
In my eyes I am blurry, clear, blurry again, not always present.
In my ancestors' eyes, I am at once away and here, home and gone, blending in and out of borders I have yet to claim as my own.
In America's eyes I am Black girl pathologized who happened to make it out. An exception.
In Ghana's eyes I am mixed, White.
In queer's eyes, I am heterosexual, uninvited ally.
In heterosexual's eyes, I am queer. Too weird, too open, too honest.

Coming out. Of what? I have been telling my secrets since I was a little girl. Simple secrets, but my secrets nevertheless. When I was a child between the ages of six and nineish, I bit my toenails and ate my boogers. I had a girlfriend, my first girlfriend I suppose, who lived across the street. She was a year or so older than me. We would sneak into her backhouse to bump uglies with our panties down. The feelings of pleasure and possibly getting caught were magnificent. Now as an adult, I still expose parts of my sexuality freely through discourse. Only now, I come out every day in ways that are deceitful, but not my fault. You see, dear reader, I pass very well for heterosexual.

Bryant Alexander (2006) tells us that passing is a performance of suppression where one exists "betwixt and between two performance communities, the point of origin and the territory of desire" (p. 73). I think of these two performance communities as existing on a continuum, a *straight* line with one point serving as the origin and the other as the territory of desire. I think of navigating this *straight* line and what it means to push or pull in one direction. My point of origin is heterosexual. That is what this world tells me; but that is what I am pushing against. I am not heterosexual. However, admitting that I have a husband serves as a sort of coming out for who I am not in a space where heterosexual registers as the normative position. I find myself having to explain myself often. But Alexander contends that passing is a product, process, performativity, and reflection of positionality (p. 73).

My position is queer, my desires are queer, but my two-dimensional family portrait speaks otherwise. And the illocutionary act of "I do" on my wedding date signifies what Ragan Fox (forthcoming), channeling J. L. Astin, calls "performative power by creating and maintaining a world of outsiders (i.e., LGBTQ people), as it celebrates heterosexuality's reiterative power." I am guilty of speaking the words, but I never claimed innocence. Again, Fox reminds us that, "queering is an act whereby a critic or consumer challenges the grammars of compulsory heterosexuality." It is up to me to tell my story and disrupt the compulsion to mark a body as explicitly heterosexual and continue to perpetuate heterosexism. Unfortunately, the way my stories are received are beyond my control.

In a conversation on sexuality, someone called me an in-the-closet-heterosexual, as if being homosexual was the cool thing to do and I wanted to be down. So I wrote a paper about my sexuality and invited others to think of queer intersectionality as a space to write our own desires free from heteronormative and homonormative scripts. One of my reviewers replied:

> [T]his reads as a straight woman feeling left out and wanting to be included, and no one ever said queer politics was a politics of inclusion. What do queers get by defining the nuclear family as a potentially queer form? I would argue that what that does is reinscribe the center, once again. This isn't to say that straight married people who take advantage of that system of privilege can't engage in micro-political practices that might be queer, or that they can't show up at a queer rally, or that they can't be good allies, but I have to wonder why someone in that position would want more than that....

Micro-political practices. Are my practices micro-political? And how does one measure micro and macro politics of the body. I felt an urgency to prove myself. I e-mailed the editor because this was important to me. I wanted her to get it. Being married to a man is tough business when you want to be considered more than an ally. You are what you answer to, right? Wrong. Sometimes there are no labels to define your identities, so you masquerade under others until you either find one that suits you more comfortably, or create a new one. I always knew I was something *more* (perhaps *else* is the better term here), so I called myself a post-heterosexual. Being married to a man, I knew there was something potentially heterosexual about me. But I never fully felt heterosexual or desired the same scripts that heteronormative

life perpetuates. I answered to heterosexual only when pressured to. Pressure pushes upon the dialectical tensions of our bodies until we either implode with new language and/or give in.
I imploded once.
Post-heterosexual.
Rigid.
Bend, twist, turn, only inside your little box.
Rigid.
English language fills my mouth forcing it into a cube.
Rigid cube.
Not plush and soft like the two-spirited.
Hard, immovable.
Rigid.
I learned to speak in silence.
Batting my eyelashes. Quietly remembering desires in public.
I learned to look for intelligence in others
as an invitation to explore the metaphors of their brains
sexually.
You want a piece of me?
Yes.
Are you gay?
No.
But you like women?
Yes.
So you're a lesbian?
No.
But you like women?
Yes.
So you aren't heterosexual.
No.
Cue the questions.
Is your *husband* okay with that?
Do you seek pleasure from women outside of your relationship?
Who all is in *your* covenant?
Rigid questions.
Rigid answers.
Who are you?
Perhaps we should try to be more open-ended
Until then, I remain silent.
I learned to appreciate skin where skin didn't matter before.
Like the wenis of an elbow.
The pressure is getting to me.
You happy now?

No. So I told pressure to back the fuck off.

Give me time to process.

To learn my body in ways that labels didn't allow.

I wanted to enter my messy intersections and learn my body from the inside out in ways only a body can. "Such broad fluidity of gender, performance, sex and orientation indicates that it is not identity that is censored and scripted, cramped by definitions, but the *performance* of identity" (Schuh, 2006, p. 48). I have to learn to perform my identities in ways that don't restrict my identities. I find being honest, open, and candid reflect who I am beyond rigid, gendered, and sexualized performances.

Eventually, I found the language. I am a sapio-pansexual who found the perfect partner in a person who happens to have a penis. And admitting that I have a husband in conversation becomes a form of origin passing, a form of coming out backwards, like stepping outside the back of the wardrobe and entering Narnia. Further admitting that I have loved lesbians and am attracted to gay men becomes my small step forward. I want people to see *me,* not a two-dimensional picture predicated on normativity.

I want to remind those who question me what Hausman (1995) so articulately describes:

> As it is currently deployed, gender is a concept meaningful only within hetero-sexuality and in advocacy of heterosexuality—after all, its signification is the heterosexual subject. It masquerades as the ground for what is ungroundable (the body) and it pretends a fixity and stability that are conferred by a cultural system desperate to maintain a "body" as its natural counterpart. (p. 194)

My gender doesn't matter. My desires don't matter. I am who I am, and rhetoric will not, and cannot change that. To place a label on the body is to create a sense of clarity, but it doesn't change the body. As much as we conform to meet our labels, we are merely hiding bits and pieces of our identities that, eventually, will leak out.

Leaking out of my own closet then is the cultural matrix that assumes heterosexuality and provides space for an epistemology of the closet to exist (Adams, 2011). I push against heteronormativity by continuing to tell my story, mark my body as queer, and search for a type of agency only begot by reflexivity and subversive bodily acts (Clough, 1994). I am not heterosexual, I am *more.*

I didn't have many options for negotiating sex at the intersections as a young Black girl. There was no middle ground between the control-ling images of the Sapphire/Jezebel and the asexual Mammy/Matriarch. Anytime I felt sexual, I felt guilty. Anytime I assumed asexuality, I felt wrong, awkward, untruthful. Commanding then drafting my own language allowed me to create a platform to talk about these things. Language is an intersection. It was much harder to negotiate my sexuality without labels. But I also recognize that my labels don't have the stigmas attached to

93

them that lesbian, gay, and bisexual do. Language is a mark of privilege. It is my *more.*

On Being Labeled Reflexive

The intersections of skin color, race, nationality, blood, beauty, hair type, desire, and *more* come together as dependent variables in the equations of our identity. The variables are dependent because they shift as we navigate and negotiate different aspects of our identities. Even bloodlines can shift as new information develops, stories are found, or confessions are made. Our identities are not fixed. They fluctuate in a constant state of negotiation. What all of these narratives highlight, then, is the siphoning through intersections that afford the opportunity for *more.* Because of my skin color, middle-class status, and command of the English language, I have been able to understand and map my own desires, sexuality, and abilities. Negotiation is a language of possibility. Soyini Madison (personal communication, September 18, 2012) reminds us that, "if we don't have a vocabulary to imagine alternatives, we don't know that there are alternatives." Language not only helps us understand our intersections, it gives us the tools to navigate them.

Note

1. Alexander and Warren draw on Michael Kirby's (1979) notion of *autoperformance,* and what Susan Huddleston Edgerton (1993) describes as *poetic pedagogy* to formulate autopoetic narratives that tap into creative and critical articulations of lived experience.

References

Adams, T. E. (2011). *Narrating the closet: An autoethnography of same-sex attraction.* Walnut Creek, CA: Left Coast Press, Inc.

Adams, T. E., & Holman Jones, S. (2011). Telling stories: Reflexivity, queer theory, and autoethnography. *Critical Studies ↔ Critical Methodologies, 11*(2) 108–116.

Alexander, B. K. (2005). Performance ethnography: The reenacting and inciting of culture. In N. K. Denzin, & Y. S. Lincoln (Eds.), *The Sage handbook of qualitative research* (pp. 411–442). Thousand Oaks, CA: Sage.

Alexander, B. K. (2006). *Performing Black masculinity: Race, culture, and queer identity.* Lanham, MD: AltaMira Press.

Alexander, B. K. & Warren, J. T. (2002). The materiality of bodies: Critical reflections on pedagogy, politics, and positionality. *Communication Quarterly, 50*(3&4), 328-343.

Anzaldúa, Gloria. (1987). *Borderlands/La Frontera: The new mestiza.* San Francisco, CA: Spinsters/Aunt Lute.

Boylorn, R. (2011). Gray or for colored girls who are tired of chasing rainbows: Race and reflexivity. *Cultural Studies ↔ Critical Methodologies 11*(2), 178–186.

Clough, P. (1994). *Feminist thought: Desire, power, and academic discourse.* Cambridge, MA: Blackwell.

Conquergood, D. (1985). Performing as a moral act: Ethical dimensions of the ethnography of performance. *Literature in Performance, 2*(5), 1–13.

Denzin, N. (1996). *Interpretive ethnography: Ethnographic practices for the 21st century.* Thousand Oaks, CA: Sage.

Edgerton, S. H. (1993). Toni Morrison teaching the interminable. In C. McCarthy & W. Crichlow (Eds.), *Race, identity and representation in education* (pp. 220–235). New York: Routledge.

Fox, R. (forthcoming). "Phags for Phelps": Exploring the queer potential of the Westboro Baptist Church. *Liminalities: A Journal of Performance Studies.*

Gingrich-Philbrook, C. (2005). Autoethnography's family values: Easy access to compulsory experiences. *Text and Performance Quarterly, 25,* 297–314.

Goltz, D. B. (2011). Frustrating the "I": Critical dialogic reflexivity with personal voice. *Text and Performance Quarterly, 31*(4), 386–405.

Hausman, B. (1995). *Changing sex: Transsexualism, technology and the idea of gender.* Durham, NC: Duke University Press.

Holman Jones, S. & Adams, T. E. (2010). Autoethnography is a queer method. In K. Browne & C. J. Nash (Eds.), *Queer methods and methodologies: Intersecting queer theories and social science research* (pp. 195-214). Surrey, UK: Ashgate.

Kirby, M. (1979). Autoperformance issues: An introduction. *The Drama Review 23*(1), 2.

Kraidy, M. (2005). *Hybridity: Or the cultural logic of globalization.* Philadelphia, PA: Temple University Press.

Langellier, K. (1999). Personal narrative, performance, performativity: Two or three things I know for sure. *Text and Performance Quarterly, 19*(2), 123–144.

Madison, D. S. (2006). The dialogic performative in critical ethnography. *Text and Performance Quarterly, 26,* 320–324.

Nakayama, T. K. & Krizek, R. L. (1995). Whiteness: A strategic rhetoric. *Quarterly Journal of Speech, 81*(3), 291-309.

Pollock, D. (2006). Marking new directions in performance ethnography. *Text and Performance Quarterly, 26,* 325–329.

Schuh, C. A. (2006). Being Lisa: Discourses of gender and transsexual identity. *Kaleidoscope: A Graduate Journal of Qualitative Communication Research, 5,* 35–56.

Shange, N. (1997). *For colored girls who have considered suicide when the rainbow is enuf.* New York: Scribner. (Original work published 1975).

CHAPTER FIVE

Performing Fortune Cookie
An Autoethnographic Performance on Diasporic Hybridity

Richie Neil Hao

SEVERAL YEARS AGO, MY UNCLE TOOK MY PARENTS, SIBLINGS, AND me to a Chinese restaurant in a suburb east of Los Angeles. After we ate our delicious Chinese meal, a waiter came over and dropped off some cookies that were strange but intriguing at the same time. Prior to coming to the US to visit my uncle and his family in the early 1990s, I had never seen these cookies before. As I reached over to get one of the light brown Pac-Man shaped cookies wrapped in plastic, I asked my uncle what it was.

He said, "Oh, these are fortune cookies."

"What are fortune cookies?" I asked with my curious 12-year-old voice.

My uncle smiled and replied, "Well, these are cookies with little messages inside that tell you some good things." As I pondered more questions, my uncle, who was seemingly frustrated, just wanted to end the conversation: "Ai-yah ... it doesn't matter. Just eat it. It's something *they* eat out here."

From that point on, I always wondered who "they" are, those who eat these fortune cookies. Was my uncle referring to US Americans in general, the Chinese who reside in the US, or both? No matter who the fortune cookie caters to, I got the impression from my uncle that these cookies are an American construction of Chineseness.

According to Lee (2008a), about 3 billion fortune cookies are made each year, almost all in the United States. In addition, fortune cookies are served in Chinese restaurants in other countries, such as Britain, Mexico, Italy, France, and India, but not in China or in my point of origin as a person of Chinese heritage growing up—the Philippines. The fortune cookie's present

Critical Autoethnography: Intersecting Cultural Identities in Everyday Life, edited by Robin M. Boylorn and Mark P. Orbe, 96–109. © 2014 Left Coast Press, Inc. All rights reserved.

form known in Chinese restaurants in the US was contested in China for its authentic Chineseness when it was introduced there in 1993 (Burke, 2002). Richard Leung, vice president of the Wonton Food Company, says, "It seemed like a good idea at the time, but it just didn't pan out. Fortune cookies are too American of a concept" (Burke, 2002, para. 5).

As an ethnic Chinese who was born and raised in the Philippines and has lived in the US for almost two decades, my diasporic experiences have shaped who I am culturally. While diaspora is often discussed in different literature as a yearning to return to a homeland or being in another location, I see diaspora the way Gilroy (1995) talks about it—as a process of *becoming* rather than *being*. And, because my hybrid identity as a Chinese Filipino is constantly located, situated, shaped, and negotiated in different cultural contexts, I consider myself a diasporic hybrid, or metaphorically speaking, a fortune cookie. Instead of using metaphors like Oreo (black outside/white inside), coconut (brown outside/white inside), and banana (yellow outside/white inside), I use fortune cookie as a metaphor, because it does not simplify the constructions of identity to fixed physical, social, and cultural variables. While using fortune cookie inevitably leads me to discuss identity and authenticity at the same time, it allows me to examine our historicities as a point of contention to question and challenge the notion of authenticity. Because the fortune cookie does not have a clear point of origin given its different versions of history, I believe that using it to represent my diasporic hybridity reinforces the point that identity is a process that shapes who we are in various locations and times.

Through everyday performances of my diasporic hybridity, I illustrate in this autoethnographic piece how my performing as "fortune cookie" has shaped my understanding of self in relationship to cultural and linguistic practices in different contexts. It is imperative for me to first provide an overview of the fortune cookie's multiple historicities. Next, I discuss how I came to understand my diasporic hybridity, specifically examining the intersectionality of racial, ethnic, national, and class identities, through my lived experiences in my birthplace—the Philippines—as well as visiting China and living in the US. Finally, I explain the tensions and possibilities I face as a fortune cookie.

Fortune Cookie: Multiple Historicities

The history of the fortune cookie continues to remain a mystery, but there are multiple historical interpretations of where, why, and how the cookie became ubiquitous in Chinese American restaurants. The inventor of the cookie has been commonly considered to be David Jung, a Chinese immigrant and founder of the Hong Kong Noodle Company in Los Angeles, before World War I (Brunner, 2005). The lore states that David Jung invented fortune cookies as an appetizer, not a dessert (Lee, 2008b). According to Jung's son, George Cheng, his father got the idea of fortune cookies from "an ancient game played among the upper classes in China. Individuals would be given pen, paper, and a twisted cake that contained a scrap of paper with a subject written on it ..." (p. 145). The players were expected to write wisdom in a narrative. Another theory is that Jung invented the fortune cookie "to cheer up downtrodden men on the streets of Los Angeles and that a minister had written the messages inside" (p. 146). On the other hand, a Japanese American, Makoto Hagiwara, in California claimed credit for introducing or popularizing the fortune cookie (Harvey, 2008). Hagiwara said that he made and served fortune cookies to visitors of the Golden Gate Park's Japanese Tea Garden in the 1890s until 1942, when he and his family were sent to an internment camp in Topaz, Utah (Lee, 2008b).

By the 1930s, Umeya, owned by the Hamano family in Los Angeles, was "one of the earliest mass producers of fortune cookies" where they distributed "to more than 120 Japanese-owned restaurants throughout central and southern California" (Lee, 2008b, p. 144). Since there was not a lot of demand for sushi at the time, many Japanese Americans opened Chinese restaurants to earn income. However, when Japanese Americans were sent to internment camps during World War II, they had to leave the equipment they used to bake the fortune cookies. By the time Japanese Americans were released from internment camps, numerous Chinese American fortune cookie makers had begun to overtake the fortune cookie market. By the 1940s, fortune cookies were widely available in California, especially in San Francisco, where soldiers and sailors frequented Chinese restaurants. The cookies soon caught on in other major cities in the US, where they were sold on supermarket shelves and customized to announce engagements and promote businesses.

Despite fortune cookies' historical presence in the US, their origin may actually be Japanese. Yasuko Nakamachi, a Japanese researcher, discovered that "many confectionery stores had offered candies that came with little fortunes inside them" during the Showa period in Japan (Lee, 2008b, p. 263). To confirm her findings, Nakamachi reviewed Edo- and Meiji-era documents that referenced *tsujiura senbei* in Japan during the nineteenth century and described them as "brittle cookies that contained a fortune in a fictional work by Tamenaga Shunsui, a humorist who lived between 1790 and 1843" (p. 261). Nakamachi also found a book that featured an 1878 print of a man grilling *tsujiura senbei*.

While reading a Japanese book on confectioneries, Nakamachi stumbled upon Japanese cookies folded around little pieces of paper as a regional snack in Ishikawa being made locally during New Year festivities (Lee, 2008b). In Kyoto, Nakamachi also saw several small family Japanese bakeries that sold a version of fortune cookies similar to those in the US. The bakers called them *omikuji senbei* ("fortune crackers"), *tsujiura suzu* ("bells with fortunes"), or *tsujiura senbei*. The Japanese fortune cookies are flavored with miso and sesame, and they are bigger, darker, and shinier than their US counterparts. Additionally, the slips of paper are placed between the cookies' outer folds in Japan rather than inside the cookies as they are in the US.

Performing Diasporic Chinese in the Philippines

Both of my parents are Chinese Filipina/o, so it is fitting that they raised my siblings and me in a household composed of both Chinese and Filipina/o cultures. When we used to live in the Philippines, my family and I would frequent Manila's Chinatown as a way to maintain our Chineseness. Every time my family and I walked down Ongpin Street, I could smell the aroma of *sho pao* (sweet pork bun), *sho mai* (dumplings), and *ma chang* (sticky pork rice) that seemed so familiar yet nostalgic at the same time. I remember eating a handful of these and other Chinese delicacies that my family and I enjoyed at our favorite dim sum restaurant. After dim sum, we typically walked down the long strip to visit familiar stores that carried artifacts, clothes, paintings, calligraphies, among other things, that represented our Chineseness.

My family and I also participated in festivities and celebrations on Ongpin Street. In particular, during Lunar New Year, we would walk around Ongpin Street and find a spot to stand and watch the fireworks display and lion and dragon dances. The street was crowded with people—young and old, Chinese and Filipina/o—who were all anticipating the public spectacle associated with Lunar New Year. Year after year, it is a tradition to see ritualistic performances of lion and dragon dances, in which a few people go under an elaborately decorated lion and dragon red/gold train and parade around Chinatown. One person holds the gigantic head, and the others carry the stretched body, using long sticks, which they carry in their hands. Each lion or dragon visits the stores along the strip to eat up the *hong bao*—red envelope with money—that is tied up in front of the store as a symbol of a prosperous new year. As these dances are going on, the booming sounds of firework displays occur simultaneously with enthusiastic spectators looking on, smiling, and clapping at these ritualized performances. Ongpin Street was a place of confirmation—a confirmation that my family and I were part of the Chinese diaspora in this Filipina/o town.

As a Chinese Filipina/o family, my parents also made sure that certain Filipina/o cultural practices become ingrained in our daily lives. For instance, we had a family ritual of performing *noche buena*, which is Spanish for "good night," on Christmas Eve. My family and I would normally go to a late night mass at a nearby Catholic church. After the mass, we would have a big feast at home that normally consisted of traditional Filipina/o and

Chinese Filipina/o foods: *queso de bola* (gigantic cheese ball), *lechon* (roast pig), *pancit* (noodles), fried chicken, *lumpia* (egg rolls), rice, *adobo* (sautéed pork or chicken), *halo-halo* (dessert drink), rice cakes, and other pastries. After eating this diasporic hybrid meal, my family and I would stay up until early in the morning to share stories with each other. Celebrating the Lunar New Year and *noche buena* are just two of many examples of ways my family and I celebrated our diasporic hybridity while living in the Philippines.

However, issues of authenticity also posed challenges to my Chinese Filipino identity. In order for one's identity to be authentic, there is an assumption that it has to be "coherent, unified, [and] fixed" (Sarup, 1996, p. 14). As an ethnic Chinese in the Philippines, I was Chinese before I could claim my Filipino identity. Even though I was born and raised in the Philippines and know how to speak Tagalog fluently, many Filipina/os couldn't see past my Chinese-appearing body as a marker of Chineseness, which made it difficult for me to identify culturally as Filipino. Despite generations of the Chinese presence in the Philippines, they are the ethnic minority in the country (See, 1997). While growing up in the Philippines, I encountered some Filipina/os who believed that Chinese Filipina/os should go back to China, even though most of us were born and raised in the Philippines. I am a third-generation Chinese Filipino, given that my grandparents (except for my paternal grandmother) were born and raised in the Philippines. In every sense of my being, I consider myself Filipino, too, since the Philippines was the only place I knew. I had never been to China until my family and I went to Guangzhou for a vacation when I was ten years old.

My experience as a diasporic hybrid in my birthplace shows how the notion of authenticity affected my sense of being, specifically how the particularity of cultural and ethnic expectations forced me in some cases to identify as Chinese as opposed to Chinese Filipino. Hall (1994) points out that diasporic individuals have the desire to return to their lost identities. In my case, I always wonder if my diasporic hybridity prevents me from claiming Filipino identity. I was sometimes forced to pick an identity—Chinese or Filipino—in order to fit in with a particular community. Even though my family and I are Filipina/o by nationality and ethnicity, our Chinese ancestry has greatly influenced much of our cultural identity. For instance, like most Chinese in the Philippines, my siblings and I attended a Chinese Filipina/o private school that emphasized the importance of Chinese history and language in addition to Filipina/o history and English language classes. In so many ways, I was privileged enough to attend a Chinese Filipina/o school that allowed me to learn about my Chinese culture and identity, but such an opportunity was also strategic to being Chinese. Most, if not all, Chinese Filipina/os I knew growing up attended Chinese Filipina/o schools at the elementary and secondary levels as a way to perform and maintain their Chinese cultural membership. Oftentimes, Chinese Filipina/os who choose to attend local Filipina/o public schools because of economic and/ or assimilation reasons are considered not "Chinese" enough. My schooling experience is one example of how I was socialized to understand that, in the eyes of my parents and others, I am Chinese. In a way, my diasporic hybridity makes it difficult for me to achieve "wholeness," as I constantly have to negotiate my identities to seek recognition from others (Bhabha, 1994, p. 10).

Finding Chineseness in the Mainland

In 1990, my family and I went to Guangzhou, China, for a vacation. We went to a street market full of vendors that sold clothes, artifacts, toys, and other things that normally attract tourists and locals alike. As my family and I walked around the market, it was a bizarre feeling. It was like having a reunion with long lost relatives. My Chinese-looking body blended in with the rest of the crowd. I felt I was one of the Chinese citizens at the market.

There was so much to see at the street market. To cover as much ground as possible, my family walked faster than usual. I followed them, but took my time to look at all the goods around me. As I walked past tables and tables of goods, a display of slippers caught my eye. I picked up the green fluffy slippers and touched them to get the feel of how soft they were. The Chinese vendor, a petite woman in her 60s or 70s, smiled at me and asked me a question in Cantonese. I believe she asked, "Do you like it?" Or, it could have been "Do you need help?" Or, maybe she was telling me how much the slippers were. Her question overwhelmed me, so I was speechless. I wanted to respond, but I could not speak Cantonese. All of a sudden, I was "caught up at the intersection of multiple, sometimes, conflicting, subject positions, and [did] not feel at home anywhere" (Shi, 2005, p. 55). I thought I was finally "home" at the market, yet I was not. I realized that not only did I have to look like them, but I had to speak like them, too, in order to be one of them.

I did not and still do not know what the Chinese vendor said. She continued to smile waiting for my response, and I smiled back and nodded my head pretending I understood what she said, just like most tourists. All of a sudden, her smile turned to an annoyed look, and I could sense she was suspicious of my Chineseness. In that moment, similar to Alexander's (2006) experience as a tourist in China, I felt that the "issue of authenticity [was] not about what [was] real as much as what [was] known" (p. 19). My Chinese body allowed me to pass as one of them, but my inability to speak the language made it apparent that I was not one of *them*. For the first time, I felt I was not Chinese. I learned in that experience that as a tourist "the struggle to find authenticity is also the struggle to avoid one's own sense of familiarity, and authenticity's pleasure is really its absence" (Alexander,

2006, p. 31). I wanted to be one of them, yet the Chinese vendor saw me as Other—the Westernized Chinese Filipino who had left his mother tongue behind. I felt like another tourist trying to get to know the culture and language I did not know. In a sense, I was in what Bhabha (1994) calls "'in-between spaces' ... that initiate new signs of identity, and innovative sites of collaboration and contestation" (pp. 1–2).

When I was in China, I thought I had found my home, where I could reconnect with my roots. Unfortunately, the street market turned out to be, what Chawla (2003) calls, just another "roof over the head. Dislocation [as] a way of being" (p. 273). The street market was a place where I fit in physically, but was dislocated for speaking like a foreigner. I did not feel at home anymore. So, where is "home"?

Home—the place where my ancestors came from?
Home—the city where my birth certificate was printed?
Home—the country of my permanent residency?
Home—the state where my family lives?
Home—the college town where I lived for four years?
Home—the country where I could vote?
Home—the city where I currently live and work?
Home—the place where personal and cultural connections are made?
Home—where is home? (see Hao, 2012)

Diasporic Hybridity in the U.S.

As a fortune cookie now living in the US, I continue to struggle in performing my diasporic hybridity. I thought coming to the culturally diverse United States would make it easier for me to perform my multicultural identities. To my surprise, many people from mainland China, Hong Kong, and Taiwan in particular that I met or interacted with saw/see me as "American-Born Chinese" or "ABC" for short, even though I was not born in the US. Is it because I am an ethnic Chinese who speaks English with somewhat an undetectable Chinese accent? Is it because I speak more English than Chinese? Is it because I watch more US TV shows than Chinese ones? Is it because I can't tell how "authentic Chinese" food is supposed to taste?

My assumed ABC-ness apparently came through when my family and I ate at a local Chinese restaurant close to where my parents live in suburban Los Angeles. That Sunday afternoon, I suggested to my dad that I would like to practice my Mandarin by ordering one dish from the menu. My dad smiled and gladly accepted my request. After having taken a few Mandarin courses in high school and college, I did not think it would be that difficult to order one dish in Mandarin. So, I picked up the menu, opened it, and flipped through the pages, which had Chinese characters on the left side and English translations on the right. My first stop: the pork section. Sure enough, one of my favorites, sweet and sour pork, was on the menu. I attempted to read the menu silently. For some reason, I could only read one Chinese character. To save myself from embarrassment with the Chinese waiter, who was staring at me, I kept looking through the menu to see what other dish I could say in Mandarin so that I could order it. My dad asked me if I was ready to order. I looked at him, signaling that I needed more time. Some more minutes passed, and I could not stall any longer. I had to order something—anything—so that the impatient waiter could be on his way to wherever he was supposed to go. I continued to look down at the menu. I felt helpless and confused. As I was attempting to order other dishes, I was once again blinded by all of these Chinese characters. So, I went back to try to read sweet and sour pork—in Mandarin—this time, out loud. Um ... Um ... *Rou* (meat). Because I could only read one of the Chinese characters, all I could do was use my index finger to point to the menu to let the waiter know what I wanted to order. "This one, please," I told the waiter while lowering my face to mask my embarrassment. The waiter impatiently took my order and shook his head before leaving the table.

About twenty minutes later, four courses of food (seafood fried rice, green beans in black bean sauce, curry chicken, and sweet and sour pork) that my family and I ordered had arrived. I picked up the off-white plastic chopsticks on the table. So, here I was attempting to pick up the green bean from the plate at the center of the table. For some reason, I could not hold the chopsticks properly. After many tries, I gave up and decided to raise my hand hesitantly to signal the same waiter that I needed my spoon and fork. The waiter approached me, and I told him what I needed in English without looking him directly in the eye. I was hesitant to leave the chopsticks on the table for fear of being perceived as an inauthentic Chinese—again. However, at the same time, I grew up in the Philippines accustomed to eating with a spoon and fork. Should I be ashamed for abandoning my chopsticks? Does that make me less Chinese? When the waiter came back with my fork and spoon, he looked at me and seemed to be questioning my Chineseness. A real Chinese would know how to use chopsticks, his suspicious eyes seemed to say. I became suspect, presumably posing as "Chinese" in this Chinese American restaurant.

Reflecting on my embarrassing experience at a restaurant, I think about how I continue to perform and negotiate my racial, ethnic, national, and class identities in the US. While living in Los Angeles, I did not have to think much about my racial identity, since I was surrounded by Asian Americans in my daily interactions at school and other public contexts. At home, I communicated with my family primarily in Taglish (a combination of Tagalog and English) and Chinese (Hokkien dialect). In addition to maintaining the languages we grew up with, my family and I continued to celebrate some of the cultural traditions and practices as Chinese Filipina/os, such as the Lunar New Year and Mooncake Festival, even though they became less elaborate than the way we celebrated these traditions in the Philippines. Both Chinese and Filipina/o foods and supermarkets are easily accessible in different L.A. suburban neighborhoods we have lived in. I also attended a predominantly Asian American high school where my body blended in with those of my peers, most of whom also came from immigrant families. If anything changed dramatically for my family, it was my family's socioeconomic status. While in the Philippines, my parents owned their own business, but in the US, despite my father's business degree from the Philippines, he continues to this day working as a gas station attendant. My mother stays at home to take care of the family. My family's change in socioeconomic status made me realize that as Asian immigrants in the US, our lives turned out to be different from what I had envisioned it meant to be "American." Despite my family's economic situation, eating comfort foods, being surrounded by my family, and living in predominantly Asian American neighborhoods allowed me to celebrate and appreciate my Asianness, and, more specifically, my Chinese and Filipino identities.

When I moved to Carbondale, Illinois, for graduate school, I could not find a lot of people who looked like me. I felt isolated and missed what I had taken for granted when I lived in Los Angeles. For the first time since living in the US, I started to yearn to know more about myself. While I had the luxury of being able to celebrate my Chinese Filipino identity in L.A., the very small presence of Asian Americans in general in this small college town changed my perspective on my identities. I no longer looked for the specificity of my identity as a Chinese Filipino, rather it was more pressing for me to (re)claim my Asian identity. While in Carbondale, where there was only one "international grocery" and decent Chinese restaurant, I was hungry to take Asian American history and culture courses, which had been readily available in the universities I attended in L.A. However, when I was in L.A., I did not take advantage of the limitless opportunities to take courses in Asian American history and culture. Perhaps a part of me believed that in the midst of other Asian American bodies in L.A., I did not need to "know" who I was racially; I already knew what it was like—my body is first and foremost marked as Asian.

Now living in Denver, I am beginning to reclaim my Asianness because of some visible presence of Asian American cultures in various areas around the city. I see Asian supermarkets again in the city and surrounding Denver suburbs, which allows me to feel at home to some extent. However, Chinese and Filipina/o communities here are small compared with what I was used to in L.A., so I always find myself longing for Chinese and Filipina/o foods, cultures, and traditions. When I go back to L.A. to see family and friends, I always make a checklist of the familiar restaurants by my parents' neighborhood and the surrounding suburbs where I can eat my favorite Chinese and Filipina/o foods.

However, living in Denver has provided me an opportunity to appreciate my Asian racialized body further. While living here since 2009, I have been involved in an Asian Pacific American community as a mentor in the Emerging Leaders Program (ELP), which is designed to help Asian Pacific American students get involved in a community outreach project that would benefit the local Asian Pacific American community. My involvement in the Asian Pacific American community in Denver has instilled in me the significance of mentoring and how that shapes my understanding of my Asianness in relationship to other mentors and mentees in ELP. From my own experience in ELP, I believe that Asian Pacific Americans in Denver are more conscious of their racialized and ethnic identities, because there are not a lot of us here compared to other major cities, such as L.A., Chicago, and New York, so there seems to be a solidarity that needs to be preserved and maintained to make our presence known. While Denver is not the same as L.A., I have gained a different appreciation of my Asianness here, specifically from a racial identity perspective.

Rediscovering Fortune Cookie: Tensions and Possibilities

Several years ago, I got to eat my very first fortune cookie. During that same time, I found out from my uncle that Chinese people do not eat fortune cookies. However, after I scanned side to side, front, and back of the restaurant, most of those people eating where my family and I were dining that day were Chinese; they just happened to live in the US. The history behind the fortune cookie's identity still leaves us with many questions. The modern-day fortune cookie we know in the US was not produced in China, but a recent discovery tells us that it could actually be Japanese. At the same time, both Chinese Americans and Japanese Americans claim the invention. No matter how we look at it, the fortune cookie that we know today has different variations, flavors, and influences.

Due to the restrictions that go along with the notion of authenticity, fortune cookies—literally and metaphorically speaking—usually face multiple tensions. Therefore, it is not a surprise that fortune cookies did not fare well in China when they were marketed there many years ago. To legitimize their Chineseness, many fortune cookies today offer Mandarin Chinese lessons to those who eat them. In 1993, the Wonton Food Company began printing "Learn Chinese" features on the back of the fortune slips (Burke, 2002). Common phrases in English, such as "I am an American," precede their Chinese phonetic translation: "Wo shi Meiguoren." It is interesting to see how the fortune cookie's identity is performed and negotiated through these texts. To me, the fortune cookie is used as a medium to teach Mandarin lessons to those who want to get (re)acquainted with their Chineseness while trying to maintain a US American identity. For other US Americans, the fortune cookie can be used to start learning basic Chinese words and phrases, but it primarily serves as part of the expected Chinese dining experience—to discover "fortunes" (through "Chinese wisdom" and "lucky numbers") that are printed on the fortune cookie inserts.

The fortune cookie's linguistic performances remind me of the Mandarin classes I used to take in high school and college as a way to perform my Chinese identity. Even though I speak Chinese (Hokkien dialect, to be exact), I felt a need to become fluent in Mandarin. For some reason, I perceived Mandarin to be an "authentic Chinese" dialect, because it is China's official language and it is used widely in the US. I enrolled in Mandarin classes the last two years of high school and during my sophomore year of college. I learned how to read, write, and speak basic words, phrases, and sentences.

After studying Mandarin for a couple of years, I started to feel more Chinese, yet at the same time I felt like a fraud. If I was really Chinese, why did I have to learn how to become Chinese? While attending Mandarin classes, I continued to make what Shimakawa (2002) calls "a movement between visibility and invisibility, foreignness and domestication/assimilation" (p. 3). Now thinking back, my enrollment in the classes compromised my diasporic hybridity. In essence, I was both visible and invisible, because, while learning how to speak Mandarin could probably mark me as "authentic Chinese," taking the classes reinforced the idea that speaking Mandarin was the only way I could be Chinese.

My in-betweenness as a fortune cookie contradicts the notion of authenticity, which is a way for people to distinguish who is culturally similar or different in order to establish solidarity (Appiah, 1996) based on "shared systems of symbols and meanings as well as norms/rules for conduct" (Collier & Thomas, 1988, p. 113). However, diasporic hybrid identities are never complete (Anthias, 2001). As Johnson (2003) states, an identity may exist as a floating signifier from one culture to another, as it is influenced by material, political, social, and cultural forces. My experiences in different countries and US locations further inform who I am based on my racial, ethnic, national, and class identities. In the Philippines, I passed as an "authentic Chinese" with flying colors; I looked, sounded, and acted the part of a socioeconomically privileged Chinese. However, I was not Filipino enough. In Guangzhou, China, I fit the look of a Chinese, but I was not considered Chinese, because I failed to speak the local dialect.

Moving to the US allowed me to think about my different identities. More specifically, in addition to my ethnic and national identities, I also began to examine my Asian body and socioeconomic status further. I never thought that my family's Asian immigrant background could be a barrier to my family having a comfortable life in the US. Despite my family's financial situation, we managed to find a Chinese Filipina/o community in suburban Los Angeles for support. Having lived in different parts of the US for the last two decades has provided me with an understanding of how my identities continue to shift as I move from one place to another. It has helped me understand, for example, when to privilege my racial, ethnic, or national identities. In Los Angeles, I was able to celebrate my Asianness and Chinese Filipino identity, because I lived in predominantly Asian American neighborhoods that provided me the comfort of Chinese and Filipino traditions and foods. When I attended graduate school in Carbondale, Illinois, I privileged my racial identity because of the limited presence of Asian Americans in the area. While living in Denver is not comparable to living in Los Angeles, it allows me to reconnect with my Asianness through the local Asian Pacific American community that I could not find in Carbondale. My involvement in the community through the mentoring program has been an opportunity for me to reflect on how I could reconnect with my Asianness—not just for the purpose of finding my racialized body again in the midst of other Asian Americans, but also to make connections with other Asian Pacific Americans in the community.

Because our identities are always changing, emerging, and constantly in negotiation, I am using fortune cookie as a metaphor for my diasporic hybrid identity, since the fortune cookie as a food product does not have a fixed historicity that specifically locates where it came from or how it originated. Instead, the fortune cookie has become a food product that is composed of many cultural influences and varieties that symbolically represent how identity, as Yep (2002) notes, is "a person's conception of self within a particular social, geographical, cultural, and political context" (p. 61). Furthermore, the function of "hybridities," as the fortune cookie symbolizes, is that "they postulate of transgressive cultural formations which in and of themselves function to dispel the certainties of fixed location" (Anthias, 2001, p. 620). In essence, my fortune cookieness has been shaped and influenced by my life experiences in the Philippines, China, and the US, where "cultural diasporization" (Anthias, 2001, p. 620) exists as new forms of identities.

From the Philippines to China and to the US, I continue to perform and negotiate my identities in different cultural contexts. I have learned and accepted over the years that it is not easy to be a diasporic hybrid. After all, I struggled to fit in wherever I was and am, based on my physical and linguistic markers. As a result, I was not "Chinese," "Filipino," or "Asian" enough. Oftentimes there are people who would ask me, "What are you?" While I am compelled to say "Chinese Filipino" every time, my answer would typically lead to other questions, such as, "Is your dad Chinese and your mom Filipina?" At times, it is convenient to simply say I am "Chinese" or "Filipino." However, by choosing "Chinese" or "Filipino," am I compromising my diasporic hybridity? Despite some challenges with my identity negotiation and legitimization, after all these years, I am beginning to appreciate the possibilities that come with my diasporic hybrid identity—as a fortune cookie.

References

Alexander, B. K. (2006). *Performing black masculinity: Race, culture, and queer identity.* Lanham, MD: AltaMira Press.

Anthias, F. (2001). New hybridities, old concepts: the limits of "culture." *Ethnic and Racial Studies, 24,* 619–641.

Appiah, K. A. (1996). Identity: Political not cultural. In M. Garber, R. L. Walkowitz, & P. B. Franklin (Eds.), *Fieldwork: Sites in literary and cultural studies* (pp. 34–40). New York: Routledge.

Bhabha, H. K. (1994). *The location of culture.* London: Routledge.

Brunner, B. (2005, May 10). The history of the fortune cookie. *Infoplease.* Retrieved May 1, 2007, from http://www.infoplease.com/spot/fortunecookies.html

Burke, K. (2002, April 3). The secret history of fortune cookies. *Columbia News Service.* Retrieved May 1, 2007, from http://www.jrn.columbia.edu/studentwork/cns/2002-04-03/320.asp

Chawla, D. (2003). Rhythms of dis-location. In R. P. Clair (Ed.), *Expressions of ethnography: Novel approaches to qualitative methods* (pp. 271–279). Albany: SUNY Press.

Collier, M. J., & Thomas, M. (1988). Cultural identity: An interpretive perspective. *International and Intercultural Communication Annual, 12,* 99–120.

Gilroy, P. (1995). "To be real": The dissident forms of Black expressive culture. In C. Ugwu (Ed.), *Let's get it on: The politics of black performance* (pp. 12–33). Seattle, WA: Bay.

Hall, S. (1994). Cultural identity and diaspora. In P. Williams & L. Chrisman (Eds.), *Colonial discourse and postcolonial theory: A reader* (pp. 392–403). New York: Columbia University Press.

Hao, R. N. (2012). Cultural reentry: A critical review of intercultural communication research. In N. Bardhan & M. P. Orbe (Eds.), *Identity research and communication: Intercultural reflections and future directions* (pp. 71–85). Lanham, MD: Lexington.

Harvey, S. (2008, June 8). Claims to original fortune cookies crumble under weight of research. *Los Angeles Times.* Retrieved June 15, 2008, from http://www.latimes.com/news/local/la-me-then8-2008jun08,1,1823605,full.column

Johnson, E. P. (2003). *Appropriating blackness: Performance and the politics of authenticity.* Durham, NC: Duke UP.

Lee, J. (2008a, January 16). Solving a riddle wrapped in a mystery inside a cookie. *New York Times.* Retrieved June 15, 2008, from http://www.nytimes.com/2008/01/16/dining/16fort.html?_r=1&scp=2&sq=fortune+cookie&st=nyt&oref=slogin

Lee, J. (2008b). *The fortune cookie chronicles: Adventures in the world of Chinese food.* New York: Twelve.

Sarup, M. (1996). *Identity, culture and the postmodern world.* Athens: University of Georgia Press.

See, T. A. (1997). *Chinese in the Philippines: Problems & perspectives* (Vol. 1). Manila, Philippines: Kaisa Para Sa Kaunlaran, Inc.

Shi, Y. (2005). Identity construction of the Chinese diaspora, ethnic media use, community formation, and the possibility of social activism. *Continuum: Journal of Media & Cultural Studies, 19,* 55–72.

Shimakawa, K. (2002). *National abjection: The Asian American body onstage.* Durham, NC: Duke University Press.

Yep, G. A. (2002). My three cultures: Navigating the multicultural identity landscape. In J. Martin, T. Nakayama, & L. Flores (Eds.), *Readings in intercultural communication* (2nd ed.) (pp. 60–66). Boston, MA: McGraw-Hill.

CHAPTER SIX

Critical Autoethnography as Intersectional Praxis
A Performative Pedagogical Interplay on Bleeding Borders of Identity

Bryant Keith Alexander

OR ME, DOING CRITICAL AUTOETHNOGRAPHY IS SOMETIMES LIKE capturing a picture of yourself in a glass borderless frame; a picture in which an image of you is represented and there are sightless borders of containment; containments called race, sex, gender, culture, and occasions of human social experience fixed in time and space, floating in a fixed liquidity of memory, giving shape to experience, structuring vision and engagement with the intent for others to see and know you differently as you story the meaningfulness of personal experience in a cultural context. For me this is the engagement of autoethnography. The critical in critical autoethnography captures a moment in that borderless frame and holds it to a particular scrutiny—intersplicing a sociology-of-the-self with a hermeneutics of theorizing the self. Yet in the process of such an engagement, there is always a feeling of risk: a risk of bleeding, in which the presumed categorical containments of your identity threatens to exceed its borders, revealing the ways in which we are always both particular and plural at the same time; never contained and always messy.

I often have used the construct of "bleeding borders" or "bleeding identities" to reference the false boundaries that limit social possibility—whether that be the migration of identities across place and space, or the limitations of what we are supposed to be, based on the materiality of bodies, the presumed fixity of sex and gender, or the historical points of origin that signal cultural and clan affiliation (see for example Alexander, 2011). I have argued that the notion of "bleeding" is not necessarily a violent metaphor, as much as the travel between permeable membranes of bordered identities within an embodied text—often when inter/intra-cultural-racial encounters force a realization of the predicament of selves. Such a construction in my engagement of a critical autoethnography also reveals the intersectional nature of identity.

In her oft-cited essay, "Mapping the Margins: Intersectionality, Identity Politics, and Violence against Women," Kimberlé Crenshaw (1995) offers the construct of *intersectionality,* which examines the intersection of race (particularly African American raced identity) with gender (particularly African American women). In her conclusions, she speaks to "recognizing that identity politics takes place at the site where categories intersect thus seems more fruitful than challenging the possibility of talking about categories at all. Through an awareness of intersectionality, we can better acknowledge and ground the differences among us and negotiate the means by which these differences will find expression in constructing group politics" (p. 377).

For me, in doing critical autoethnography you always experience odd moments of catching a glimpse of yourself in a glass borderless frame; images of yourself reflecting back from the gloss and glean of a polished surface layered atop the fixed image *of* yourself, a potentially reified rendition caught in time; a ghosting, if you will, that when viewed, forces a critical reflexive moment of searching for the missing pieces of yourself that the shutter of the lens did not capture but only critical autoethnography can recover—revealing the dynamic of politics at play in the scene that at once appears fixed but in actuality bleeds the lives narrated in the picture and the very moment of viewing the picture itself. So, it is in this way that I want to begin this exploration of critical autoethnography as intersectional praxis, and as a particular pedagogy of doing.

Trying to Tell the Story of a Borderless Frame

There is a story that I want to tell. No, there is a story that I *need* to tell. A story claimed by others that will be told, whether I like it or not, but it won't include my voice. It won't include my side. It won't include me in the manner that I want to be re/presented. It won't include me trying to make sense of the story in the process of thinking and writing the story. It won't include the story of me stepping back to see the story with perspective; the story of me stepping back from the picture to see me in the picture of the story trying to get perspective; the story of me stepping back to critically see me and others in the story I tell, knowing that it is not exclusively my story (nor theirs). In this moment I am not staging a moment that reifies a given reality, but taking stock of how I am implicated in the scene of a happening. Maybe I will be "read" in this story. Maybe the story is really in that photo. That photo that sits on the shelf in my living room that everyone makes comment about. That photo of my three brothers and me, the one from the wedding:

His wedding, and
His wedding, and
His wedding, but not my wedding.
That photo.

That *queer* photo of three straight Black men dressed in white tuxedoes and one queer Black man dressed in a tan suit. Me, still with long hair that they joke makes me look feminine, in relation to their own performed masculinity in which the length of hair becomes a politic of gender. It's not a joke, it is a critique and one that in my childhood far preceded the dreadlocks that later grew as an act of resistance from my head.

Brothers.
Brothers?

That photo that *I* staged and had someone take. That photo that *I* gave a copy of to each of them, pressed behind a prism of glass with a borderless frame, implicates me. It implicates them. A borderless frame, as if there are no limits to its containment or limits to the interpretations by which every brother tells a story.

It is a wedding photo.
It is a photo taken at a wedding.
It is a photo of my three brothers and me.
It is a photo that weds us to each/other.
It is a wedding photo that I am allowed to be in but I can't be part of the wedding.

Each of the brothers in white is married. Each of the brothers in white invited the other brothers to be in their wedding. I received no such invitations. This picture is performativity; the iteration of an iteration, of an iteration, maybe of an intention. But that's my story. The story that I gave them in a borderless frame. In the picture I am the anomaly. I am the irregularity. I am the peculiarity. I am the queer. Invited to attend the wedding, but not to be in the wedding.

Not invited to wed.

That photo of my three brothers and me, the one from the wedding; from the symbolic weddings:

His wedding, and
His wedding, and
His wedding, but not my wedding.
Invited to attend the weddings, but not to be in the weddings.
Not invited to wed.

I staged this photo as I am staging this story to document our brotherhood, not realizing that the abject body in the photo (and maybe in the story) would be mine. The queer brother in tan also standing in place for the absent queer brother, a fifth brother, who died from AIDS before the weddings; another tan suit? We called him Tanny, which was short for Nathanial. I am implicated in the staging of this photo. I am implicated in the telling of this story. I am implicated in this story through a complicity of blood, gender, race, and writing. This story is not apolitical.

It is a story about brothers and gender performance.

It is a story about the heterosexual privilege to wed.

It is a story about inclusion, exclusion, and bordered and borderless identities that bleed in the banal moments of weddings, and photos, and the mixed identities of brothers (biological, cultural, racial, or spiritual). It is a story about the intersectionality of identity; a meeting place of race, sexuality, culture, and gender; co-informing, co-narrating and co-performing identities that become something altogether different, more. I don't know their stories.

It is a picture that I love.

It is a picture that I hate.

It is a picture that I hate to love.

It is a picture that I study with critical intent to find my selves floating in a fixed liquidity of identity politics.

In the presence of my brothers I am the same and not the same. I am a Black man linked with other Black men by biology and heritage. Yet the particularity of sexuality, their heterosexuality and my homosexuality, becomes the perceptual variable that marks our difference—in that way in which our relational dynamic is both intraracial and intercultural at the same time.

***

In using autoethnography as a critical methodology in performance studies classes and even classes like interpersonal, relational, and intercultural communication, I have often asked students to engage in an explication of lived experience in a cultural context; exploring themselves in relation to and in the context of cultural communities. But in particular, I have asked them to do a performed close analysis of their identity as a critical nexus. Following Crenshaw (1995), I am asking students to not easily settle on the particularity of their race, sex, and gender or even the more amorphous constructions of culture and class in which they glom onto a collective sense of self as practiced in alignment with others. I ask them to address the bleeding borders of their identity that place them betwixt and between; places and times in which the seeming singularity of their identity becomes plural. In an autoethnographic assignment, I ask them to speak to variables of personality, positionality, and the politics of being that dynamize their sense of self in relation to culture and society.

Hence, Crenshaw's construction of intersectionality is helpful as an analytical tool in teaching this approach to autoethnography without the limitation of only focusing on race, sex, and gender. In some ways, maybe I am engaging what Wenshu Lee (2012) references as a *critical intersectionality* that expands the "holy trinity of identity markers, race, class and gender" to such variables as "age, religiosity, ideology, and party identification" and more (p. 922). And while Lee does not cite Crenshaw, the intentionality of her reference is implied. And while Lee does not offer a particular definition of *the critical* in her construction of *critical intersectionality*—such a meaningful definition is at the core of my own orientation (in this approach) to teaching autoethnography and the evidenced student enactments as response to this assignment that I include in this essay.

The notion of "critical" is an engagement of discernment of the deep meanings in any given situation with the potentials and possibilities of transformation. In approaching a critical autoethnography, I often use D. Soyini Madison's orientation to doing critical work. In her construction, Madison (2005) writes that critical work seeks

> to articulate and identify hidden forces and ambiguities that operate beneath appearances; to guide judgments and evaluations emanating from our discontent; to direct our attention to the critical expressions within different interpretive communities relative to their unique symbol systems, customs, and codes; to demystify the ubiquity and magnitude of power; to provide insight and inspire acts of justice; and to name and analyze what is intuitively felt. (p. 13)

Madison's construction is aptly applied to engaging a critical autoethnography because it asks deep questions and demands rigorous considerations. In teaching critical autoethnography, I often frame each of her definitional components as questions that students must ask themselves, thus forestalling the tendency to simply tell a good story, but to tell a critical story of meaning situated in a cultural context with potential to transform self and society (Spry, 2001). So with this framing of a critical autoethnography as intersectional praxis, I want to share with you samples of student work in a junior-level performance studies class at California State University, Los Angeles. I present two pieces with the students' permission. Each of the student efforts follow a form that might be described as a *poetic autoethnography*, both in the form of engagement as well as in that way in which poetry is a liquidity of emotion that fuses the politics of story and form.

"Advocate of Hope" by José "Pepper" Jimenez Quiroz

I was brought to a land where I had no identity, got my ID for about a dollar 20,
so technically I was conceived at the corner store,
I never gave a damn before,
so why start now,
look into my past,
see I was born,
as an outkast,

everything I do is so unconventional,
I miss a lot of church so the music is my confessional,
it's a shame I focus on me try to make the right move,
in a year or two u gonna see me on the breaking news,
either talking recklessly,
probably making history,
doesn't really matter,
my pops facing repo,
I connect to the people standing at home depot, just like prostitutes,
tryin a get a buck or two,
tryin a get a meal,
I was born a dirty immigrant I learned to work the field,
I aint no sergeant but yea I know the drill.
My life is like a movie I just wanna see the reel.
They label me an alien,
I'm just tryin a phone home,
Look where I went wrong,
Look at my mistake,
Born in the wrong place.
Aint that a shame, my whole damn life's like Obama's campaign,
Advocate for hope, hoping for some change.
Bring it back to suspense this is just like the show,
black swan flow,
got the academy owned,
my globe aint gold,
and oscar owes more than he could afford, that's just how it goes,
stress does linger,
smiles do vanish,
every hustler on the corner first language is Spanish.
I don't smile at cops,
I hardly laugh at all,
racism hurts,
but I just laugh it off.
I been numbed by the world,
real life vicodin,
fell on the 3rd,
got right back up again.
I gotta play my cards,
there is no fold,
no bluffing when the truth is exposed,
so here I go as I testify, on my every day life, looking at me like your life's like mine,
but you're judging from the outside,
look inside of mine.
They label me an alien, I'm just tryina phone home,
Look where I went wrong,
Look at my mistake,
Born in the wrong place,

Aint that a shame, my whole damn life's like Obama's campaign,
Advocate for hope, hoping for some change.
People where I come from usually become crooks,
they don't even see success they're scared to look.
I know about the immigrants,
didn't need to read a book,
at the age of 16 that's when my whole world shook
every moment past that, man I fully understand all the obstacles in my path,
so I rarely show pity,
I'm labeled as a stranger in my own damn city, treating government like my God,
I hope he forgives me.
I swear this right here is torture, me I'm the reason for the fence along the border,
Mexican champ but I aint talking cainvalasquez,
anybody touching me on the mic, nonsense.
Mexican in the blood I can name some cartels, but me I will never never ever tell,
not an ounce of a snitch,
I'm tryin a get big,
literally like opera.
I'm rocky balboa when it comes to tasting victory,
sorta like cesar chavez yea I'm making history.
I was born with this burden it's my original sin, green card or not I gotta win, life's
like that, gotta face facts, I put actions in my dreams, now that's my dream act.

***

"We Will Beat Discrimination" by Daisy Evelyn Muñiz

So something happened at 18, as I got ready for college,
It messed with my head, couldn't explain it with my own knowledge,
You see, border patrol planned raids all over my small town.
For about a month, they targeted anyone they saw was brown,
Pulling people over, even those walking the streets.
In Lake Elsinore there was a border patrol fleet
Never had I seen the town look so deserted, no one walking out their doors,
And the thought of this, man, it shook me to my core
Man, I was scared and I was born in this nation.
But, my parents weren't, yeah, I'm the first generation
La migra took friends, co-workers, and neighbors
Good people I knew, who only wanted labor.
And I thought
We can make it through with the help of God and with determination.
Even with the odds against us, we will beat discrimination (2x)
I closed my eyes and opened them every morn' at 3am
Wondering who else is having to do the shit I am.
Hugged and kiss my dad, we each got in our car.
Then I'd drive behind him, looked up, and wished upon a star
Daddy's little girl was now protecting him.
But, I didn't mind, yeah, I'd do it all again.

When we had driven out of town, Daddy would pull up to my side,
Turned on the light so I could see him, smiling, he'd wave bye-bye.
I'd turn mine on, wave back and smile,
releasing all the stress I'd gained with every single mile.
If I didn't do this, they might pull him over, taken him there and then
just as they had done with many other men.
As I drove home, I'd pray: God get him home safe and sound
And wondered what would happen when I moved, when I wouldn't be around.
Oh, and I didn't mention my mom, who was basically on house arrest
'cause going out risked getting deported, just like all the rest
So that left me to take and pick up the kids, to go buy all the groceries.
Inside the stores were Catholic women, whispering, holding rosaries.
I'm not Catholic but I'm sure our prayers were much the same,
Lord keep us safe, we beg this in Jesus' name.
I wanted to tell them,
We can make it through with the help of God, and with determination
Even with the odds against us, we can beat discrimination (2x)
When BP drove behind me, my heart would sink.
When I got home, I would just lay there and think,
How the hell can I be proud to be American like this,
I felt so illegal, though and American miss.
I was so ashamed of being from the USA,
And I felt horrible for feeling this way.
But, it's hard when you're living like a pigeon while you're dreaming like an eagle,
Because there's no good jobs if you are an illegal.
Things were getting outta hand, something had to be done.
So, a group of us decided to march under the IE sun.
We needed to show ICE we wouldn't take this lying down.
So, with picket signs and loud voices we marched throughout the town.
Town hall, the mayor couldn't even show his face,
All we wanted was for him to put himself in our place.
Sheriff's department, a deputy came out,
Said "sorry, this is something we can do nothing about."
The rage grew inside me; I wanted to defend my kind.
Let this border patrol pull me over, I'll give him a piece of my mind.
It frustrated me that you can stand up and be proud of that red, white, and blue,
But, if you're not the right color, it might not be so proud of you.
Watched the news, every Spanish channel addressed the issue at least a bit each day.
But, flip the channel to English news, and not a damn station had a thing to say.
Did they not know, or did they simply not care.
Promoting the American dream, but they're not even playing fair.
My parents left it all for a better opportunity.
So, someone tell me why we've been suffering an eternity.
It was for me and my siblings that they stayed even when the going got tough.
Persecuted like criminals, never once heard them say "enough is enough."
How had they endured this for so long, after 2, 3 weeks I was falling apart.
There had to be something I could do, some way to do my part.

I sat and realized I had two options; act or pout.
I could sit and cry and whine that there was no way out,
Or, I could get up, wipe my face, and take some action.
But, I was only one of two; God was the rest of that fraction.
And I thought,
I will make it through with the help of God and my determination,
Even with the odds against me, I will beat discrimination (2x).
I had to show my parents the worth of their sacrifices.
So, I prayed that God would deliver us from this crisis.
I promised myself I'd graduate from a university,
And that I would show the world that good can come from diversity.
So, now I sit in class, less than six months to go.
Then, I can work more and provide my family with dough.
We've applied for residency, but that's also expensive.
And the background investigations, man those things are extensive.
But hey, we've got nothing to hide, so we should be OK.
But this process takes forever, wish it was complete today.
And it's $200 to process the first three forms.
Make sure to bend our knees and pray there's an immigration reform.
'cause if this process isn't over before there's a new president,
The new one might revoke any chance of becoming residents.
So, I've got to hurry up, so I can pay these fees
Because this lawyer doesn't get paid with only thanks and please.
Tell me getting a job isn't easy, yeah, it's rough out there
I won't accept the pessimism
I just crack my knuckles and, uh, flip my hair.
I declare my family's success, won't take no for an answer.
Gotta fight back, 'cause discrimination is like cancer.
Don't get me wrong, I love the U.S. come what may,
But I don't wanna live with the fear of losing my parents every single day.
You need money, a good lawyer, blah blah, I've heard it for so long,
Obstacles like broken records, playing the same old songs.
And I got people asking, "Why'd you choose, instead of working, to go to college?"
I'm not doing it for me, not just to gain knowledge.
I do it so at grad I can say "good job mom and dad,
You got me here because you gave everything you had.
My degree is for you, so are the blessings that come from it.
It's because of you I'm on top. It's because of you I've reached the summit."
So, now I'm looking up, and so darn optimistic.
Got a smile on my face, been so long, I surely missed it.
I embrace the discriminated, hyphenated me,
The Mexican-American my parents soon will be.
And as for our future,
We will make it through with the help of God, and with determination,
Even with the odds against us we will beat discrimination. (2x)

***

José's and Daisy's performances work to fulfill qualities of effective auto-ethnography and critical work. Each is self-reflexive of their sociopolitical interactivity placing their bodies on the line of border politics. Each is a provocative weave of story and theory that moves both emotionally and critically as they narrate lived experience in a sociocultural context. Each performance works through and emboldens the varying modes of using autoethnography as methodology (e.g., mode of research/inquiry, mode of re/presentation, mode of critique and resistance, mode of activism).

Each of the performances engages in a systematic unpacking of experience as a form of social criticism; each offers clear conclusions not designed as controls, but as possibilities of knowing and engaging the social world. And each is aesthetically pleasing and intellectually astute, demanding that the audience use these contributing qualities as information gathering, truth seeking, action steps, and templates for engaging their own situatedness of being (See Alexander, 2009). And maybe, more importantly to the par-ticularity of this exploration—each critical autoethnographic exploration illuminates a complex intersectionality of being and becoming.

Both José and Daisy explicitly frame their autoethnographic performance as political, activist, and resistive. Daisy marks a struggle against discrimina-tion and her particular involvement in political protest against Immigration and Customs Enforcement (I.C.E) in the Inland Empire (I.E.) of Southern California. José discusses his Mexican American masculine identity con-struction and the iterations of discrimination he experiences as a result. Each of these performances was a partial and self-referential tale that connected with other stories, ideas, discourses, and contexts of these performances, as well as being delivered in a class at a predominantly Hispanic Serving campus—with many first-generation, and a number of "undocumented" students in the class, who, at the end of these performances, began to narrate aspects of their own experiences. Each performance created a plausible and visceral lifeworld and a charged emotional atmosphere as an incitement to act within and outside the context of the work.

These performative engagements sought to articulate and identify the hidden forces and ambiguities that operate beneath the appearance of their story as well as keying in the nexus of the broader politics of immigration and border rhetorics. Each excavated the critical expressions and conditions of living within their interpretive culture, inspiring acts of justice; and by virtue of their first-person subjective location, they sought to name and analyze what is intuitively felt and expressed in the narrative. And both of these autoethnographic performances engaged in a critical dialogue with history, social structure and culture, which the performances help to foreground as always and already dialectically revealed through action, feeling, thought, and language—with an embodied critical intersectionality of their own predicament. And maybe therein lies the complicated beauty of critical autoethnography as intersectional praxis. Both José and Daisy engage in an argument of intersectionality not exclusive on a bodily or cellular level, but acknowledging the social construction of identity—as historical, social, locational, and cultural—their bodies meeting at the borders and politics of time and place; bodies on the line in public debate of value and territorial imperatives that have human consequences (see Alexander, 2009).

The Classroom as a Border/less Frame: A Conclusion

My purpose in this short essay was to explore an approach of teaching critical/autoethnography as an exercise in intersectionality and the ways in which the borders of identities bleed. In the process, I offered you two student examples undergirded by principles of theory that define my approach to a critical autoethnography and critical intersectionality with allusions to effective qualities in each. The work of my students engages a level of complex theorizing that forestalls, and at times brings into sharp contrast, the facile and reductive orientation of intersectionality limited by just race, gender, and class to address a more complex critical intersectionality that speaks to the politics of bleeding identities that includes, among others, national and international politics of citizenship, issues of desire and disdain in which the body is revealed as always and already a political location; a nexus of being, as well as a literal and figurative border crossing. In fact, each performance is an act of resistance and a struggle for self-definition that bleeds the borders of the expected and the known—voices struggling to be heard between complex and overlapping borders of identity.

My own autoethnographic entry was presented as an intersectional study of my race and gender, the politics of legalized same sex marriage, and the bleeding borders of "brother status" in a fixed liquidity of time and space. But while I situate my autoethnography in an analysis of a photographic image of my biological brothers and myself—these variables of race, sexuality, and gender are always and already present within the dailiness of my life. They often become palpable in the classroom. The classroom as a confluence where bodies and lives, cultures and curricula often encounter in a clash of determinations and destinations. The classroom, where historically, only particular stories have been told in a linear fashion that resist cultural variations of situated tellings; stories told of conquest that do not recognize the bodies of students that refuse to be colonized over and over again through someone else's narrative authority. The classroom, where the body of the teacher becomes reductively representative of the curriculum; ahistoricized, dera(c)ed, and neutered, talking a talk that often threatens to perpetuate self-oppression. And alike, the complex lives of students are made generic for the ease of transmitting a particular knowledge, often void of a critical application and recognition of how students resist facile explanations of compartmentalized realities, because often their lives, as does our own, intersect and straddle multiple bordered realities.

In the classroom, I often flaunt my particularity as a teacher—as a Black/gay/male teacher in the ivory tower. I flaunt it, not as gaudy evidence, but as a dissenting member to professed social constructs; like that picture of myself captured in a borderless frame standing in a tan suit next to three white tuxedoes—presumed difference in relation to orthodoxy; a photo that I staged to commemorate a moment so that I could consistently critique that reality from the inside out and from the outside in. In the classroom, I often engage in a critical show and tell. The materiality of my body and manner captured in the gaze of students, shows a sense of who I am—so I follow up with telling; critical tellings of lived experiences of growing up in the south; critical tellings of my life with my partner of 15 years—tellings of our talks about our marriage as a resistance to public propositions that would deny us such a right. I metaphorically share with students who we would invite or not invite to our wedding, to be in our wedding, to be the best man, and why. I tell intimacies of the personal, not to titillate, but to tease at what should and should not be spoken of in the classroom—thereby sanctioning students to also tell; to tell of their tales, to tell of their travels, to tell of the tensions and the tensive aspects of their lived experiences that bring them to this current moment; experiences that cross borders but always carry the residual tracks of where they come from and how they live between worlds and realities. I like the idea of tracking and trafficking stories across the borders of the classroom.

The classroom is like a borderless frame; a series of contextualized engagements that offer the allusion of possibility but contains a particular territory; a particular reality. Critical autoethnography as critical praxis bleeds what Roger I. Simon (1992) refers to as the *horizon of possibility*, creating an "openness of expression of capacities encouraged in a free society and the normative, regulating forces of those social forms which define the terrain on which everyday life is lived" and storied (p. 28). It becomes what Aronowitz and Giroux (1991) might call a *border pedagogy* that helps students to understand that "[o]ne's class, race, gender, or ethnicity may influence, but does not irrevocably predetermine how one takes up a particular ideology, read a particular text, or respond to particular forms of oppression" (p. 119). It becomes what Paulo Freire (2002) references as praxis, reflection and action upon the world in order to transform it.

In the photographic image of my brothers and me, it may appear that I am held in a particular stasis of that relational dynamic, but that is just a photographic image. My life is much more expansive, and I wear multiple suits of different colors. I offer my students the possibilities of seeing themselves and showing themselves in such ways, in the classroom—bleeding the borders between the present and the possible.

References

Alexander, B. K. (2009). Autoethnography: Exploring modalities and subjectivities that shape social relations. In J. Paul, J. Kleinhammer-Tramill & K. Fowler (Eds.), *Qualitative research methods in special education* (pp. 277–334). Denver, CO: Love Press.

Alexander, B. K. (2011). Bordered and bleeding identities: An autocritography of shifting academic life. In S. Jackson & R. G. Johnson III (Eds.), *The Black professorate: Negotiating a habitable space* (pp. 14–31). New York: Peter Lang Press.

Aronowitz, S., & Giroux, H. (1991). *Postmodern education: Politics, culture & social criticism.* Minneapolis: University of Minnesota Press.

Crenshaw, K. W. (1995). Mapping the margins: Intersectionality, identity, politics, and violence against women of color. In K. W. Crenshaw, N. Gotanda, C. Peller, & K. Thomas (Eds.), *Critical race theory: The key writings that formed the movement* (pp. 357–383). New York: The New Press.

Freire, P. (2002). *The Pedagogy of the Oppressed.* (B. Ramos, Trans.). New York: Continuum.

Lee, W. (2012). For the love of love: Neoliberal governmentality, neoliberal melancholy, critical intersectionality and the advent of solidarity with the other moments. *Journal of Homosexuality.* Downloaded 28 August 2012. http://dx.doi.org/10.1080/009183 69.2012.699830

Madison, D. S. (2005). *Critical ethnography: Methods, ethics, and performance.* Thousand Oaks, CA: Sage.

Simon, R. I. (1992). *Teaching against the grain: Texts for a pedagogy of possibility.* New York: Bergin & Garvey.

Spry, T. (2001). Performing autoethnography: An embodied methodological praxis. *Qualitative Inquiry, 7.6,* 706–732.

SECTION III

༄

Negotiating Socially Stigmatized Identities

*T*HE THIRD SECTION OF THE BOOK EXTENDS THE SECOND SECTION by focusing on the negotiation of constructions of identity that are marginalized within larger social structures. These four chapters highlight the similar and different ways in which diverse stigmatized identities (based on race, class, gender, sexuality, nationality, disability, and body politics) are experienced across contexts. In addition, each of the chapters demonstrates the need to understand how marginalization is enacted on multiple levels simultaneously—something that becomes apparent through intersectionality. *Standpoint theory, co-cultural theory,* and *cultural contracts theory* function as insightful theoretical frameworks to contextualize these chapters.

Standpoint Theory

Standpoint theory is based on one simple idea: Life is not experienced the same for all members of any given society. In explicit and implicit ways, our *standpoints*—determined by our social/cultural group memberships—affect how we communicate as well as how we perceive the communication of others. Standpoint theory is established in the work of many feminist scholars (e.g., Harding, 1987, 1991; Hartsock, 1983; Smith, 1987). Although it has traditionally been used as a framework to study the lives of women, it can also be applied to the perspectives of those marginalized in terms of race, ethnicity, class, religion, and so forth (Wallace & Wolf, 1995). Through

Critical Autoethnography: Intersecting Cultural Identities in Everyday Life, edited by Robin M. Boylorn and Mark P. Orbe, 123–128. © 2014 Left Coast Press, Inc. All rights reserved.

the exploration of the lived experiences of persons in subordinate positions (Smith, 1987), standpoint theory focuses on the subjective vantage point from which persons interact with themselves and the world around them. Moreover, standpoint theory acknowledges the specific societal structures that influence such vantage points. Recognition of the impact of a person's field of experiences, according to this perspective, is critical in understanding how she or he perceives daily communicative experiences.

Standpoint theory is grounded in several epistemological assumptions. First, research that seeks to understand the standpoint of persons in subordinate positions must be grounded in the lived experiences of such individuals. Second, the inclusion of these experiences in the research process is essential, since those without societal power often have conflicting worldviews with those with societal power. Overwhelmingly, existing scholarship presents only the dominant perspective (Orbe, 1998). As it relates to this notion, standpoint theorists subscribe to the notion of alternative understandings of the world that are situated in the daily experiences of both marginalized and dominant group members. A third assumption posits that the value of these co-cultural perspectives is crucial, since marginalized group members have the ability to see dominant societal structures from the positioning of an *outsider-within perspective* (Collins, 1986).

Given the four chapters in this section, standpoint theory appears especially suited to assist in our exploration of similarities and differences among traditionally marginalized groups. Although traditional [feminist] standpoint theorists focused primarily on sex identity (e.g., Harding, 1987, 1991), our interest here is more heavily on work that has focused on how a person's standpoint reflects an intersection of race, gender, class, and other identity markers (Allen, 1996). Standpoint theory also informs another relevant theoretical framework, co-cultural theory.

Co-Cultural Theory

Co-cultural communication refers to a particular form of intercultural communication research that centers on issues of societal power and dominance within different societies (Orbe, 1998). Co-cultural theory helps us understand the ways that persons who are traditionally marginalized in society communicate in their everyday lives. Grounded in muted group (Kramarae, 1981) and standpoint theories (Smith, 1987), it represents a relevant framework for studying the experiences of people of color, women, people with disabilities, and gays, lesbians, and bisexuals (Cohen & Avanzino, 2010; Orbe & Roberts, 2012).

Co-cultural theory is based on the idea that because of their marginalized societal positioning, certain individuals have to develop certain communication orientations in order to survive and/or succeed in their respective societies (Orbe & Spellers, 2005). However, it is important to recognize the vast diversity within and among different co-cultural groups. Therefore, the adoption and maintenance of certain orientations—as well as the rationale behind such decisions—varies greatly. Six interrelated factors reportedly influence such decisions. *Field of experience* relates to the sum of lived experiences for an individual. Through a lifelong series of experiences, individuals learn how to communicate with others. Based on a unique field of experience—which is simultaneously similar to, yet different from, others'—an individual comes to recognize that *perceived costs and rewards* are associated with different communication practices. In some instances the advantages and disadvantages are clear, in others, they are not. A third factor is the *ability* to enact certain strategies that work to establish and maintain a specific communication orientation. All co-cultural group members do not have the same capabilities in terms of their communication. Much depends on individual skills and the specific dynamics inherent in any given *situational context*. This includes where the interaction takes place, other parties who are present, and the particular circumstances that facilitate the interaction. It should be apparent that situational context, like the other five factors, intersects in highly complex ways (Orbe & Roberts, 2012).

The final two factors are communication approach and preferred outcome. *Communication approach* refers to the specific "voice" used by co-cultural group members. Is the communication approach aggressive, assertive, or more nonassertive? *Preferred outcome* relates to the ultimate goal that the person of color has for the interaction: Are they trying to fit in (assimilation), work with dominant groups to promote change (accommodation), or focus on strengthening ingroup community (separation)? Note that no one approach or preferred outcome is most (or universally) desirable (Orbe & Roberts, 2012). Much depends on how the other factors influence the person's perceptions.

Cultural Contracts Theory

Cultural contracts theory, as articulated by Jackson and colleagues (Hecht, Jackson, & Ribeau, 2003; Jackson, 2002a; 2002b), is a framework that says "that intercultural relationships may or may not be coordinated, depending upon the dynamics involved (such as power, boundaries, cultural loyalty, group identification, maturity, etc.)" (Jackson, 2002a, p. 361). Succinctly put, the theory facilitates an understanding of how diverse individuals negotiate their identities through everyday discourse (Drummond & Orbe, 2010).

Cultural contracts theory follows three premises (Hecht et al., 2003). First, identities require affirmation, something that is gained through communication. Second, identities are constantly being exchanged, reflecting a dynamic process of activity. Third, and finally, identities are contractual. By definition, *cultural contract* is used to reflect "an agreement between two or more interactants who have different interpretations of culture and have decided whether to coordinate their relationship with one other so that the relationship is deemed valuable to both" (Jackson, 2002b, p. 49). According to Jackson and Crawley (2003), many people fail to recognize the cultural contracts that they have unknowingly signed; they also do not understand all of the implications of having signed them. Three specific types of cultural contracts exist: Ready-to-sign, quasi-completed, and co-created.

Ready-to-sign cultural contracts are pre-negotiated agreements designed to promote assimilation and maintain the status quo (Hecht et al., 2003). From the perspective of the person in power, this type of contract suggests that "I am not going to change who I am, so if you want this relationship to work, you must act like me" (Jackson, 2002b, p. 48). The second type of cultural contracts are those that are *quasi-completed* (Hecht et al., 2003). Partly pre-negotiated, and partly open for negotiation, quasi-completed cultural contracts attempt to "straddle the fence" in terms of maintaining the status quo and asserting one's identity within existing structures (Jackson, 2002b). Consequently, commitment to quasi-completed cultural contracts involves active negotiations of power in terms of individual and social change (Jackson & Crawley, 2003). *Co-created cultural contracts,* the third category in Hecht et al.'s (2003) typology, are agreements that are "fully negotiable, with the only limits being personal preferences or requirements" (p. 49). This type of cultural contract is different from others in that individuals acknowledge and validate the cultural differences of all parties; because of this, co-created cultural contracts are motivated by mutual satisfaction and respect—and not obligation (Jackson, 2002b).

Theories as Lenses

Each of the three theoretical frameworks described here provides a productive lens through which to understand the communicative experiences as described by each author featured in this section. As you read through each chapter, think critically about the following questions:

- What cultural standpoint(s) is each author writing from? How are their standpoints similar to, yet different from, others in their cultural groups?
- How do reading these chapters help you understand their lived experiences *and* your own as a member of different social/cultural groups?
- Within their respective chapters, how does each author's communication choices reflect the six co-cultural factors? Do you see their communication as consistent across contexts, or different depending on different situations?

- What commonalties do you see across the communication of the different co-cultural groups represented in the section? How would descriptions of your own co-cultural communication compare with those of the authors featured here?
- Given their marginalized cultural identities, what types of cultural contracts does each author employ in their interactions with others? What would you describe as the advantages and disadvantages of negotiating each type of cultural contract?
- Based on the insight gained from the content of this section, what types of cultural contracts would you say that co-cultural group members would use if they were seeking a preferred outcome of assimilation, accommodation, and separation? Do you see how cultural contracts can also be associated with different communication approaches (nonassertive, assertive, and separation)?

References

Allen, B. J. (1996). Feminist standpoint theory: A Black woman's (re)view of organizational socialization. *Communication Studies, 47,* 257–271.

Cohen, M., & Avanzino, S. (2010). We are people first: Framing organizational assimilation experiences of the physically disabled using co-cultural theory. *Communication Studies, 61,* 272–303.

Collins, P. H. (1986). Learning from the outsider within: The sociological significance of Black feminist thought. *Social Problems, 33*(6), S14–S23.

Drummond, D. K., & Orbe, M. (2010). Cultural contracts: Negotiating a ubiquitous U.S. dominant worldview on race and ethnicity. *Communication Studies, 61*(4), 373–390.

Harding, S. (Ed.). (1987). *Feminism & methodology.* Bloomington: Indiana University Press.

Harding, S. (1991). *Whose science? Whose knowledge?: Thinking from women's lives.* Ithaca, NY: Cornell University Press.

Hartsock, N. C. M. (1983). The feminist standpoint: Developing the ground for a specifically feminist historical materialism. In S. Harding & M. D. Hintikka (Eds.), *Discovering reality: Feminist perspectives on epistemology, metaphysics, methodology, and philosophy of science* (pp. 283–310). Boston, MA: D. Reidel.

Hecht, M. L., & Ribeau, S. (1991). Sociocultural roots of ethnic identity: A look at Black America. *Journal of Black Studies, 21,* 501–513.

Jackson, R. L. (2002a). Cultural contracts theory: Toward an understanding of identity negotiation. *Communication Quarterly, 50*(3/4), 359–367.

Jackson, R. L. (2002b). Exploring African American identity negotiation in the academy: Toward a transformative vision of African American communication scholarship. *Howard Journal of Communications, 13,* 43–57.

Jackson, R. L., & Crawley, R. L. (2003). White student confessions about a Black male professor: A cultural contracts theory approach to intimate conversations about race and worldview. *Journal of Men's Studies, 12*(1), 25–41.

Kramarae, C. (1981). *Women and men speaking.* Rowley, MA: Newbury House.

Orbe, M. (1998). *Constructing co-cultural theory: An explication of culture, power, and communication.* Thousand Oaks, CA: Sage.

Orbe, M., & Roberts, T. L. (2012). Co-cultural theorizing: Foundations, applications, and extensions. *Howard Journal of Communications, 23,* 292–311.

Orbe, M., & Spellers, R. E. (2005). From the margins to the center: Utilizing co-cultural theory in diverse contexts. In W. B. Gudykunst (Ed.), *Theorizing about intercultural communication* (pp. 173–191). Thousand Oaks, CA: Sage.

Smith, D. E. (1987). *The everyday world as problematic: A feminist sociology of knowledge.* Boston, MA: Northeastern University Press.

Wallace, R. A., & Wolf, A. (1995). *Contemporary sociological theory: Continuing the classical tradition.* Englewood Cliffs, NJ: Prentice Hall.

CHAPTER SEVEN

∽

A Story & A Stereotype
An Angry and Strong Auto/Ethnography
of Race, Class, and Gender

Robin M. Boylorn

A Story of Stereotypes

She is the amalgamation of centuries-old assumptions and enduring comfort. She is a cultural enigma, parading dual identities at once and challenging notions of class, race, and sex stereotypes that have existed since the beginning of time (Parks, 2010). She presents herself in a way that centers her strength and suppresses her anger. Her strength is a combination of historical and cultural requirements, wrapped in faith and selflessness. Her anger rises when the strength subsides, an inevitable switch because the two prevailing tropes involve a lot of code switching. She is financially disadvantaged, even when she makes a good living, because she is often the breadwinner and primary caregiver of those in her family and community who need help. She is oftentimes blamed and vilified for emasculating men and intimidating women, even though those characterizations and accusations are not legitimately based on her actions or intentions.

She is "the mammy figure, the suprahuman endurer, and the Christian hard worker" (Harris, 2001, p. 1). She is "dark-skinned, ever-smiling, diligent, and doting" (Beauboeuf-Lafontant, 2009, pp. 28–29). She "confronts all trials and tribulations ... is a source of unlimited support for her family ... [and] suppresses her emotional needs while anticipating those of others" (Harris-Perry, 2011, p. 21). She is self-sacrificing, self-supporting, and rebellious. She is "too domineering, too strong, too aggressive, too outspoken, too castrating, too masculine" (Wallace, 1999, p. 91). She is "shrill, loud, argumentative, irrationally angry, and verbally abusive" (Harris-Perry, 2011, p. 87). She is "the Dark Feminine" (Parks, 2010).

She is belligerent, bossy, fiesty, insatiable, exotic, dangerous and hypervisible. She is also asexual, happy, smart, and deferential. She comes in all shades, from coconut-colored to mahogany brown; all sizes, from paper thin to country thick.

She is mad as hell sometimes, but not perpetually angry. She is resilient and longsuffering, but not inherently strong. She is compliant and willingly submits without complaint. She is a perpetual giver and transforms herself as a surrogate to meet the needs of others. She is often silent, but when she speaks, her voice reverberates and either causes calm or disillusionment. Her protests are unspoken, and she is known for swallowing her screams.

She is fiercely independent and doesn't need help. She is a problem-solver. A way-maker. A miracle worker. A sinner, a saint, and a savior (Harris, 2001), but she's not Jesus.

She exists in the public imagination but lives in private realities.

You've seen her on the cover of pancake boxes and at the box office featured behind the white heroine she saves. You know her, she silently concedes when you make unreasonable requests for which she will not be compensated or rewarded. You've heard about her lazy lascivious ways that are thwarted by the open doors that are only open because she is a minority, a leach, a pariah, a homewrecker, an affirmative action acquirer. You overlook her when she is serving food, cleaning rooms, sometimes struggling to get by. You don't pay attention to her when she is the only one in the room, the only one at the table, the only damn one. You see her, smiling on the outside, dying on the inside, but you can't tell the difference. She stands on invisible pedestals that set her up to fail.

When she doesn't smile, you ask her why she's so mad. When she doesn't concede, you throw accusations of bias and unfairness at her feet. When she makes babies, you shake your head in disapproval, when she is unmarried, you blame her for her undesirability. She cries in secret, and you are hopelessly unaware. You think telling her she is strong makes up for the circumstances that require strength.

She seems invulnerable when she's not mad.

Safe when she's not strong.

And poor.

*

The stories told about black women are often stories of stereotypes and contradictions disguised as truth.

*

The lives of black women, including "myths, mystiques, sincere fictions, or controlling images" (Beauboeuf-Lafontant, 2009, p. 152) inform and are influenced by larger cultural narratives that dictate their personal identity and interpersonal relationships. Black women routinely face negative stereotypes and limited representations that are popularized through media and myths. When black women internalize stereotypes, it can limit their self-presentation and lower their self-esteem (Thomas et al, 2004). Two stereotypes in particular are pervasive of black women: Mammy and Sapphire. The Mammy stereotype is seen as selfless and nurturing. When a black woman internalizes this stereotype, she may support others to her own detriment and present a "facade of strength" for the benefit of others. The Sapphire stereotype is shrill, loud, hostile, and aggressive. When a black woman internalizes the Sapphire stereotype, she may feel limited outlets for self-expression and communicate anger in order to be heard (Thomas et al., 2004).

According to social constructivism (Berger & Luckmann, 1967), concepts of personal identity are socially and culturally constructed. For some populations, like black women, the social constructions are overwhelmingly reliant on stereotypes, which cause problematic and one-sided perspectives about identity. Auto/ethnography can speak back to stereotypes and provide insight into the cultural milieu of black women in the US.

In this auto/ethnography, I juxtapose the Mammy and Sapphire stereotypes together with a class analysis to investigate the layered-ness of race, class, and gender/sex identities. I use stereotypes to show how external labels of black women's identity are often used to limit and police their emotions and behavior. I also look at the interpersonal implications these restrictions have in their emotional and social lives and discuss how class informs black women's communicative performances of self. I offer personal stories and popular culture discourse to make sense of stereotypes as stories (of identity) and stories as stereotypes (of identity).

Intersectionality

Intersectionality offers a multidimensional way to think about how black women are often seen in contradictory ways because of their lived experiences as members of marginalized social groups. Crenshaw (1989) argued that black women experience discrimination simultaneously in at least three distinct but overlapping areas: race, class, and sex. Intersectionality speaks to the intersection of multiple forms of discrimination and the inextricable connection between them. Due to the simultaneity of oppression that black women experience, it is impossible to distinguish one form from another. When black women experience discrimination, it is often unclear if it is because of their race, sex, class, or all three at the same time. Additional factors that may contribute to intersectional subjugation include ability status, age, sexual orientation, and education[1].

While not a primary mode of intersectional analysis, I believe we can use intersectionality to consider how identity factors, both together and separate, are informed by stereotypes. By using an intersectional approach to discuss black women's lived realities, we can better understand how and why black women are often limited by the collective stereotypes attached to their social identities.

How we see ourselves and how we perceive ourselves as being seen and understood by others is largely influenced by cultural factors (including stereotypes) and our relationships. Hundreds of times, as a child, I was warned before going in public that my behavior and actions were a direct reflection of my mother, my family, and anonymous black folk I had never met. I was taught that it was important that I carry myself in a respectable manner and was hyperaware that I was being watched and judged as a *blackgirl* (a lesson that has stayed with me into adulthood). I was not warned explicitly about stereotypes, but I was told how to behave like I had home training, to resist retaliation even when warranted, and to be prepared for racism. When applicable, my mother would point out someone else's child whose bad behavior seemed to both inspire collective shame and offer evidence to outsiders that "we" (read black folk) don't know how to act. The ways I was conditioned to resist those mischaracterizations were also opportunities to challenge larger injustices linked to black culture. My blackness and femaleness were linked to my identity, my identity had intersectional aspects, and those intersections influenced current and potential relationships. I knew the assumptions others held about (rural, poor, dark-skinned black women like) me carried consequences. I also understood that those assumptions were informed by larger cultural narratives (stereotypes) of black women, narratives (stereotypes) that we sometimes resisted and sometimes reiterated. Therefore, the link between my behavior and perceived intent was important, because black women, I was taught, relied on multiple relationships and institutions to survive. Beyond family, there was the church, my mama's work networks, nonbiological kinships or chosen kin, and friendships. We all, intentionally and unconsciously, represented each other.

Strong + *Angry* + *Poor* =

While stereotypes are pervasive in several categories, the implications of stereotypes on the lives of people of color and women includes further stigma, especially when those positionalities are jointly combined (Combahee River Collective Statement, 1982; Crenshaw, 1989; Lorde, 2007). I distinguish between strength and anger, later combining them, to discuss the ways that they inform one another in the public imagination about black women's cultural performances.

> When strength is attached to black womanhood it is (mis)interpreted as a compliment.
> When anger is added to black womanhood, it is (mis)recognized as an inalienable truth.

When poverty precedes black woman, it is seen as a lasting and sometimes inevitable reality.

Confronting these myths, assumptions, and occasional truths of black womanhood is challenging. As a black woman who knows black women who are strong, angry, and/or poor, and knowing myself, at various times in my life, as all of the above, I sometimes struggle with the ways that those labels impact my identity. There have been times I have held fast to the strongblackwoman myth while rejecting my working-class roots and denying my anger. It has taken me years to flip the switch on the expectations of my performance of black womanhood, to embrace the anger and resist the strength (Morgan, 2000) instead of the other way around.

The opening prose defines black womanhood in its various manifestations, blending myths and truths to show how indistinct they are made to seem. Missing from the larger hegemonic narrative and (mis)representations of black women is an acknowledgment of discrimination, exploitation, and oppression. We oftentimes overlook the pain black women are forced to endure in order to be strong. bell hooks (1989) states,

> It is not that black women have not been and are not strong; it is simply that this is only a part of our story, a dimension, just as the suffering is another dimension—one that has been most unnoticed and unattended to. (pp. 152–153)

In other words black women live with circumstances that require strength for survival, and they endure structural oppressions that justify anger, but that does not mean their strength is impenetrable or that their anger is ongoing.

Stereotypes shape realities, but they don't always represent reality. By looking at the historical implications of strong and angry figures of black women, I can look at stereotypes as cultural constructions rather than realities and discuss the social and intersectional implications of these characterizations and how they are influenced by time (nineteenth, twentieth, and twenty-first centuries), linked to culture, and affiliated with class. Further by using auto/ethnographic stories to challenge perspectives of black women from an inside/out view rather than an outside/in view (Sigelman & Tuch, 1997), I can critique how racial assumptions of women's communicative behavior work with stereotypes to police black women's public performances.

A Stereotype: Black Women Are Angry

Sapphire

The angry black woman stereotype became popularized in the late 1920s on the *Amos 'n' Andy* radio show, which was later a short-lived television show (Harris-Perry, 2011; Morgan & Bennett, 2006; Sapphire Caricature, n.d.).

The black woman character, Sapphire Stevens, was known for her abrasive treatment of her lazy, unemployed, and ruthless husband, "Kingfish." While both characters were largely stereotypical, and Sapphire's frustrations were targeted at her husband for his irresponsible choices, the name came to represent black women's so-called indiscriminate anger. The Sapphire image, unlike other stereotypic images of black women, requires the presence of a black man, who is usually the victim of her verbal vehemence (Jewell, 1993). The Sapphire characterization has survived various transformations in media representations and has been uncritically accepted as truth (Morgan & Bennett, 2006).

A Story: I'm Mad as Hell

Bluntness runs in my family. I grew up watching two distinct responses to injustice. My grandmother, who had a reputation of not taking any shit, was quick to seek retribution from those she felt had wronged her or those she loved. My mother, on the other hand, was a soft-spoken saint, who was quick to forgive and who consciously forgot. When I suffered mistreatment at the hands of peers, my mother would encourage me to "turn the other cheek," while my grandmother warned me on the first day of every school year that if somebody hit me, I had better hit them back (or face her wrath). Over the years, I internalized both of those strategies for tempering my anger and frustrations.

Anger swells in my belly and continues to expand until I can feel it in every crevice of my body, particularly my fingers and toes. It makes my face feel flushed, and I can hear my heart beat. I can sense my jaws clench, my lips tighten, my eyes squint, and my posture straighten. Anger grips my tongue in silence and numbs hurt feelings, weakness, or fear. My hands feel heavy, my mind often spins, and I feel an urgency for release, to scream, or swing, or shake, or swallow. I can feel my blood pressure rise, and I feel full and enormous. In many ways, anger manifests itself in my body as if I were preparing myself for a discursive fight or bracing myself to receive a physical blow.

I am not easily angered, but in many ways I feel that by the time I get mad, I have been provoked aggressively. I think of myself as mild mannered and easygoing, so if someone pisses me off, it usually feels intentional, the result of a barrage of ongoing slights and moments of disrespect or challenging. Countless times my kindness has been mistaken for weakness, but if I give in to my anger, if I speak my mind or rally in response to instigation, I lose. Black women cannot afford to be publicly angry. The consequences are ongoing. So I bury my malevolence and carry it with me, fully aware of the ways that my reaction to mistreatment is a corporate reflection of black women. Microaggressions and insults happen every day. I have taught myself to overlook slights because if I had a visceral reaction to every attack on my personhood I would be exhausted from being angry. Though mammying (a term I use as a verb to describe the expectation that black women acquiesce to disrespect and duplicity) is no less laborious.

*

I am speaking to a black male student in my office, careful to smile after every few words, because I don't want to come across as angry. I tell him I am writing a paper about black women's anger. I don't say that I am writing about *my* anger, because I don't generally bring anger with me to the workplace (though there have been times when it meets me there). Black women, it seems, can't get mad at work. It's a job hazard.

The student sits down and says, "My dad told me once that when a white woman is upset, people think she is having a bad day, but if a black woman gets upset, people think she has an attitude problem." I nod, agreeing, wondering if I have ever heard someone accuse a white woman of being "angry." He went on to say, "I think people are genuinely afraid of black women's anger."

Reflecting on his words, I realize that I oftentimes avoid my anger and suppress expressions of it in fear that I will be viewed as an "angry black woman." Perhaps I am just as afraid of my black woman anger as everyone else.

*

Mammies are strong, accommodating, eager to help, and always smiling. Many times black women's elevated voices, default expressions, and lack of interest in coddling strangers is seen as attitudinal and abrasive. Black women are expected to suppress their anger and "mammy" their way through oppression, injustice and critique. It seems black women's anger is only acceptable in private.
Behind closed doors
in the car on the way home
talking to myself or
on the telephone with a homegirl
or sitting across from someone I trust
I can fully and finally express what I don't always recognize as anger.
My anger disguises itself as frustration, exhaustion, disenchantment, sickness and solemnity out of the fear of appearing stereotypical. The only escape is through unintentional tears and angry, harsh rhythmic words I save for someone who looks like me and understands I am more than my temporary emotions. And we can talk back and forth, roll our necks and our eyes, speak in our outside voices, cuss and shout when we have to, knowing we are angry but not at each other.

The Angry Black Woman: Deconstructing Anger

"Her anger is usually compassionate, protective, and retributive—you have to do something to her or those under her protection first—but once she is angry, offenders need to get out of her way.... Her anger is not out of control; it is strategic" (Parks, 2010, p. 110).

Black women are without social protections around their emotions. As Parks (2010) notes, "the image says that anger is the black female default emotion, and anytime a black woman is not smiling, she must be angry" (p. 115). Anger is generally attributed to men, as a masculine emotion, so when attached to womanhood, it is seen to be unfeminine and dangerous.

Often missing from the discussions of black women's assumed anger is the ways in which anger is not a negative emotion, nor is it an unreasonable reaction to the discriminations black women are forced to endure on a daily basis. Unchecked racism, sexism, poverty, and oppression are reasons to be angry, but miraculously, black women resist persistent anger. As Harris-Perry (2011) explains, the angry black woman stereotype

> does not acknowledge black women's anger as a legitimate reaction to unequal circumstances; it is seen as a pathological, irrational desire to control black men, families, and communities. It can be deployed against African American women who dare to question their circumstances, point out inequities, or ask for help. (p. 95)

Parks (2010) describes a positive and negative version of the angry black woman. The positive version is linked to anger that protects others. The negative version is the more popular one "of a woman who is permanently furious and dangerously ready to act out her anger on innocent—read white—people" (p. 110).

Black women's anger is oftentimes in response to specific and continuous racial microaggressions[2] that oftentimes leave them feeling vulnerable, disempowered, and voiceless (Solorzano, Ceja & Yosso, 2000; Sue, Capodilupo, & Holder, 2008). Their anger, which many times they have been conditioned to hide, is the only thing they have left, but they struggle with the implications of what it means to be an angry black woman. While black women's anger can be seen as constructive (Griffin, 2012), "when [a black person] speaks directly and is also critical, it is likely to be seen as being an expression of hostility" (hooks, 1989, p. 154).

There are, however, positive possibilities for interpreting anger. It can be seen as an aesthetic that is at the heart of women's truths (Grasso, 2002). It can be seen as a catalyst for activism (Lorde, 2007). It also can be seen as a legitimate and justified response to injustice (Harris-Perry, 2011). A reimagination of anger, beyond the stereotype, can help black women engage their emotions and interrogate what it means to be angry. If we saw anger as powerful rather than mythical, what would happen?

A Stereotype: Black Women Are Strong

Mammy

While many scholars distinguish the strong black woman as separate from, but sometimes connected to, other controlling images of black womanhood, Beauboeuf-Lafontant (2009) offers the strong black woman as a current rearticulation of the mammy stereotype. She says,

> Black women too often are treated as modern-day mammies, prized for their fortitude, caring, selflessness, and seeming acceptance of subordination. Like their historical counterparts, contemporary mammies are quintessentially beings designed to invisibly and uncomplainingly support a social order that regards them as an exploitable source of labor. (p. 29)

Mammy is the original strong black woman. According to Harris-Perry (2011), the strong black woman is a racial and political construct. The strong black woman archetype disguises itself as a compliment and emerges from various versions of black womanhood and masculinized circumstances. Ironically, the strength affiliated with Mammy was her ability to endure the hardships of slavery (including prioritizing the needs of white families over her own) and sustain her biological family after slavery (oftentimes as a matriarch and in the absence of black men). The superwoman label made her "a magnificent stereotype" (Parks, 2002, p. 51).

A Story: Breakable

The first time it happened I felt like a failure.

Sure as the sunrise I knew something was not right with me. I had grown up watching the women around me move mountains and shit, and there I was falling apart over a mole hill.

Black women in my world were stoic amazon women whose coconut skin and wide arms could equally intimidate and comfort. They were strong and willing women who spoke their minds, waved their fists, and never cried. They used words and stories to make sense of the things that didn't make sense. The way hereditary diseases swooped in and took away the lives of their loved ones too soon, the way making ends meet was always so hard, and paycheck-to-paycheck was a normal way of living. They always seemed to shake off the messiness of life. Hurt feelings from failed relationships was not worthy of too much attention because there was always a better looking man with better loving looking for a good woman. There was no sense in wasting time crying or worrying or waiting over things you could not control or change. They were emotionless, the women and men of the house, taking on every gender script required to get by. They struggled, but it never looked like struggling. It looked like living, like thriving, like surviving.

I had never seen them cry, but I couldn't stop crying. I had never seen them break, but I felt broken. They were strong black women, but I wasn't. They were standing over me, staring, praying, shaking their heads, confused, conflicted, and worried. I was ready to stop breathing, and they were willing to give me their last breath.

"Is she gone crazy?" my grandmother asked half-concerned, half annoyed. She didn't have time for my antics, no time for tears, no time to worry about something that she couldn't fix. When I said I hurt all over, but on the inside, they decided I needed to go to the doctor. The diagnosis, intermittent bouts of depression, was so un-blackwomanlike that my strong black women didn't know what to do with me. I wasn't like them. I wasn't strong enough.

Mental illness was like a secret we never talked about. I thought it was just me, buried under the weight of sadness I couldn't explain and an inability and disinterest in pretending I was always all right. In retrospect, I wonder if we all were not suffering from some form of depression, mine diagnosed and theirs buried beneath pseudo-anger and aggression. Without many options, and because we were unpracticed in talking through our problems (we were more versed in talking about things and/or people) we suffered in silence. I suffered in silence. I felt that strength, like curly hair, skipped a generation. Everybody had it but me.

The Strong Black Woman: Deconstructing Strength

"[I]t continues to be difficult to let the [superwoman] myth go. Naturally black women want very much to believe it; in a way, it is all we have."
—Michele Wallace

Equating black women's strength with fallibility, Michele Wallace (1999) exposed the myth of the black superwoman by explaining that just because some black women emerge as mythical does not make strong black woman-hood glamorous. Wallace said that black women's strength was imaginary, temporary, and dangerous. For black women, strength is a by-product of survival and a self-defense mechanism against the tyrannies of racism, classism, and sexism.

Referencing the "Propaganda Mammy" figure as the personification of strong black womanhood, Parks (2010) explains that these images, often tied to Aunt Jemima, were strategic versions that commercialized pro-slavery images. These so-called strong women were perhaps angry black women in disguise, but the cost of expressing their anger was often more than they could afford.

Lorde (2007) speaks of using anger for strength. Morgan and Bennett (2006) explain that characterizations of black women as angry and strong disregard their emotional complexity and humanity. Harris-Perry (2011) believes that the strong black woman may be a way to reimagine the angry Sapphire as socially acceptable. The angry black woman and strong black woman stereotypes influence each other and are largely influenced by cultural norms that dictate how the representations are interpreted.

Social class offers an interesting lens through which to interrogate the angry and strong tropes of black womanhood. Class identities, though fluid, tend to remain intact based on original circumstances. For example, I self-identify as working class based on my upbringing, even though as a college professor I am currently comfortably middle class. However, my early gendered and raced experiences were strongly influenced by my class circumstances, which gives me an insider/outsider perspective of how and why class matters in terms of how black women are rendered. While class privilege does not protect black women from racial and gender discrimination, it does impact how it is experienced.

The stereotypes of successful black women, especially those who have overcome class disadvantages, may sometimes be used to support claims of meritocracy and exceptionalism, using one black woman's success against other black women who are not afforded the same options or opportunities. This realization, which upwardly mobile black women are usually conscious of, is problematic. Our relative class privilege comes with an experiential knowledge of how oppression works in our lives and in the lives of other disenfranchised folk (of color). Accordingly, I believe middle- and upper-class black women remain seen as inherently angry/strong, because we understand that our class circumstances offer an additional layer of stereotype privilege not afforded to other socially stigmatized groups.

Black FLOTUS: A Class Critique

Michelle Obama, the first First (black) Lady of the United States, was immediately heralded as a both a strong black woman and an angry black woman within public discourse (Cooper, 2010; Lightfoot, 2009; Moffitt, 2010). It was clear that despite her upper-class status and position she was not exempt from the racist insinuations of conservative extremists who decided that her blackwomanness made her a fair target. Critics sought opportunities and reasons to attach her to stereotypes. Labeled everything from "angry" and "anti-American" to "ghetto" and a "baby mama," she was attacked with negative characterizations of black women as if they were weapons (Cooper, 2010; Harris-Perry, 2011; Parks, 2010).

The attempted stigmatization of Michelle Obama prompts a focused discussion on the differences between anger and strength in the presentation of black women. As one of the most elite, educated, sophisticated, and visibly upper-class black women in the country (who rose from humble and working-class roots to the top echelon of national politics), she represents both the poor black woman and the rich black woman. She has personally experienced poverty and prosperity. Her class circumstances do not, however, protect her from racism and sexism (Cooper, 2010; Lightfoot, 2009; Moffitt, 2010).

The FLOTUS (First Lady of the United States) offers an interesting example of how class is trumped by race and sex politics. While working-class or uneducated black women may be expected to be strong, angry, and aggressive, upper-class and elite black women are brushed with the same stroke. Class privilege is often rendered as less salient than the penalty that comes from race and gender (Collins, 2009). Obama's social capital and bank account does not guard her from the raced and sexed stereotypes attached to black women (Harris-Perry, 2011).

Collins (2009) discusses the "black lady" as a class-specific image linked to successful and professional middle-class black women. The "black lady" is compared to both the angry black woman (for her assertiveness) and the strong black woman (she is deemed a modern Mammy) because she is hardworking and masculine-identified in the workplace. Class mobility, then, offers no protection for the problematic guise of black women's demeanor.

Despite the different economic conditions and circumstances of black women's lives, they are still subjected to essentialism and binaries. Bad black women are those who embody negative stereotypes, and good black women are those who don't. All stereotypes, even those that are disguised as positive (strong black women), are problematic. If good blackwomanhood is linked to the politics of respectability and employability (Beauboeuf-Lafontant, 2009) and bad blackwomanhood is linked to negative interpretations of stereotypes, then the mischaracterizations of the FLOTUS don't make sense. The case of FLOTUS Michelle Obama provides a telling illustration that while class is a factor in black women's lives, and can sometimes be a buffer to racism and sexism, it does not offer protection from negative labeling.

Stories as Stereotypes and Stereotypes as Stories

"This is not to be confused with being strong, black, and a woman. I'm still alla that."

—Joan Morgan

In *Getting Off of Black Women's Backs: Love Her or Leave Her Alone*, Morgan and Bennett (2006) challenge the angry black woman myth explaining that the danger of stereotypes is not that they represent reality, but that they are used to shape reality. They state:

Stereotypes are powerful and pernicious ideological devices designed both to maintain social and cultural structures and, perhaps most importantly, to silence those whom they target, trapping them beneath a relentlessly confining and contemptuous gaze. Stereotypes do not merely tell us how a culture "sees" a group of people; they also tell us how a culture controls that group, how it bullies them into submitting to or evading the representations that haunt them. (p. 490)

Speaking specifically of the angry black woman stereotype they say, "[it] goes unnamed not because it is insignificant, but because it is considered an essential characteristic of Black femininity regardless of the other stereotypical roles a Black woman may be accused of occupying" (Morgan & Bennett, 2006, p. 490).

Stereotypes are effective and pervasive because they are sometimes reinforced by our lived experience and not challenged in our everyday lives. When we are used to black women being some combination of angry and strong, the trope becomes ingrained in the cultural narrative of black womanhood. We forget that Mammy and Sapphire are stereotypes and not truths. While black women generally reject negative cultural images and redefine and reconstruct them for themselves (Jewell, 1993), and black women do not necessarily use stereotypes to define themselves (Collins, 2009; Harris-Perry, 2011; James, 2007), stereotypes are regularly used against them. By using stories to confirm and resist stereotypes and looking at stereotypes to frame and tell our stories, black women can move beyond the emotional ambiguity that one-dimensionality causes. Stories may not always successfully challenge the myths and stereotypes of black women, but personal narratives guarantee that black women have agency about how they are represented beyond stereotypes. Stories allow black women to show vulnerability alongside strength, and justification alongside anger.

On Being Seen: An Angry & Strong Poem

I see you
invisibly disguised
like a walking stereotype
raised rural and working-class
working
on living
a life that would make your mama proud
you make five times the salary of your grandmother
who worked in factories, houses and hospitals
cleaning up after other folk
like a Mammy
you are (strong) like her
I see you
hidden behind stories people tell about you

dark-skinned and brown
blackgirl beautiful
with child-bearing hips
but no children
and insecurities you bury beneath ambitions
I see you
smiling to cover up fear
doubt
pain
and anger
so deep you worry it will swallow you whole
if you let it
sassy like Sapphire
you are secretly afraid
you will never be
enough

Notes

1. Due to the focus of this chapter on stereotypes, I consciously focus on the ways stereotypes are used against black women. I am, however, aware of the ways that black women experience privilege and penalty due to their race and gender, especially in relation to intersectionality. For example, a black woman can experience heterosexual privilege and racial discrimination, or able bodied privilege and gender discrimination.

2. Racial microaggressions are commonplace behaviors and/or indignities that communicate hostility and/or subtle insults towards people of color. Microaggressions are often unintentional, and those who commit them are often unaware of the implications of their communication. For more on microaggressions, see Solorzano, Ceja, & Yosso (2000) or Sue, Capodilupo, & Holder (2008).

References

Beauboeuf-Lafontant, T. (2009). *Behind the mask of the strong black woman: Voice and the embodiment of a costly performance.* Philadelphia, PA: Temple University Press.

Berger, P. L., & Luckmann, C. (1967). *The social construction of reality.* Garden City, NY: Anchor.

Collins, P. H. (2009). *Black feminist thought: Knowledge, consciousness, and the politics of empowerment.* New York: Routledge.

Cooper, B. (2010). A'n't I a lady?: Race women, Michelle Obama, and the ever-expanding democratic imagination. *MELUS: Multi-Ethnic Literature of the US, 35*(4), 39–57.

Crenshaw, K. (1989). Demarginalizing the intersection of race and sex: A black feminist critique of antidiscrimination doctrine, feminist theory and antiracist politics, *University of Chicago Legal Forum,* 138–167.

Grasso, L. M. (2002). *The artistry of anger: Black and white women's literature in America, 1820–1860.* Chapel Hill: The University of North Carolina Press.

Griffin, R. A. (2012). I am an angry black woman: Black feminist autoethnography, voice, and resistance. *Women's Studies in Communication, 35*(2), 138–157.

Harris, T. (2001). *Saints, sinners, saviors: Strong black women in African American literature.* New York: Palgrave.

Harris-Perry, M. V. (2011). *Sister citizen: Shame, stereotypes, and black women in America.* New Haven, CT: Yale University Press.

hooks, b. (1989). *Talking back: Thinking feminist, thinking black.* Boston, MA: South End.

James, N. C. (2007). When Miss America was always white. In A. Gonzalez, M. Houston, & V. Chen (Eds.), *Our voices: Essays in culture, ethnicity, and communication* (pp. 61–65). New York: Oxford.

Jewell, K. S. (1993). *From mammy to Miss America and beyond: Cultural images and the shaping of U.S. social policy.* New York: Routledge.

Lightfoot, E. (2009). *First lady of hope.* Guilford, CT: The Lyons Press.

Lorde, A. (2007). *Sister outsider.* Berkeley, CA: Crossing. (Original work published 1984).

Moffitt, K. R. (2010). Framing a first lady: Media coverage of Michelle Obama's role in the 2008 presidential election. In H. E. Harris, K. R. Moffitt, & C. R. Squires (Eds.), *The Obama effect: Multidisciplinary renderings of the 2008 campaign* (pp. 233–249). New York: SUNY Press.

Morgan, J. (2000). *When chickenheads come home to roost: A hip hop feminist breaks it down.* New York: Touchstone.

Morgan, M., & Bennett, D. (2006). Getting off of black women's backs: Love her or leave her alone. *Du Bois Review, 3*(2), 485–502.

Parks, S. (2010). *Fierce angels: The strong black woman in American life and culture.* New York: One World Books.

Sapphire Caricature. (n.d.). Retrieved October 18, 2012 from *http://www.ferris.edu/htmls/news/jimcrow/sapphire/*

Sigelman, L., & Tuch, S. A. (1997). Metastereotypes: Blacks' perceptions of whites' stereotypes of blacks. *The Public Opinion Quarterly, 61*(1), 87–101.

Solorzano, D., Ceja, M., & Yosso, T. (2000). Critical race theory, racial microaggressions, and campus racial climate: The experiences of African American college students. *Journal of Negro Education,* 60–73.

Sue, D. W., Capodilupo, C. M., & Holder, A. (2008). Racial microaggressions in the life experience of black Americans. *Professional Psychology: Research and Practice, 39*(3), 329–336.

The Combahee River Collective. (1982). A black feminist statement. In G. T. Hull, P. B. Scott & B. Smith (Eds.), *All the women are white, all the blacks are men, but some of us are brave: Black women's studies* (pp. 13–22). Old Westbury, NY: Feminist Press.

Thomas, A. J., Witherspoon, K. M., & Speight, S. L. (2004). Toward the development of the stereotypic roles for black women scale. *Journal of Black Psychology, 30*(3), 426–442.

Wallace, M. (1999). *Black macho and the myth of the superwoman.* New York: Dial. (Original work published 1978).

CHAPTER EIGHT

∞

Caught in Code

Arab American Identity, Image, and Lived Reality

Desiree Yomtoob

Prelude: An Intersectional Identity

*T*HIS PIECE IS WRITTEN AS A BEGINNING EXPLORATION OF THE experience of intersectionality in my life. I am the daughter of Iraqi-Iranian Jewish parents who immigrated to the United States in 1963. My parents came to the United States during the period when the Shah was in power and US relations with Iran were much different than they are now. My family is Iraqi and Iranian Jews. This is a fact that somehow surprises people in the United States. This surprise gives me pause. What is it about the perception of the Middle East that makes this ethnic configuration so difficult for people to perceive? Most likely it is the layers of Orientalism (Said, 1978) that are present in popular and high-culture textual representations of the Middle East (Shaheen, 2009). Even I make reference to stereotypical pop culture images of "the place I have come from" when trying to understand and place my cultural understanding and image of myself. Orientalism, alongside other racial and ethnic stereotyping, has been present for a long time in the United States (Prashad, 2000; Shaheen, 2009). This ongoing activity has been compounded by the current wave of prejudice against the group of people put together under the category of "Arab" in the United States. While more concrete forms of prejudice occur, in the form of unnecessary detentions, racial profiling, and so on (Bayoumi, 2008), the textual forms created by the mass media have produced a newer meaning of the racialization on the "Arab" body, affecting the mapping and configurations of race constructs in the United States.

Critical Autoethnography: Intersecting Cultural Identities in Everyday Life, edited by Robin M. Boylorn and Mark P. Orbe, 144–158. © 2014 Left Coast Press, Inc. All rights reserved.

The following work speaks from my standpoint as someone who has experienced the US process of orientalization from childhood and who now experiences this new wave of racialization. The experience of understanding a process of racialization that is shifting and growing should not be underestimated.

The process of writing standpoint epistemology (Denzin, 1997) brings particular insight. For example, the value of interrogating the subjectivity of the author is invaluable towards understanding the particular accuracies of any work. While there are many critiques of autoethnography, I believe one of its many values is that it allows us to access the experience of discrimination and understand it from the perspective of the person it is happening to. While someone can take care in understanding and expressing the process another person is going through, nothing can take the place of someone speaking from their own position. Autoethnography can also give insight into embodied experiences (the way it feels, what is important, and what can be understood in a whole body sense). In this chapter I share an understanding of the way the process of orientalization and racialization feels and the knowledge that I bring to the spaces where I understand my own experience. I also offer insight from the knowledge of my experience.

Intersectionality suits my experience of lived reality, and certain themes I address could occur in the lives of other Arab Americans. However, we are much more than the lumping together of characterizations. We, Arab Americans, are people with multiple identity locations who are hurt by the misrepresentations and misrecognitions that occur through stereotyping. My identity, as understood from both the inside and out, is characterized by multiple layers of definitions and experiences as a gendered, ethnic, classed, and racialized person. I am defined by the intersections of my Jewish Iranian American self, my queer Third World feminist self, my working class living among the academic elite self, and my recognized/unrecognized light-skinned racialized self. I understand and speak from my intersections. I am also defined and understood by others through a lens of stereotypes. This work is about how I experience myself in those moments.

At the Borders—On the Television Screen

There are times when you watch your own life like you are watching a sports event, or your favorite Olympic gymnast vying for the gold medal. It is not the fun kind of watching, like when you wonder what kind of eye training those top notch Ping-Pong (table tennis) players use to know where the ball is in a quick flash (the way they locate the ball has to be sound based) or when you check out the female footballers for their power and grace. Instead, it's the kind of watching where you are rooting from the deepest part of you for your side, or your hero to win, to win just this round, so they can stay in the game.

I watch the Olympic gymnast on the balance beam with the same kind of attention I give my own life, these days. I watch my own life with the same kind of attention that I give the Olympic gymnast, these days. Each move executed accurately, gracefully, a win, a pass, a chance to go on to the next move with no points taken off. Every falter, a flinch, and move on to the next move, knowing that there is no time to spend thinking about the last move. A nervous exhaustion at the end of each run, when you wait for your score, out of breath, tooth clutching lip, in nervous anticipation (Fanon, 1967).

I watched the 2012 Olympics, televised from Britain, in a local bar and at the student union in my central Illinois town. I watched for many reasons. I almost exclusively watched for women athletes. I also liked watching the male divers. At the local bar I watched alone, sitting at the bar drinking Cherry Pepsis. I watched, and because I cannot help it, I noticed the reaction of the people, almost all men, who were sitting alongside me.

I watched the men, as I watched the images of the adolescent women on the parallel bars, young and balancing and bending and twisting, on the television screen. I flinched, as I both anticipated and heard the men's comments, as the young women, who worked at the parallel bars, providing performative labor in countless ways in that moment to the global community, were being watched by their family, their coaches, the audience, the cameras, and the world. I couldn't hear exactly what the male spectators were saying, but they were lewd and leering at the television and snickering in a way that made my stomach curdle. I heard one of them say something to the other about the gymnasts' ages. None of the gymnasts were over 18. A similar thing happened when I was watching at the student union, always the women gymnasts, a group of young men slapping each other on the back, laughing and congratulatory, when together noticing the moves of a gymnast doing the floor exercises. Not with an eye of appreciation, or even an eye of enjoyment, but with a lewd eye, and a feeling of camaraderie because they had succeeded in a way of looking that is a way of taking. Their gaze was objectionable objectification.

* * *

I walk through the mall in a hurry to make my acupuncture appointment. I am thinking about intersectionality and wondering about the way I am perceived. I often have unexpected trouble in the town I live in and at the university I am affiliated with, trouble that I don't expect, trouble that seems to come from nowhere. I think about how I am often afraid. I think about how I complain to my loved ones, that I never know what the rules are. Today I am wondering if this is because of the way I am read as a body. I wonder if it is the class culture of my body movement and appearance, or some kind of combination of the way my age and race/ethnicity and perhaps education, are read as I move through the world. I am thinking of this as I notice a man, who seems to be of European descent, walk by looking at me with an eye of anticipation. I don't think, as I glare at him, about how often I get these kinds of looks from men who appear white, or men in general. There were days last summer when I wouldn't leave the house if I didn't have to, because I had had enough. Men who not only look but would come stand next to me to talk, or act as if they know me from across a public space. They behave as if they are just being "friendly" and are offended when I don't return their interest; they are younger and older, and well-dressed or not so well-groomed, they are richer or poorer, and it doesn't seem to matter at all to them if I return their interest. It is all about what they want. They stare at me while they stand next to their girlfriends or wives, who seem hurt and offended. If I am alone, this evokes fear in me. I often wonder what I did to attract this kind of attention, or who I might resemble that may welcome these exchanges, but I brush it off as bad manners. They are just impolite, I think.

This summer I memorized some of my reactions from similar encounters with men, always too close, and always acting like they were entitled to their behaviors and I should enjoy the attention. Some would be angry if I didn't notice them or appear hurt if I did not return the gaze. I don't like the games they play, with rules they assume I will follow. There on public sidewalks and in store aisles, I was getting information I did not understand, and it was getting in the way of the comfort and freedom of my everyday movement in public spaces. Being a woman, especially a woman who is attracted to women, feels dangerous.

"They do not understand that I am not interested in men. Do I have to tattoo a rainbow on my face to get them to leave me alone?" These experiences were hard on my queer coming outness, which has taken five-plus years to happen. It made me afraid of what might happen if I kissed a woman in public.

* * *

After my acupuncture session, I went to the food co-op. In line, I saw an older lesbian couple. They looked at the people around them with discomfort. I smiled at them with my soft post-acupuncture eyes, and there was ease. I realize that who we are and how we think and feel about the ways people perceive us are legislated by the gaze in public spaces. Our sense of safety and possibility, our sense of belonging, our sense of power is oftentimes silently spoken with our eyes. I do not say, "stop" to the men who look at me, I simply do not look back at them. There is a whole dialogue and vocabulary in the way we look at one another.

I am so bothered by the way men stare, at me, at young gymnasts on the television screen, at lesbian couples in the food co-op line, that I start to look at the way that men look at women in general. I pay attention when I see a man in his car, his own personal viewing room, staring out his front window at a large group of young women walking across the street. When I am with men friends who look at women in ways that make me uncomfortable I ask them about it. I even tried an experiment at a conference once. I stared at a very handsome close acquaintance of mine. He didn't notice, and I felt very uncomfortable looking at him in this way. There is power in the ways we look at each other. At best being looked at in this way, I feel noticed and erased at the same time.

I Am, Born to, Raised in

I am a queer Iranian-Iraqi Jewish American, born to Iranian Jewish and Iraqi Jewish parents on US "soil," in Chicago. I was born in a hospital and raised in an immigrant neighborhood, alongside Dominicans and Japanese and Danes. Later I lived in an assimilated European Jewish neighborhood that was solidly middle class, except for those people who weren't, and assimilated, except for the people who weren't, and Jewish, except for the people who weren't. I somehow passed for "white" (whatever version that assimilated American Jews carry), but I never really did. It was sort of a free pass that the people from the dominant culture gave some of us, to signal inclusion, but it never really did. Sort of like the family discount they gave us at the synagogue, where I had my Jewish education. I learned to read from the Chumash in Hebrew and had a Bat Mitzvah, where I chanted a Torah portion. We were 11 years old. It was from there I learned, every year, about the story of the founding of Israel, but I never heard about the Palestinian people until I went to university. I am as Jewish as the next Jewish person, and it was there in this community where I marveled along with the rest of us, at the fact that there were Jewish people living in Ethiopia.

* * *

At holidays our family, unlike the other practicing Jewish people, would go to large bodies of water to pray. There were other practices our family observed differently than the people at our Ashkenazi synagogue. Later when my family attended the Sephardic synagogue, their traditions seemed more similar to the Jewish traditions of my family, but still some were specifically our own. I have not had the time or energy to learn more about my Mizrahi background. I know that in Iraq we lived as part of tribal groups, but I still haven't talked to the family member who can give me information about what tribal group I come from. I also know that our family traditions have an earth-based feel to them, tossing green onions at each other during certain parts of religious celebrations, walking together to bodies of water to observe certain religious rites. I wonder about this difference in the ways my family practices Judaism and wonder what if this points to something significant. It's something I have to do more research on. My background is something I always have to do more research on. Often I think about the difference between the people whose cultural backgrounds are more available to them, whose histories are "common" knowledge, whose histories are written down, whose histories have been passed down through generations by storytelling, and whose histories cannot be traced. I understand there is politics involved in this.

* * *

I am walking in the neighborhood where I spend much of my time, and I am watching to see who seems like they are on the inside, and the others, who seem like they are on the outside. It's a marked difference to me, qualitatively.

I think about myself, my struggles.

It feels as if what I want doesn't matter at all. It is a constant struggle to get the good things I deserve. It is as if my subjectivity is invisible.

I feel as if I am hardly seen or heard.

I think about how I feel I might do something "wrong" at any moment, about how I don't know the rules.

I know that others feel this way. I wonder if I can tell by looking who does and does not. I wonder if I can tell by the way others look at me, who does and does not.

I feel seen and unseen. Looked at and not seen.

The Crisis in New York City

Airplanes crash into the buildings in the busy metropolis of New York. The planes explode. Tall buildings go down, many die. We see on split screen television, televised again and again, burning buildings with people jumping out of high story windows, alongside small photos of men with bearded faces, and brown skin.

* * *

"Behrooz, listen to your father."

"Listen to your father," the dark haired woman on the television says to her son. She has hair like my mother did when my sister was born. She is living in a house that is decorated the way my aunt's house is, my aunt who lives in the valley. This female character has the high cheek bones and large dark eyes that I am so used to seeing reflected back to me in the faces of women of my family. The actress who plays the character is named Shoreh Anghdashloo. She is an Iranian actress who has played the role of a Middle-Eastern woman in many films and television programs I have watched. From Iran, from the US, she plays the wife of the terrorist, she plays the wife of the disaffected man from the Shah's regime now living in California. The man kills her and then kills himself. The man is part of a terrorist organization that plans to blow up Los Angeles, Teherangeles, with a briefcase sized nuclear weapon. He loves his family and expects their loyalty. He is emotional and angry. He expects his son to join him.

For two episodes his wife, played by Shoreh Anghdashloo, drives around Los Angeles, injured by a bullet to the arm. Her long brown sultry hair, while a little mussed, seems sweaty but lays nicely along her face. I yell at the television, "What woman, when shot, would not put her hair up in a ponytail?" My long brown sultry hair goes up (in an unconscious move) into a bun when I am trying to get anything done. My aunt's house in Los Angeles, in the valley, is decorated on the inside in the same way the terrorist family's is. None of the men in our family are terrorists. As a matter of fact, I know a lot of Iranian men who are not terrorists. In my experience, Iranians are generally not terrorists. I met a terrorist once, actually he was an ex-guerrilla fighter; he was not Iranian. But living in houses that look generally like my aunt's house are men who are married to women who look generally like me; men who are terrorists that want to blow up Los Angeles with nuclear bombs that are the size of a briefcase. That is if you believe what you see on TV.

A new kind of stereotyping has begun. I can follow the implications of this along with stated political actions of the government. I wonder how the production of culture seems to work so explicitly with the nation's political goals.

* * *

A stereotype is when specific details describing a group of people are taken, and particular meanings are attached to them. Women from unspecified Middle Eastern descent have long sultry hair that stays nice, no matter what kind of trouble they are in, and they are usually in some kind of trouble, not because of their own doing, but because of the men they are married to, and they live in houses that are decorated the way my aunt's house is. These houses are in the valley, as they are shown in the television series *24*.

At the Borders—In the Airport Security Line

I am taking a plane for the first time in a long time. I have my passport instead of a state issue ID card. I am mildly nervous. I wait in a long zig-zaggy line that is held in by ropes at the airport. I am dragging my suitcase along with me. I stand there for so long that I become bored, and my nervous expectation of some kind of racist-inspired-airport drama lessens. When I finally get to the checkpoint, the man sitting at the entryway to the terminal takes my passport. I am nervous even though I am a US citizen. He looks at the passport and then checks my name against the ticket. Then he takes a look at my face, and compares it to the photograph on the passport. "Pretty picture," he says and waves me in.

* * *

I am running late to catch the plane. I am not used to airport security. I have worn the lightest and simplest clothing possible so that there will be no belt buckles or jewelry to untangle at the security line. I walk confidently through the security gates. I am signaled to move behind the gate. I wait. I can't imagine what the problem could be. A woman waves a wand over me. It beeps when it goes over my head. "Oh, my hairpins," I say to the security officer. She looks sternly at me. I start to take out the 30 or so hairpins I have used to fasten my updo. It's my new look. I find the situation funny. She signals to me to stop. They put me in a three-sided transparent Plexiglas case. It is right behind the checkpoint. Now I am the one everyone sees. A large African American man is blocking the exit. He gives me a tough look. He is assisted by two shorter African American women. I wait in the Plexiglas holding space for longer than is comfortable. I start to feel cagey. I say to the guard, "Is this about race?" He and his coworkers become angry; they think I am talking about their race. I say, "I am Iranian American." His face softens.

* * *

I am at the airport. I am in line for security in a cramped area improvised for the occasion. We, the passengers, are in a long line that snakes around an area that has security gates and conveyor belts in the center. As I reach the front of the line I see an older gentleman struggling to get his shoes off. He puts them in the bin on the conveyor belt that will take them past the security monitor. The bins have advertising on them. They have been provided by Zappos. The older gentleman has a young man with him who tries to help. We are all waiting in line and watching as a young woman from the airlines brings four hip–looking rock star-type young men to the front of the line. They are quickly waved through security. They look like they are having fun. A young, modest, but well-dressed couple with small children looks worried as they are pulled out of line. They stand to the side as the airport security guard scrutinizes their passport booklets. The booklets are dark green with the words *Mexico Passaporte* embossed in gold. We are in Southern California, USA. The security guard has them wait as he sends a few more people through the line. When it is my turn, he glances at and gives me and my US passport an easy pass. I say to him, jokingly, "That is an Iranian last name you know."

He looks as if to say, don't tell me that.

* * *

In the years after the Bush administration's reaction to the events occurring on 9/11, I found myself in a process of being continually racialized. One layer over another. To go from someone who never felt racially profiled to being someone who is, is a shock to the system.

I now wonder if when I need to look for an apartment or a job, how my name, Desiree Yomtoob, will be read. I wonder how my name will influence who I am understood to be.

When I was in elementary school my name was always the last one on the alphabetical class roster. At the beginning of the school year I would have to teach the teacher how to pronounce my name.

I am dismissed by Iranians because I don't speak Farsi. I am dismissed by Iranian Americans because I wasn't raised with other Iranian Americans and because my mannerisms and behaviors are so clearly Midwestern. To Midwesterners from the US, who would be willing to engage with me, I don't really fit.

* * *

I lie to the bank manager when he asks me as a part of "friendly" banter where I am from. I tell him I am from Turkey. I have never felt the need to not disclose my background before. He is confused later when he mentions that his family, who lives in Germany, goes to Turkey for vacation, and I say I have never been there. It is a conversation I would have preferred to not have in the first place.

I falter when speaking to the Paris-educated Iranian feminist scholar who visits our campus. I talk to her about my family and our many Persian rugs. She says that we have them because we like to show off our wealth. I explain how my parents found them at garage sales and mended them. She tells me certainly that they were collected as a symbol of wealth. I tell her that I think it was more a signal that would allow my parents a feeling of nostalgia. She tells me, once again, that they were displayed as a sign of wealth, then turns her head to speak in French with another scholar, and in Farsi with another, and then in English with a third, and I think to myself, if there was wealth to be shown, surely my parents would have taught me to speak Farsi when I was a child, instead of carefully speaking to me in English, so I would not grow up with an accent.

The accent of the standard American English I speak signals privilege in the world I live in. The undergraduates at the Big Ten school I work at have no claims to "not being able to understand me" because of it. For the years that I taught English as a second language, I taught "unaccented" English, studying together with my students the way the sounds were formed by my tongue as they came from my mouth. I would listen for the vowels and consonant sounds that could be "improved," make a list of words with them, and have the student read them. Then, when I would hear a "mistake,' we would stop, and I would say the word, and they would repeat it, and I would listen carefully for the "problem," I would say the word myself and study the shape of my mouth, the action of my tongue, where the sound was being made in my face, and explain it to them, saying the word, making the sound, and explaining it, using parts of my own face to demonstrate, and leading the students into copying, from my face onto theirs, until they knew it well enough so that it could become their habit.

Noting that my constructed race and ethnicity has a different kind of visibility than it had before is not necessarily a complaint. I can tell that the reactions and expectations that others have of me are clouded by who they think I am. I am fascinated by how the public discourse shifts who I supposedly am, opening some doors if I position myself one way, and closing other doors if I am positioned in another (Sandoval, 2000). What is most fascinating to me are reactions that I encounter in public places, on the street, on the bus, by strangers, acquaintances, and even people I call friends. I am sure I do the same thing. We react in particular ways when we encounter what we understand as difference, but to sense your difference intensely on an everyday level is exhausting. I am part of several communities, each of which could out me for any reason (Anzaldua, 1999). I travel in several spaces where I am misunderstood, as a woman who might be interested in men, as a person from the United States who has no minority status, as a Jew who could not be an Arab, and when I open my mouth to talk about my research, I scare myself because I fear I will be profiled for writing on US prejudice against Arab Americans. In certain groups I could be dismissed because I am a woman who is almost 50 years old.

A Woman of a Certain Age

Please dismiss me because I am almost fifty. Please, gross men who stare and expect me to talk to you, ignore me! Sometimes, I look forward to the invisibility I imagine comes with growing older.

"She is that way, cause she is an old woman," says one of the younger freedom fighters I know. She is in her mid-thirties, smart, and hates prejudice, and she calls someone "an old woman."

This "old woman" happens to be one of the people dearest to me, who is in her late sixties. I see her, this so-called old woman, and I watch her. I watch for when she is happy, and sad, and strong, and weak, because she is important to me and has taught me a lot about the world and how to be a person in it. She has given me many gifts. She is my friend.

Being a woman at 49 is complicated. I would like to imagine it is easier if you have some money and some steady lovers, but I have a feeling it is complicated for all of us. Quickly, the physical characteristics we counted on—as we understood (or did not understand) our gender throughout the years—change. The ways we found our pride, the ways we masked our insecurities—shift. Sometimes, I find myself wondering about the length of my eyelashes. I never watch broadcast television, only TV shows when they come out on DVD, but once when I made the mistake of doing so I saw a commercial for a pharmaceutical that grows your eyelashes. It was being marketed to "older" women. The commercial ended with the eyelash woman reading to a child she loved and then looking lovingly into his eyes. Was this woman supposed to be an older woman who had a child late in life and wanted to be able to still love her child with her loving older woman's eyes?

Sometimes when I wonder how I am changing as I grow older, in the middle of the night when I wake up in between dreams, I bring the side of my index finger up to gently brush up against my eyelashes. I wonder if they are shorter than they used to be. I do not know, because I never measured the length of my eyelashes. I think they are shorter than they used to be. That's ok, they were already pretty long in the first place, I reason. I look in the mirror, and I confirm, they are shorter than they used to be. I am sad for a minute, and then I think, "Yay, now maybe the gross men will stop looking at me and trying to talk to me! Come on gross men, notice the eyelashes," I hope.

* * *

My hips grow wider and move more sensually. I am happier and more comfortable knowing that I love women. I feel lucky that I know spectacular queer women my age. No one is more fascinating or sexy than a fifty-year-old queer woman you are interested in.

I understand that as we grow older we become more delicate and more vulnerable and somehow finer. I hate it when younger men make jokes about me, "looking not a year over thirty, wink, wink." The implications that they think I would laugh at this puts their desire central. I love the sweet and interesting thirty-year-old men who earnestly flirt with me. They are polite and not pushy. They are curious and relatively respectful. Still, I think about what they might have seen on television about "cougars" on commercial breaks from major sports events, and how this colors who they might think I am.

This beginning of aging feels to me like going behind some kind of magic curtain, where there are certain things that happen that only people who are aging can understand. My friends who are older, almost lose their temper with me when I talk about aging. I know there are things I do not understand (yet).

We Live Together/Because It Left a Space in the Sky

We live together and apart. We live in groups that we name and that are named for us. As "Arab" Americans, we are a diverse group. As Iranians, we are a diverse group. As Iranian Americans, we are a diverse group.

Growing up, I knew I wasn't the same as the people around me. I knew we were different. When I was young and lived with other immigrants, we were all different, and the whole thing was wonderful, and things like Christmas happened. Santa Claus was as important as the Japanese Bead Flower arrangements that my mother was learning to make from her friend who was visiting from Japan. We had a Chanukah tree in our house, and I totally flipped because there was a present for me under the tree on Christmas morning. We were Jewish, so that meant that there was a Santa Claus for sure. On Christmas, my Japanese best friend from nursery school and I made Christmas cookies with our Danish Grandma, Karen, who was our grandma and our babysitter. She used a cookie press, and we put sprinkles on them. They were melt-in-your-mouth delicious. Later when my Iraqi-Jewish grandma made those kinds of cookies for us in her tiny kitchen off of Queens Boulevard, they were made with a cookie press, decorated with chocolate chips, and melted even better in our mouths. She made them, and it wasn't even Christmas. The dominant culture was so mixed up in the multiple celebrations of our everyday culture that we became central. The strong, brilliant, and loving women in my everyday life ensured it.

***

I often wonder about my own transnationalism. If you can be a transnational subject without traveling around the globe. I wonder what that looks like.
I was an ethnicity that was not usually identified in the United States.
If people were curious about where my family came from it seemed like it was from a goodwill kind of curiosity, to learn about me.
Then planes crashed into the buildings and the angry man we saw on television made some choices about war.
The buildings are gone from the cityscape that was part of my family home in New York City. Those buildings that my uncle showed me with pride, pointing with his fingertip to the Twin Towers, when they were first built, are gone.
An empty space is now there. That space that my sister later showed me with her fingertip, "See the sunlight on the other side of the street, it wouldn't be there, but the towers are gone," she said.
The towers are gone from the cityscape that I viewed from the balcony hallway in Queens that we walked across to go from outside, the city, to Grandma's door, to the inside of her house, where my large extended Iraqi Persian family was waiting to greet me.

The planes hit the towers, and everyone became more
afraid and suspicious, and we became more suspect.
Especially men with a certain skin color and hair color and hair
growth were profiled and profiled and profiled and profiled,
and some people said, now you know how it feels.
And most of us try to ignore it, because what can we do about it anyways,
but we always know it's there. And the ones who look like the ones being
profiled are upset, and the ones who are being profiled are angry.
Two wars were fought on this production of fear and anger,
especially the strange anger of the people who fight the
war for reasons, we can guess, but they don't tell.
And this affects mothers and fathers and grandmothers and
children and coworkers and jobs and homes and medical care
And lives,
And lovers.
Images created to support these actions spring from the depth of people who
produce our culture and let the whole thing make a kind of sense (Said, 1978)
that it would not otherwise. So it can continue without interruption.

In the meantime, the Iranians and the Transnationals, and the "Arabs" and the Iranian Americans and the Arab Americans, and the Jews indigenous to Iraq, who now live in the United States, live in levels of meaningful and identity displacements, one two three four and more layers strong.

The US "Arabs" who are not Saudi Arabian blame the "real Arabs" in their telephone calls to family, and the Iranian men are blamed on the radio. In certain Iranian American communities, they claim model minority status. Some Iranians mix with Dominican and Puerto Rican street culture, while others make so much money that they can buy flights to the moon. The Iranians in the US are rich and educated, they are heads of businesses, they are excellent doctors, they are not like the minorities.

The lump sum category that racial and ethnic prejudice and profiling creates blurs our boundaries and imposes new ones on top of them as we struggle to redefine ourselves against what really amounts to nothing but a pack of lies. It is like sinking in quicksand, when you struggle to get out, it makes things worse.

I have always wondered about my skin color. My skin does not look "brown." It does not look "white." I look across the room at the skin color of a Palestinian man I know. His skin is lighter and has an undertone that is darker. I wonder if this is how my skin is. I wonder if this is where it is at, in the undertones. I remember how beautiful the skin color of my friend's face is. Her skin color is very dark with light undertones.

Conclusion: Caught in Cultural Code/s

My experience with cultural identity has been difficult during this media saturated period of globalization in the United States. I draw cultural understanding and live in many different kinds of meaningful communities, but my cultural location is not as cohesive as one might imagine cultural communities to be. While my sense of myself feels whole to me, the sense that I take from others' response to me is shattering. Clearly, to many others with whom I move in and out of a spatial community, I am positioned as a person who is embodied and imbued with meaning, meanings that make me foreign to them, other. My otherness is not organized in a clearly consumable package that meets their apprehensions and expectations. My otherness, like their reactions to me, causes some kind of erasure. In so many ways, my different cultural locations create the illusion of somewhat irreconcilable positions because I appear to be from traditionally marginalized communities and my concerns and stances appear to be at odds, foreign, or erased from what appears to be the everyday center. But these conditions only occur under the illusions that hegemonic factors negotiate. And so while certain types of people understand that their gaze, judgments, and preferences are central and can bring their gaze to notions of who I may or may not be, and how our differences position me as the "other," this is only from the perspective that hegemonies have created. Who is at "center" and who is at margin is changeable.

Certain appearances of multiple cultural locations occur because of the ways that symbolic codes of "who is who" have been produced and digested. They come down in the ways we treat one another, and how we are read, a kind of cultural code. Other experiences of multiple cultural locations come from each person's understanding of where they have been and what they have experienced, a different kind of cultural code. Structural forces such as law, gateways to institutions, and resource allocation have a hand in activities of marginalization that have different avenues of mutability and involve to a greater extent the first kind of cultural code. The fact that I pay attention to this at all, while it doesn't seem like a problem to others, whose identities are from cultural locations that are situated more centrally, is a problem. The time and energy that is expended dealing with issues of marginality is enormous. But for those of us who have our teachings and our pens and who appear to be at the margins but are at the center, we who appear to be fragmented but are whole, will prevail.

References

Anzaldua, G. (1999). *Borderlands/La Frontera: The new mestiza.* San Francisco, CA: Aunt Lute Books.

Bayoumi, M. (2008). *How does it feel to be a problem?* New York: Penguin.

Denzin, N. K. 1997. *Interpretive ethnography: Ethnographic practices for the 21st century.* Thousand Oaks, CA: Sage.

Fanon, F. (1967). *Black skin white masks.* New York: Grove.

Prashad, V. (2000). *The karma of brown folk.* Minneapolis: University of Minnesota Press.

Said, E. (1978). *Orientalism.* New York: Vintage.

Sandoval, C. (2000). *Methodology of the oppressed.* Minneapolis: University of Minnesota Press.

Shaheen, J. (2009). *Reel bad Arabs: How Hollywood vilifies a people.* North Hampton, MA: Olive Branch Press

CHAPTER NINE

Lather, Rinse, Reclaim

Cultural (Re)Conditioning of the Gay (Bear) Body

Patrick Santoro

I am caught, tethered to the system of my own and others' making.
(Pelias, 2011, p. 107)

THE FOLLOWING IS AN AUTOETHNOGRAPHIC SOLO PERFORMANCE
depicting how I have become caught in a pervasive mediated consciousness, ever navigating and negotiating body image amidst a del-
uge of culturally "acceptable" images of gay men and masculinity. Specifically,
it represents my experience as a Bear—a member of a gay subculture generally thought of as celebrating larger body sizes and/or significant amounts
of body hair—lost among the portrayals of thin and hairless gay men that
have become standard imagistic fare in mainstream media. Weaving forma-
tive moments of my childhood and adolescence with those of my adult life,
"Lather, Rinse, Reclaim" reveals a developing identity through time to il-
luminate how the media and culture, as mutually informing entities, attempt
to condition my "abject" body—a lathering in which I have succumbed to
shame and guilt over my uncontrollably growing, differently marked flesh.
Seeking assimilation in lieu of isolation, I adopted everyday performances
of self that were attempts at silencing my body for the sake of social and
cultural conformity—rinsing myself in a perpetuating, exclusionary system.
While I may have heeded the expectations of "beauty" infinitely outlined
and enforced throughout US culture, I have come to loosen the grip culture
has had over me and heed the power of autoethnographic performance as
an agent of personal change—a transformative act of reclaiming the self.

Critical Autoethnography: Intersecting Cultural Identities in Everyday Life, edited by Robin M. Boylorn
and Mark P. Orbe, 159–175. © 2014 Left Coast Press, Inc. All rights reserved.

But autoethnographic performance is a methodology that resonates beyond the self, positioning lived experiences of life on and from the margins as activism with the potential to create social, cultural, and political change.[1]

* * * * *

[*In darkness, projected images of shirtless male bodies appear—the repertoire of typically buff, hairless men—one slowly dissolving into the next for a minute or so. The stage still dark, I walk upstage center into the projection of bodies, wearing a buttoned-down shirt with the top three buttons undone, my hairy-chested body flooded by theirs.*]

Would you die early for the perfect body?

Would you?

How early? How perfect?

A sampling of my British gay brothers from across the pond reveals that more than a decade-earlier demise would be all too sweet a sacrifice for a life of physical beauty—the privilege that comes with [*Holds arms outstretched.*] flying through the world on the wings of defined arms, with sinewy, gym-born musculature, in streamlined, smooth flesh, within the wonder of bodily, social, and cultural ease. [*Drops arms.*] While they were only 10 percent of the almost 400 surveyed, a larger number of men—48 percent—would give up one year or more for the same privilege, for the comfort, confidence, and cultural cachet of—quote—"a constant desire to look tall, lean, and muscular with clear skin and a full head of hair."[2]

Ahhhh, the power, illusion, and elusiveness of perfection …

[*Projection shifts to footage from the following described television episode, intercut with footage of men walking a fashion runway—muted and in slow motion. With stage lights up to half, not competing with projected media, I walk out of the image to downstage left.*]

Once, as a child, I found myself in the viewing shadows of the daytime talk show *Donahue*, where shirtless men paraded around the stage in some beauty pageant ritual, and I sat transfixed by the image on the screen, dwelling on the differences of my husky build (thank you, Sears, for the memories!) and already-significant body hair alongside their thin, muscular, smooth physiques. I envied their perfect bodies, the physical refinement, grace, and power bestowed upon them by the overwhelmingly raucous approval of the all-female audience. I desired their bodies. As a young boy assured of his attraction to other boys, I was eager to explore what that meant, what it would look like, and how it would feel. [*Beat.*] I wished I could be *like* them. I wished I could be *with* them.

[*Projection fades to black before shifting to an unfocused still image of a male model wearing a tight T-shirt, sleeves hugging his bulging biceps, the front reading: "NO ONE CARES WHAT YOU THINK."[3] While the image is indistinct, it gradually comes into focus as the performance progresses, approximately 30 minutes, until reaching its greatest visual clarity and impact, noted later in the script.*]

But envy and desire were fleeting, turning into anger and fear. I wished that my body would stop growing like it had. I wished that the teasing at school would stop, that I could get through one day without being bullied because of my poorly behaving and oafish-looking body. I wished I could turn a blind eye to the consequences, to stop caring what others might say, do, and think. I wished that others would view my body with the same overwhelmingly raucous approval. I wished there was a way to lessen—erase—bodily difference. I wished.

[*Walks downstage center.*]

We live in an image-conscious society, a body-obsessed culture, where certain bodies matter more than others, and the ones that matter most are those that have been plastered across mainstream films and music videos and billboards and magazine covers, bodies that signify cultural ideals, bodies that function as enforcers of hierarchical flesh, bodies that cause fragmentation among individuals trying to decipher between flesh that is imagined and flesh that is real, bodies, apparently, worth dying for.[4]

You know the type.

The media, and its trickle-down effects on popular culture texts of all kinds, floods us with a nonstop barrage of bodies that show us how to look—from the shape of our bodies to the clothes that adorn them—knowing well that bodies are our interface with the world; that flesh is the most visible marker of bodily differentiation; that enfleshment is not without politics, power, and powerlessness; that bodies and identities and desires go hand in hand; that bodies constantly rub up against other bodies and their accompanying politics, power, identities, and desires; that cultivating a sense of self through bodily (dis)identification is never an isolated act, but, rather, relational—a sense-making process understood in the presence of other similar and dissimilar bodies. The media inundate us with a revolving door of beauty products and procedures that will purportedly provide us with transformative remedies, bringing us one step closer to a more satisfying body, a more satisfying embodiment, complete with the promise that we, too, can look and feel just as alive as the well-constructed and adapted images in front of us, that the best iteration of one's self is yet to come, that the qualities currently missing from one's life are [*Holds arms outstretched.*] simply waiting in the wings of possibility. [*Drops arms.*]

Though we may know better, though we may remind ourselves that their propaganda reflects an alternate reality motivated by profit, that such advertisements shouldn't matter, that they don't matter, that the only thing lurking within their neatly wrapped, bedazzled ideological packages are broken promises and probable heartache—"gifts" that never let us forget that with privilege comes oppression, with visibility comes invisibility, with presence comes absence, with promise comes failure, with wholeness comes fracture, with ideals comes imperfection, with hope comes disappointment, with heroes come villains, with*out* options comes otheredness—the effects of the system are no less real, no less consequential.

Siiiiiiiiiiigh.

[*Walks downstage left.*]

Picture it: An unsuspecting woman of size standing in line at a fast food counter, looking on at her out-of-frame meal preparation, accompanied by a caption reading: "Your ass … It's on backwards." Got it? Well, so do the 438,749 who have viewed this Internet meme, including those who felt compelled to take their own shot at her by commenting:

"Soo much awkward body in this picture, makes me shudder."
"how does this even occur in nature … ?"
"Yeah, that's it, go buy yourself some more fat."
"I'VE BEEN TRYING TO DESCRIBE PEOPLE LIKE
THIS TO MY FAMILY. Now, I can show them."
"Somebody 'fix' it!"[5]

As an impressionable adolescent growing up with and in a mediated consciousness of constrained rigidity, aware of right and wrong, yet too insecure to remember the difference, I disassociated from *my* overweight, five-foot-eleven-inch, 240-pound, high school body and focused on other bodies. I engaged my body in a performance of distance, avoiding any possibility of fat by bodily association. This woman became the target, fodder for one-line zingers that could be shared among friends in the mall while throwing back buckets of popcorn and Auntie Anne's pretzels. This woman's body became the target, the subject of communal scrutiny over dinners of burgers and fries and shakes while she dined alone in an adjacent booth. This body became the target, an object of fascination, an image of internalized disgust, while I locked myself in my room at night, stuffed myself with the evening's leftovers, and contemplated our bodies—hers and mine—before drifting off to sleep. There is truth in what Carter, the culturally complicit character in Neil LaBute's play *Fat Pig*, says: "People are not comfortable with difference. You know? Fags, retards, cripples. Fat people. Old folks, even. They scare us or something.... The thing they represent that's so scary is what we *could* be, how vulnerable we all are.... We're all just one step away from being what frightens us. What we despise. So … we despise it when we see it in anybody else."[6]

While laughing at her, I laughed at myself, knowing full well that her presence could be my presence at some unsuspecting point in my life. While waiting for *my* supersized meal, always a guilt- and paranoia-laden purchase, I, too, could become bodily fodder for public consumption. Who's to say

I hadn't already? At some level, I must have been aware that my thoughts and behaviors were defense mechanisms, deflection from and projection of my own insecurities, my own present and future fears about my body. As a 13-year-old, projecting my shame onto her was an opportunity to belong, and become, like everyone else, to beat others to the punch before I got punched. Yet again.

[*Walks center stage.*]

In a recent interview, entertainer Hayden Panettiere spoke about her struggles with body image, and in conclusion she said: "But I remember reminding myself that beauty is an opinion, not a fact. And it has always made me feel better."[7] While I praise Panettiere for her uplifting insight, the reframing of her relationship with the media juggernaut and her refusal to allow an industry to dictate her understandings of her body and her sense of bodily acceptance and happiness, I yearn for more than another distilled declaration. While it is *not* unfortunate that she and so many others find liberation from their struggles with body image, it *is* unfortunate that beauty is often chalked up to being mere individual opinion, without taking the media to task as a cultural machine that addresses bodies in and as fact. Let us not forget the media as oppressor, the ultimate gatekeeper, the most invasive of storytellers spinning tales of bodily inequality—a system that, no matter how hard I try, no matter how much I acknowledge it as a myth factory, I cannot escape. And while dismantling such a time-honored tradition is no easy task, we should not let the media off the hook. Because to live in a world—with any degree of complacency or resistance—means to always live by its rules.

I know the media's rules well, especially as they apply to commercial gay representation. Every day I feel the weight of bodies, how flesh positions one's self along a continuum of desire, how flesh can dictate one's desire for self and others.[8] Flesh is social capital for gay men, the currency of sexual longing, where bodies are no throwaway commodity, and capital *gains* [*Gestures a larger body size and tugs chest hair.*] are ungainly. The media's formulaic image for gay representation is straightforward: young, thin, smooth, feminine bois—B-O-I-S. Cute, huh? The closer one is to fulfilling this bodily template, and identifying with its accompanying ideology, the more personally grounded and sexually satisfied one is. So the promise of cutedom goes.

Gay men who give in to the media's demands, who become perpetuating puppets to the discourse of privilege, who buy into the beliefs that such a system promises, uphold a hierarchy of beauty reifying body fascism.[9] And they do it for many reasons. I mean, who doesn't want to belong? Who wants to be marked as different, especially within a marginalized community? Who doesn't want to live in a body that is recognized—and desirable? Who can always shun the persuasive messages that surround? While some bodies conform naturally, and others go to great lengths to appear so, both parties become oppressors, everyday citizen-cops who, knowingly or unknowingly, keep gay men's bodies and their sexual desires in check, downtrodden, and in a state of bodily insufficiency and personal shame. Though there is no guarantee that men who fit this mold of [*Uses voice to indicate air quotes.*] "perfection" are actually happy, there must be validation in seeing one's self represented, in being granted a public stamp of approval. In this widely circulated, yet narrowly minded, prescriptive portrait of gay men, what becomes of the misrepresented bodies, the underrepresented bodies, the silenced bodies, the young and developing bodies who search for a sense of self but are met with and in an imagistic void, an absence of options? A corporeal crisis, indeed.[10]

[*Walks downstage right.*]

While viewing the video recording of my most recent solo performance, my filmed body turned profile to the camera, lit only by projector light and spawning a multiplicity of profiled shadows upon shadows upon shadows against the cyclorama, I saw … a hump. I saw a hump on my twenty-nine-year-old mid-back. A hump *so* defined that I panicked. I panicked because, in an instant, I could envision a lifetime ahead of spinal disfigurement, of further physical detraction. [*Beat.*] I never said I wasn't dramatic. I panicked because, without thinking clearly, it seemed that my body was once again a site of trauma, marked yet again as different. And I panicked some more, horrified that my back could [*Gestures the curve with hand.*] jut out in such an abnormal-looking way. I panicked.

[*Moves body as described, the audience as the referenced mirror.*]

Before I could pick up the phone to make an appointment with a diagnosing doctor, I ran to the bathroom mirror, turned sideways, and elongated my posture, pulling my shoulders back, attempting to undo whatever I thought I saw. With the fullest stretch, I could feel tightness in my back, exactly where I saw the hump in the video. I didn't want to deal with this. I didn't know how to deal with this. Maybe I imagined it? Maybe it was a light trick, just a shadow? But I knew better. I knew of the subtle pain in my back, which I chose to dismiss. I knew what I saw. But I had to be sure. I stood as upright as possible—an elongated body of posture-perfect verticality—and slowly… rolled … my … shoulders … forward … [*Hump fully accentuated.*] until the mass of my chest disappeared into my body, no longer independently defined, but an amalgamation of flesh that united with my belly, my nipples no longer able to poke through the fabric of my shirt. With my chest's temporary disappearance, my hump became pronounced. Through this kinesthetic engagement with my postural past, I felt bodily familiarity, as not only did this position feel comfortable—natural—but it provided a release of body memory: flashes of strategically walking the junior high and high school corridors of many years ago with the intent to dissolve my body and its then-48-inch chest into the background of other, smaller bodies that I felt claimed, and that deserved to claim, the space.

[*Readjusts to regular posture and previous orientation to audience.*]

As a chubby kid, perhaps like so many overweight boys, I had to deal with the stigmatized "moob": the man boob. In a strategic move to lessen my flabby, womanly chest, to avoid the ridicule, to look less apart *from* and more a part *of,* I learned to deemphasize that part of my body by turning my shoulders inward.[11] Since I also went to great lengths to conceal my stomach by sucking it in, it turns out that depriving myself of diaphragmatic breathing gave me no choice but to take shallow breaths through my chest and, ultimately, cause greater pain in and damage to my back. Standing in front of the mirror, my hump accentuated, my body felt at home—a position that didn't hurt as much as when I attempted to sit or stand upright. While I did not know the significance of my body's sedimented behavior until this moment, I knew that my present-day hump was the result of posturing for bodily, social, and cultural complacency and approval—the aftereffects of a disciplined body through time.

[*Walks center stage.*]

Walking the streets of Chicago's Boystown neighborhood in late summer, I stumbled upon a salon's prominently displayed banner of a young, shirtless, six-pack-sportin', smooth stud resting comfortably in a chair, his brown leather belt snugly wrapped around the jeans of his lean and muscular waist, as he tugs, with both hands, a white hand towel wrapped around his bare shoulders. He is, after all, an image of [*Uses voice to indicate air quotes.*] "perfection," the man all men should aspire to look like, and to become. Centered above his body on the vertical banner is the attention-getter: "got hair?" Below his body is the word *Restoration* and an elaborate six-part definition:

1. The act of restoring; renewal, revival, or reestablishment
2. The state or fact of being restored
3. A return of something to a former, original beauty
4. Restitution of something taken away or lost
5. Something that is restored, as by renovating
6. A putting back into a former position, dignity, etc.

No doubt this salon caters to gay men; besides the banner, its Boystown address reveals that much. And I suppose that I'm expected to swoon over this man, to locate him—his body—as the object of my desire, to heed its [*With a deepened, fearmongering voice.*] rhetorically cautionary tale that body hair is the enemy—an unwelcoming presence functioning as the polar opposite of the grandeur that is restoration.

Siiiiiiiiiiiigh.

Will someone please tell me how I can get to Mantown? Because I am no boy, and I do not have a boy's body, though I am certainly some*body*.

I am a *man* who defines himself as a Bear—a member of a gay subculture of often larger-sized, typically hirsute men, and admirers of heft and hair.[12] The Bear movement began out of a need "to create a new way to express and find intimacy, emotional and sexual,"[13] and has further become a reaction to and against commercialized imagery of bodies and attitudes that seeks to paint gay identity with limited strokes—pastel watercolors of pansies and fruit. Of course, I recognize the dangers of reduction and stereotype, but I also understand the need for playfulness—fat guys, after all, are usually funny guys. Bears represent and embrace the everyday man, the man who has grown a bit too much around his waist, who has failed to groom himself as often and thoroughly as popular taste dictates, and who rejects sexuality as solely the effeminacy of boyish pleasures. Bears dance to the beat of their own drum, as Pixie Herculon, comedienne Margaret Cho, and a den of plaid-wearin', singin' Bears reveal: "No one'd call me a sissy, no fuckin' way / In Wasilla or Juneau, they'd take me for straight / In my lumberjack shirt and my working man boots / not just a beard but completely hirsute."[14]

Rawrrrrrrrrrrrr!

Bears exist in and as a dual marginalization—a community of gay men perceived by both straights and other gays as outliers who resemble very little, if anything at all, of the recognizable and understood gay bodies and personalities situated center stage. As visual and behavioral contrasts to the dominant identities that exist in the media, Bears are often storied as novelty, memorable for their campy embrace of manhood and masculinity, along with their refusal to adhere to the rigid body standards placed upon them.[15] Yet, as playful and nonthreatening as Bears can be, they are a threat to the larger communicative system at play. As such, they are often relegated to the margins, mainstream media choosing either to story them as comical characters and, therefore, too animated for reality, or leaving them unstoried altogether. We live in binaristic times, and Bears challenge the either/or logic, refusing the label of commonly identified effeminate fag in favor of a masculine counterimage. Since the media prides itself on polarization—a dichotomy presenting *a* desirable body that speaks of a less desirable one, privileging visible bodies over invisible ones—it is easy to see why Bear representation is absent. Bears don't fit—ironic, eh?—and not fitting makes representation a challenge.[16]

[*Walks downstage center.*]

Upon removing my shirt and revealing my upper body on stage[17]—purposefully untrimmed for over a year, chest, back, and shoulders covered in dark, shag carpeting—a female audience member came up to me in the charged space of post-performance, thanked me for sharing my story, applauded my disclosure, leaned in, and—without taking her widened eyes off my chest—revealed in a hushed tone: "It was like seeing your winky ... without seeing your winky." Suddenly, it made sense: My bare/Bear body and its imagistic antagonism became clearer. You see, my body is an anti-commercial body that grows and communicates ferociously, provocatively, dangerously. It may seem that my body makes a bid toward normative sexuality—that is, a non-effeminate heterosexuality—but I am a body of signifying excess, a man who "makes language like hair."[18] I am a man who, with or without consent, produces a hypermasculine, hypersexual discourse that counters the safety and innocence of the preferred gay bodies seen throughout the media: the men who manscape above and/or below the belt as if it were an Olympic sport, a training rite to keep up with the pre-pubescent fortune and glory of the pumped and hairless Joneses. While a site of pleasure, of "woof"-inducing approval within the Bear community, my hairy body—capital H-A-I-R-Y—is *too much* for the majority—too revealing, too obscene, too suggestive, too dirty[19]—and it is assumed that I will either oblige to restore my body to its former state of grandeur with perpetual salon treatments or donning a permanent shirt, or resist as a public outcast enduring the backlash of criticism that comes my—its—way.

[*Walks downstage left.*]

The Internet was my preferred avenue for meeting men as a recently out, nineteen-year-old coming of age in the late 1990s. While I have always valued face-to-face encounters, the Internet lessened the anxiety and threat I experienced with gay men in my younger years, a transaction where I knew my body would be subject to their gaze and interpreted in ways I could not control, in ways that made it possible for them to readily dismiss me on sight. Sadly, this is not negative speculation; this is fact, having been rejected on my physical appearance alone more times than I care to remember.

I passed my time online in the various chat rooms of America Online. AOL, or AOHell as referred to by so many, was one of the first Internet providers to introduce online chat. The rooms were rarely dull, unless you lived in a remote area and it was the middle of the night, but even then they could provide some spice. While communication in a live room ran the gamut, becoming a scrolling marquee of website advertisements, casual chitchat, and sexual solicitations, public introductions many times led to private messages, which paved the way for actual dates, physical rendezvous, and, for the romantic, possible love. If I were not in a room designated for Bears, it was not uncommon to come across images of men showing off their [*Uses voice to indicate air quotes.*] "prize-winning" bodies, flexing muscles, grinning with lust, accompanied by profile text that made their desires known:

> *Athletic* man looking for *younger, smooth,* and *fit*
> Not into *chubby* or *hairy* guys, so please *don't bother*
> *Gym bodies are A++++++*

While the computer allowed me a departure from my body, the ability to communicate my body as I wished—storied manipulatively through my profile description along with a tightly cropped image of a floating head without a body—I still felt the significance of the body, the body never completely lost in written text, the rigors of bodily obsession still kickin'.

Then his private message popped up. Tony was sweet, a sexy Mediterranean-looking, local Bearish guy with dark hair who liked stocky men on the lightly fuzzy side. [*Beat.*] Not all Bears like 'em fully Bearish, or Bearish at all, perhaps preferring an image unlike themselves—a more mainstream image of desire. I was certainly stocky, though anything but lightly coated in fur. Our conversations were engaged, meaningful, so full of life and the promise of genuine connection. After several weeks of online banter, we transitioned to the phone, a progression that included conversations into the early morning hours. I looked forward to our nightly time together.

With 20 or so miles separating us, he suggested dinner, naturally so, though I wasn't ready. I could already sense his disappointment upon our meeting. I had, after all, misrepresented my body. Though he was happy to send photos of himself, to talk and share pictures of his body, I concocted a story that I didn't have other photos, and when asked about my body, I would tell him not to be fooled by my bearded face, suggesting that everything below was only slightly furry.

A month since our first conversation online, I worked up the courage to meet Tony at a local restaurant. My mind was a mess—a wildly spinning overanalysis of consequences. So many questions presented themselves: Would he spot me from across the parking lot and drive away? Would he introduce himself and promptly leave? Would he stay through dinner out of courtesy? Would he look past the image in front of him and stay because I was still the same man he had connected with? So many answers eluded me. My conscience was guilty; I had misled him, and I didn't know how to save face.

While dressed for the date an hour before our meeting, anxiously pacing around my apartment, I was desperate. I quickly undressed, throwing my clothes on the bedroom floor, walked my naked body to the bathroom, plugged in the electric clipper, and with buzz and vibration, placed it on my chest, inch-long hair dropping to the cold, tile floor, fashioning myself to suit Tony's desires. Pass after pass, the hair fell, my chest looking more and more like a surgical site. There was so much hair, so I shaved faster, and more feverishly, contorting my body, able to reach only parts of my back's dense coating of fur. I was a striped mess.

I finished just as I imagined Tony pulling up to the restaurant and asking for a table for two. I looked in the mirror and couldn't believe what I saw: my bare skin. It had been years since I had seen the baby-smooth flesh of my body, and I was disgusted with the image of the added weight staring back at me. It was painful—so unbelievably painful—confronting my unruly waistline, my pasty white, moley, flabby, stretch-marked skin. This was no *Donahue*. It was the most exposed I had ever felt. And I vowed never to shave my body hair again.

I never met Tony, and while he called and sent e-mails for a week, I disappeared. I went into hibernation—like a good bear—awaiting the regrowth of my body hair, awaiting my armor, my mask, because, unknown to me until that very moment, my hair had become just that: a means of shielding myself from others, and from myself. It seemed that, with or without body hair, conforming or nonconforming, mine was a body without an easy fix.

[*Walks downstage center.*]

My gay Bear body—as I have understood it in the presence of individuals both gay and straight, friends and strangers alike—is marked as different, contested enfleshment. Unless depicted in niche venues with specialized marketing (and while they do exist, they are obscure but to those who actively seek them), my body is absent from the media's agenda. And, quite frankly, that pisses me off! I want representation in Hollywood films and television shows without one-dimensional, stereotypical depictions, without the fat joke subtext, without being relegated to a five-minute *Where the Bears Are*-type of existence.[20] I want a Bear to walk the fashion runway, his shirt buttons undone—if not completely shirtless—and his shameless chest hair on display. I want to see stocky, fur-covered arms, legs, and faces on the covers of non-alternative magazines and throughout their full-sized colored pages in grocery store checkout lanes, in publications that aren't deemed [*Air quotes.*] "pornographic" and preach solely to the devoted choir, alongside their partners and their children (but that's a cause for another performance). I want widespread images of men with furry faces to kiss, with bellies to hang on to, with masculinity that isn't banished to dungeon-like bar backrooms and the anonymous secrecy of bathhouses—perhaps safer havens for Bears (and not just Bears) who seek to explore sexuality and intimacy in the wake of a troubling representation.[21] I want the media and its just-following-orders minions to stop cleaning me up, domesticating me, clothing me properly, grooming me, taming me,[22] claiming me—as is—unfit for public consumption and mainstream sexual desire, and undeserving of personal acceptance. I want culture to embrace my body, to abandon fear and welcome possibility, so I, too, can embrace my body *without* fear, *with* possibility.

[*Projected image of the model whose shirt declares "NO ONE CARES WHAT YOU THINK" has come completely into focus. I turn to face him and walk upstage.*]

But I do. *I* care. Finally ... I care.

After years of your well-cast spell, basing my happiness on the juxtaposition of your body and mine, of what's yours and mine, of Abercrombie &

Fitch and Big & Tall, of dancers and linebackers, of swimmers and lumberjacks, dwelling on the differences of our bodies, hoping that one day, someday, I could—and would—fit ... no more.

After years of adopting an if-you-can't-beat-'em-join-'em philosophy; perpetuating and celebrating a blinding, binding discourse of destruction; enacting demeaning, unfair, and cruel behaviors on others and on myself that left me feeling ashamed, numb, and hungry for more; abusing my body because my body was denied ... no more.

[*Turns to the audience, projected image slowly fading to black.*]

I turn to the page—to autoethnography. I turn to the stage—to performance. I turn to autoethnographic performance—to writing and performing this collision of self and culture, to explore my body as a battleground, a site/sight of rupture and critique, at war with others and within myself. I turn to autoethnographic performance to narratively and viscerally locate the catalysts of this tug-of-war that has proven so consequential, a body muddled and weighed down by disciplining power systems in mediated multitude. I turn to autoethnographic performance to suture the wounds of fractured and fragmented remains, to re-member flesh, to initiate recuperation. In turning, I stand at the confluence of a critical and reflexive methodology—this body, this paper, this stage[23]—a poetic and performative praxis of voice and body in the service of reimagining embodiment,[24] of learning what it means to embody without burden, without guilt, without fear, without shame, because "the story comes, after the accident, to identify the body."[25] I stand—an aesthetically constructed bodily self, a self-in-process, yet so much more than my self. I am a transformative body, an intervening body,[26] a body of possibilities.[27] I stand—with, in, and by my body—summoning the heart to hope, a man reclaiming his body, reclaiming his self—all that has been lost, and all that has yet to be found.

[*Projection shifts to images of shirtless Bears—hairy and beefy men. Walks center stage.*]

I am a text that "does not act alone," that "does not speak alone," that "is not a text alone," that "is not meant to be left alone"[28] but that speaks in collaboration with other bodies, other politics, others powers, other identities, other desires. Representation (or lack thereof) always comes at a cost. Body image, gay identity, and masculinity are complex topics, fraught with nuance, and while it is my intent to use my experience as a means of providing insight into their interrelationships, my goal is not—and cannot be in one performance—to claim a comprehensive investigation of each. Locating and speaking on behalf of bodies—specifically, positioning one body type in relationship with another—is dangerous, as it implies a value judgment of one body over the other, a perpetuation of the same hierarchical system of bodies that I am against. But does a body on the margins not have a right to speak against an existing imbalance of bodily representation, to advocate on behalf of oppressed bodies, to reposition representational power? It is not my attempt to disrespect some bodies in an effort to bolster my own subjectivity and others who share a similar perspective. Nor is it my goal to offer a blanket attack against the bodies that fit the description of the cultural mainstream, bodies that may be allies to the cause, that may understand the necessity of thinking critically about bodies and representation of bodies in the media. But my narrative *is* a critique against the media itself, the culture-creators, industries, and everyday enforcers of communicative messages that oppress individuals whose bodies do not, and cannot, conform to such mythic images. If in my story I am able to allow others to think about the production of bodily privilege, to question how it is that we know what we know, to think twice about the media and popular culture texts that surround, to introspect upon their own bodies and the experiences allowed them because of their bodies, to allow another to feel less alone,[29] then I suppose I have done my job.

While I remain broad-framed and far from toned, I am 70 pounds lighter today than my 300-pound past—still medically obese. Some have questioned—myself included—if I am able to legitimately speak on behalf of overweight bodies, whether or not I am still able to claim a Bear identity. Though the size of my body has shifted, I am still the memory of weight. It is no easy task to abandon the hyperawareness of and critical engagement with my body that I knew for so long, and while I may always suffer from dysmorphia, I am making greater strides at what it means to live more comfortably in my body without comparison to other more prominent bodies. Weight aside, I am still an extraordinarily hairy body—an aging body that now grows with and in silver—so I speak from the perspective of a man whose body is still stigmatized, whose public life and body still revolves in and around visual signifiers of difference, but who, in the assuredness of his wiser thirties, is learning to rely less upon the trickery and deceit of a mediated, not-so-real reality.[30]

[*Projected images fade to black. Walks downstage center.*]

I find myself in the men's grooming aisle of Target, on a quest for body wash ... because even without too much hair on the top of my head, there is still a lot elsewhere to clean, so much that has been conditioned, so much to recondition. There are bottles upon bottles of shower gel specifically for men—growing in number by the year—appealing to masculine sensibilities with their woodsy smells and their sporty packaging. Oh, masculinity in a bottle! But across the aisle, staring at me from behind, beckoning me to acknowledge its anchored presence, is where my eye is led: a display, at least ten feet long, of electric clippers—a bounty of brands and types promising me a well-groomed, *smooth* look. I am intrigued by one clipper in particular: the Braun Cruzer Body shaver for $59.99. I pick up the box, hold it in my hands, stare at it for a moment, study the sleek package and the image of what seems to be an underwear model in classic-Calvin-Klein black and white, and I think about the men who will buy this razor, who believe in the promise of brawn, who will deny their naturally growing bodies for the "Perfect Body" advertised on the box.

I hold the underwear model in my hands, continue to stare, and consider whether or not to make this purchase. While I have become more at home in my body, welcome to my body, appreciative of my body, I still wonder about the ease of my identity if I looked less like Harry and more like every other Tom and Dick. I still wonder if it would be easier to wear a fictional hairless flesh instead of the hirsute one of my reality.

I hold the cultural model in my hands, continue to stare, and consider whether or not to make this purchase. While I understand the politics of body hair, the necessity for activism, I still wonder how my body would feel shirtlessly traversing the shores of a coast or while swimming at the public pool, whether or not I want to position my body as a discursive centerpiece, wishing for a moment when taking off my shirt wouldn't require contemplation.

I hold the possibility in my hands, continue to stare, and...
[*Blackout.*]

Notes

1. In an effort to honor the feel and prosody of live performance, meeting performance on the page as fully and experientially as on the stage, endnotes are used to provide citation and further explanation.

2. Ragan (2012, para. 2).

3. Image retrieved from http://25.media.tumblr.com/tumblr_m4r9d7m24K1rswm-vlo1_250.png

4. See also Giles (1997).

5. "Your ass" (2012).

6. LaBute (2005, pp. 71–72).

7. Krumboltz (2012, para. 2).

8. See Santoro (2012).

9. See Mann (1998, pp. 347–349).

10. Pope, Phillips, & Olivardia (2000) refer to the crisis of men and their perceived bodily imperfection as the Adonis Complex. Named after the Greek mythological character (coincidence it derives from myth?), Adonis is said to embody the ideal of masculine beauty. Their research includes a chapter devoted to gay men (pp. 213–225), in which they acknowledge a number of studies that reveal "gay men are more dissatisfied with their bodies than straight men" (p. 214).

11. Durgadas (1998) views overweight men as "automatically suspect: they are visibly, palpably soft and round, neither lean and lithe, nor robustly muscular, enjoying a physically questionable male status, upholdable only through boisterous clownishness or blustering bullyhood provided by sheer girth. Fat men are already suspiciously womanish" (p. 368).

12. Defining what constitutes a Bear is a precarious endeavor, as "the very undecidability of identity is a prominent subcultural feature of the Bear community" (Hennen,

2008, p. 96). While it is not my intent to reduce Bear identity to a singular type, privileging (a certain) physicality over another, or perpetuating the notion that Bears are merely their bodies, conceptualizing Bear identity at the physical level serves to frame how Bears represent stigmatized bodily excess and, conversely, cultural lack.

13. Wright (1997, p. 9).

14. See Sobule (2010).

15. While the Bear community appears to be a gay space of nonconformist ideology and inclusivity, an internal hierarchy still exists. The commercial image of the Bear world, or what Wright (1997) refers to as "glamor bears" (p. 9), is of mainstream appeal: muscled, moderately hairy, stern-looking, white men. Although meeting few of these criteria, I find it necessary to address the privilege of my white body, both inside and outside of the Bear subculture, in an effort to acknowledge other men's bodies and their struggles for representation and locating community.

16. See Suresha (2009).

17. See Santoro (2009).

18. Gingrich-Philbrook (2001, p. 3).

19. Warren (2009) shares his struggle with body hair: "My hair made me feel dirty. And without any way of maintaining the dirt, I always felt I had to cover my body up with the hope that no-one would see me (p. 246).

20. *Where the Bears Are* is a semi-regular scripted Web series, part comedy, part mystery, following the lives of three Bear roommates. The five-minute episodes are not presented on commercial television, but available only online: http://wherethebearsare. tv/

21. For an account of a gay man's experience negotiating his body in a bathhouse, as well as a brief history of bathhouse culture, see Berry (2007).

22. Sullivan (2003) uses this language to describe how television programming, such as *Queer Eye for the Straight Guy,* has stripped men of "the essence of maleness" (para. 11) in favor of a "squeaky clean and feminized version of manhood" (para. 12).

23. I borrow the linguistic markers body, paper, and stage from Spry's (2011) book of the same title, in which she addresses autoethnographic performance as a process of "putting the body on the page, lifting it to the stage, and then understanding that body and paper and stage *are* one another, that there is no purity of text or hierarchy of embodiment.... Our bodies are inherently part of the meaning making process, how the meaning making process is inherently tied to language and writing, and how performance operates as the dialogic process within and between the body and language" (pp. 26–27).

24. Miller (2001, p. 286).

25. Gingrich-Philbrook (1998, p. 298).

26. Pelias (2008) describes an intervening body as that which "sees performance as an opportunity to work for social justice. It is politically engaged, committed to productive change" (p. 192).

27. Madison (1998) frames "the 'possible' as suggesting a movement culminating in creation and change. It is the active, creative work that weaves the life of the mind with being mindful of life, of 'merging text and world,' of critically traversing the margin *and* the center, and of opening more and different paths for enlivening relations and spaces" (p. 277). See also Holman Jones (2005).

28. Holman Jones (2005, pp. 763–764).

29. Pope, Phillips & Olivardia (2000) state that, to combat the Adonis Complex, the first step "is to help men understand that they are not alone with these feelings, that millions of others share the same concerns and tribulations. It is time to help men appreciate the underlying social forces that contribute to their negative feelings about their bodies" (p. 26).

30. Whether my queer body is interpreted against the rigid cultural standards of what it means to perform "man" and "masculinity," or as desirable within the gay community,

I recognize that I embody everyday marginality, existing with/in a system of interrelated oppression at the nexus of gender and sexuality.

References

Berry, K. (2007). Embracing the catastrophe: Gay body seeks acceptance. *Qualitative Inquiry, 13*(2), 259–281.

Durgadas, G. S. (1998). Fatness and the feminized man. In D. Atkins (Ed.), *Looking queer: Body image and identity in lesbian, bisexual, gay, and transgender communities* (pp. 367–371). New York: Harrington Park Press.

Giles, P. (1997). Better dead than ugly. In R. E. Penn, *The gay men's wellness guide* (pp. 330–333). New York: Henry Holt.

Gingrich-Philbrook, C. (1998). What I "know" about the story (for those about to tell personal narratives on stage). In S. J. Dailey (Ed.), *The future of performance studies: Visions and revisions,* (pp. 298–300). Annandale, VA: National Communication Association.

Gingrich-Philbrook, C. (2001). Bite your tongue: Four songs of body and language. In L. C. Miller & R. J. Pelias (Eds.), *The green window: Proceedings of the giant city conference on performative writing* (pp. 1–7). Carbondale: Southern Illinois University.

Hennen, P. (2008). Bear bodies, bear masculinity: Recuperation, resistance, or retreat? In *Faeries, bears, and leathermen: Men in community queering the masculine* (pp. 95–133). Chicago, IL: University of Chicago Press.

Holman Jones, S. (2005). Autoethnography: Making the personal political. In N. K. Denzin & Y. S. Lincoln (Eds.), *The SAGE handbook of qualitative research* (3rd ed., pp. 763–792). Thousand Oaks, CA: SAGE.

Krumboltz, M. (2012, September 17). Hayden Panettiere opens up about body issues in Women's Health. Retrieved from http://omg.yahoo.com/blogs/balancedliving/hayden-panettiere-opens-body-issues-women-health-183511524.html

LaBute, N. (2005). *Fat pig.* New York: Faber and Faber.

Madison, D. S. (1998). Performance, personal narratives, and the politics of possibility. In S. J. Dailey (Ed.), *The future of performance studies: Visions and revisions* (pp. 276–286). Annandale, VA: National Communication Association.

Mann, W. J. (1998). Laws of desire: Has our imagery become overidealized? In D. Atkins (Ed.), *Looking queer: Body image and identity in lesbian, bisexual, gay, and transgender communities* (pp. 345–353). New York: Harrington Park Press.

Miller, T. (2001). Suck, spit, chew, swallow: A performative exploration of men's bodies. In P. Lehman (Ed.), *Masculinity: Bodies, movies, culture* (pp. 279–299). New York: Routledge.

Pelias, R. J. (2008). Performative inquiry: Embodiment and its challenges. In J. G. Knowles and A. L. Cole (Eds.), *Handbook of the arts in qualitative research: Perspectives, methodologies, examples, and issues* (pp. 185–193). Thousand Oaks, CA: SAGE.

Pelias, R. J. (2011). Making my masculine body behave. In *Leaning: A poetics of personal relations* (pp. 107–117). Walnut Creek, CA: Left Coast Press, Inc.

Pope, H. G., Jr., Phillips, K. A., & Olivardia, R. (2000). *The Adonis complex: The secret crisis of male body obsession.* New York: The Free Press.

Ragan, S. (2012, January 8). Would you die early for the perfect body? Retrieved from http://www.gay.net/hot-topics/2012/01/08/would-you-die-early-perfect-body

Santoro, P. (2009). Bear-ing my body. *Rocky Mountain Communication Review, 6*(2), 56–57. Retrieved from https://www.humis.utah.edu/humis/docs/organization_951_1256149852.pdf

Santoro, P. (2012). Relationally bare/bear: Bodies of loss and love. *Cultural Studies ↔ Critical Methodologies, 12*(2), 118–131.

Sobule, J. [JillSobuleDotCom]. (2010, April 6). *Pixie Herculon: The bear song.* [Video file]. Retrieved from: http://www.youtube.com/watch?v=dN_8LRgu6_4

Spry, T. (2011). *Body, paper, stage: Writing and performing autoethnography.* Walnut Creek, CA: Left Coast Press, Inc.

Sullivan, A. (2003, August 1). I am bear, hear me roar! *Salon.com.* Retrieved from http://www.salon.com/news/opinion/sullivan/2003/08/01/bears

Suresha, R. J. (2009). From cult to subculture to couture: Evolving bear community. In *Bears on bears: Interviews & discussions* (Rev. ed., pp. 117–124). New London, CT: Bear Bones Books.

Warren, J. T. (2009). It's back again. *Trunk, 1,* 244–247.

Wright, L. (1997). Introduction: Theoretical bears. In L. Wright (Ed.), *The bear book: Readings in the history and evolution of a gay male subculture* (pp. 1–17). New York: Harrington Park Press.

Your ass .... it's on backwards. (2012). Retrieved on November 27, 2012, from http://imgur.com/QYYyY

CHAPTER TEN

The (Dis)Ability Double Life

Exploring Legitimacy, Illegitimacy, and the Terrible Dichotomy of (Dis)Ability in Higher Education

Dana Morella-Pozzi

Introduction

O
UR EVERYDAY INTERACTIONS ARE SHAPED BY MANY FACTORS, THE
most significant of which originate within us. The intersections of
our identities, personalities, and past experiences form a lens that
affects how we see and experience the world and how we think about ourselves and others. Our thoughts about our intra-cultural and intercultural
experiences shape our feelings, which form the most basic bonds of our
relationships with one another and with ourselves. These thoughts are also
what form our relationships with our culture(s). Though these two ideas of
communication, cultural and personal, currently exist as separate, but perhaps
related disciplines, they are intrinsically connected by our experiences. Our
relationships with culture and with one another inform how we react to,
cope with, and internalize our thoughts and experiences.

What follows is an exploration of what I call the terrible dichotomy, the
idea of being legitimate and illegitimate all at once, and the conflict that
stems from it. This dichotomy occurs when parts of our identities are validated and other parts are oppressed. This stems from the intersectionality
that exists when multiple parts of our identity are at play at once, for example
our culture and our gender. My il/legitimacy centers around the ideas of
ability/disability and my social roles as student/faculty, but they can exist in
any parts of our identity, including for example age, spirituality, nationality,
gender, race or socioeconomic status.

Critical Autoethnography: Intersecting Cultural Identities in Everyday Life, edited by Robin M. Boylorn and Mark P. Orbe, 176–188. © 2014 Left Coast Press, Inc. All rights reserved.

A good friend of mine is Native American, but looks Caucasian. He doesn't like celebrating Thanksgiving and takes offense when he hears Native American words used out of context. People are often offended by his objection to holidays and words that have become second nature in American culture. This is his intersection of cultural and personal relationships. When someone calls him Chief, he takes offense to it, just as I take offense when someone uses the word "retarded" to describe a redundant or frustrating situation. The rejection of our offense (despite the difference in situational context) is often the same.

"Don't get so worked up! It's just a word."

In this chapter, I explore the idea of the terrible dichotomy and intersectionality in interpersonal and intercultural contexts. First, I will look at the oppressed or illegitimate part of my identity as a student with a disability. Next, I will look at how the terrible dichotomy exists within the legitimacy of my identity as a faculty member. Finally, I will discuss how the culture of disbelief influences how people with disabilities are mistreated both culturally and personally. The conflict described in the following pages affects both my relationships with others and how I relate to the culture of my people, those with non-visible disabilities or disabilities not marked on the body. My learning disabilities (dyslexia and dyscalculia) are typically seen as childhood conditions that can be easily overcome. The cultural thoughts about this create conflict for me as an adult student and as a professional faculty member.

Student

"You seem upset, what happened?" Ruby asks me over lunch. She is my best friend and knows when I am hiding something, especially something unpleasant.

"I'm having more problems with grad school. I can't explain how insulting they have been and how much I have come to resent the administration, especially my disability advisor."

"Tell me what happened ... all of it."

"It was all over the phone, I was expecting a call to resolve a debacle over a textbook. I ended up filing a complaint about my disability advisor." I take deep breaths between words, "I resent that I have no say in how they deal with my disability. I mean, the term *disability advisor* implies that I need to be advised about my own disability, which I have had all my life, by someone who is not disabled! My advisor, April, wouldn't give me access to a textbook I needed, and today her supervisor called me to follow up."

"What's the supervisor's name?"

"Sharon. She was already convinced that I was wrong. Here's what happened ..."

I relay the following conversation to Ruby with as much clarity as I can.

"Dana …" Sharon sounds upset saying my name. "I'm calling about the issue *you* recently had with April." She is playing up her role as legitimate since she is a supervisor and employed by the university. She is also reminding me of my illegitimacy as a student who, apparently doesn't know better than to talk back to staff members.

"Okay." The "issue" she is referring to is the fact that I need my textbook in a readable format that has not been provided for me. My class is progressing without me, and I am falling behind.

"April is doing her best to help you."

"Okay." I don't give a shit what April is *trying* to do. I just want my textbook.

I listen for an explanation or apology, which I know will not come. Silence. She's trying to make me feel guilty, but it's not working. I need April to do her job so I can do mine.

"You need to understand that what she is doing, she is doing because she wants to help you."

Now I'm really pissed off. All I hear is bad grammar and blame. So much wrong has been done to me in the name of help, and each time all these people accomplish is further marginalizing me by not letting me make my own decisions. It doesn't matter what her intentions are, I'm failing out of grad school because she cannot get me access to the course material. This is the definition of her job, and Sharon expects me to backpedal because she has good intentions.

"Okay, that's all well and good, but I need my book. She keeps pushing back the date when I can get it in a readable format. I've done everything asked of me. I purchased the book, submitted it weeks ago, and now the class has started, and I need the book. I'm already late on an assignment."

"Well she's doing her best."

At this point it becomes clear that Sharon is more concerned about her coworker than me. I want a transaction, Sharon wants a reckoning.

"April and I are trying to help you, but it is clear you don't want help." Ruby interrupts my story …

"Help you? Didn't your undergraduate counselors try to help you, but advised you to take the wrong classes to deal with any accommodations you might need?"

"Yes, it nearly prevented me from graduating! If I had a nickel for every person who tried to 'help' me …"

I feel my blood pressure spike, again. Retelling the story is like reliving the pain all over again. I see nothing and no one, I just feel rage. Ruby fades away, and what comes into focus is one clear, simple notion: oppression. The room gets darker, my blood gets hotter, and my vision narrows. The heat from my veins feels like they will boil the tears accumulating in my eyes.

"So what did you do? What did you tell Sharon?"

I snap back to the restaurant, to the present, to Ruby and her inquisitive look of concern. "I turned on my heel, slammed the mailroom door, and gave her a piece of my mind. —

"How dare you …" I whispered in a low rage. "How dare you say that to me? Do you have any idea the hell I have gone through to get this degree?"

"I …" She starts, but I cut her off.

"No! No, you don't!" I'm getting louder now. "You have no idea who I am, what I want, or how much I sacrificed to be here!" Now I'm yelling.

"Dana." She uses my name partially as a vocal filler, partially as a reprimand. Either way, I have never felt like someone doesn't deserve the privilege of my name, my identity coming out of their mouth, until now. "You are in violation of the student code of conduct."

Now the tears come like water discarded from car windshield wipers, fast and haphazardly. I try my best to choke them back but it is futile. I cry a lot more than I like. Tears seem to come every time I have to ask for something.

"Your whole department has violated the rules of the university and broken the law!"

"Dana, you are out of line. I can have you kicked out of school for this outburst." Her words are slow and steady. They are calculated. I hear a smile grow in her voice. Now when she says my name, it is no longer filler. Now she uses it to target her threats. The person with the most power in these conversations is the person who (seems) to have the most control. I have heard this threat before from others, mostly when they want to silence me or want me to go away.

"Well, you can try! Good luck with that."

"Wow." Ruby says, deliberately trying to sound underwhelmed. "That's some bullshit." Our normal friend protocol dictates that we both editorialize the situation. We talk about why we are right and the other person is wrong. We make each other feel supported and understood. We banter about the clever remarks we could throw back at our adversaries. But today, I'm too upset for that. Ruby lets me sit in silence for a while.

***

This instance is reminiscent of so many other instances where I suddenly found myself fighting for my legitimacy, fighting against oppression misinterpreted and trivialized as a mere interpersonal conflict. Usually, these situations progress normally, without conflict of any kind, until I reveal that my needs as a person with disabilities are different from those who have the power to grant, or keep me from my least restrictive environments. This is every time I have asked a professor for an electronic copy of the syllabus, each time I need an extension or extra time on tests. The repetition is exhausting.

Recently, someone said to me that people are socially conditioned to accommodate disabilities marked on the body, those that are visible to the naked eye. I disagree. We have accommodations for people with visible disabilities only after decades of social, political, and legislative struggle. Further, I have issues with referring to disabilities not marked on the body as invisible. They are most certainly visible to those of us who live with them. To refer to them as invisible is to deny a part of our identity.

Should Sharon and I have handled the situation differently? Absolutely. Ideally, I would never have spoken to Sharon, because April would have been able to listen to my needs and been able to accommodate them. Ideally, even if she couldn't accommodate them, she would have validated my needs, my identity, who I am. Instead, April and Sharon came to the situation with preconceived notions of what non-visible disabilities are, how they should be treated, and how to talk to people with disabilities.

Sharon mishandled the situation, and it made me angry. Truthfully, I'm still angry. The problem is that Sharon's poor handing of the situation is a reflection of a much larger systemic problem. There is a distinct lack of inclusiveness and accommodation in the way we look at disabilities.

Reflexivity

Autoethnography involves the study of human experience data (Lakoff & Johnson, 2003). My experience as a student with a disability shows a side of illegitimacy that does not exist for people without disabilities. Those of us with disabilities, both visible and non-visible, are more at the mercy of bureaucracy and administration. Those of us with disabilities are more at risk. Bureaucracies of education hold the power over students, for example, placing holds on student records, keeping those records up to date and accurate, and managing student money accounts. These are factors that add (or do not add) to the legitimacy of students. Those of us with disabilities have more bureaucratic exchanges (establishing a file in with disability services, gaining accommodations, accessing the right technology), meaning there are more places for the bureaucracy to take away our legitimacy.

My experiences shape my identity. My relationship to the data and my disability is more than anecdotes from bad days on campus. These experiences are reminders that I am not normal.[1] While normalcy is difficult to define for anyone, people with disabilities face assumptions of abnormality. My disabled identity has splintered off from who I am. In some ways, I still try to hide this part of my identity. I would rather be seen for any other part of myself, or even misunderstood than labeled as disabled.

These experiences tell me that the relationships I hold with others in the context of higher education are complex and highly variable. These relationships are full of risk, and they can strike the sensitive areas of my disabled identity and culture. The encounters are difficult, but they are also necessary. As humiliating, upsetting, oppressive, and frustrating as they are, they allow me to better understand myself and deepen my connection to the culture of disabilities.

My experiences as a student with a disability in the academy resulted in an academic crisis for me. As a result of my treatment, I became defensive, distant, and distrustful of others. This distrust is a result of a flawed system. It's true that many people tried to help me, but none of them sought to empower me. If they had helped me to stand on my own, instead of just helping me be disabled, we could have developed a trusting and respectful relationship. At the center of the communication dilemma is a struggle for power and legitimacy.

Non-visible disabilities are socially constructed, more so than visible disabilities. Unlike medical accommodations, there are no ICD-9 codes referenced by medical doctors needed to receive accommodations in the classrooms. The social construction dictates how we (educators, students, administrators, and witnesses) respond to moments of oppression. The suspicion of the non-visible disability, or more accurately, the person who is claiming to have a non-visible disability, lingers in the minds of all present. It is this suspicion, this piece of the social stigma and the social construction of disabilities, that needs to be eradicated. Why is this suspicion so prevalent? There are no good answers, but I can tell you that in my experiences, it is often because those without disabilities often think non-visible disabilities do not require any accommodations, especially in adulthood.

Faculty

It's 7:30 a.m. on a steamy Friday in August as I carefully don my favorite hoop earrings in the bedroom mirror.

"Where are you going so early today?" My partner rolls over and mumbles to me.

"I have that workshop on campus today, remember?"

"Oh, yeah. Why are you upset?"

I don't know what I'm doing to communicate my anxiety to him, but he tells me his husband sense is tingling.

"I just have this feeling that they aren't going to have these documents for me. They don't allow laptops in this workshop, but I sent Polly an e-mail telling her that I needed my laptop to use my screen reader. She said that was fine, so I have permission to use my laptop, but I have this feeling that she won't have the documents I need in an accessible format. She said they mostly used handouts."

"Don't go into it with your mind pre-blown." This is both his advice for me and a reference to a sitcom we saw last night. He's trying to advise me on a very serious situation and lighten my mood at the same time.

I'm reminded of some other advice I received from the president of the Disabled Services Center. Never judge. She was referencing a student with a disability who accused her of not having any sensitivity for disabilities, since she herself had none. What that student didn't know was that she successfully advocated for her son's rights and accommodations through his entire primary and secondary education.

**

It's 8:25 a.m. I grab my pastry from the catering table and take my seat, and suddenly my anxiety swells in my chest again. I have a sense that things aren't going to turn out well here, but I remind myself—don't judge, don't go into this with my mind made up (or pre-blown). A pre-blown mind can be a self-fulfilling prophecy. I shake my head to loosen the negative thoughts and let them escape from my brain, out my ears, and off my shoulders.

After the introductions and what I interpret to be some verbal ego stroking, the two proctors (a mentor and a protégée) do for one another, we begin. The mentor, Maggie, reminds us all to turn off our cell phones. She begins in on a tangent about technology.

"I don't allow my students to have cell phones or laptops in class. I just straight-up ask them to leave. What do you do?" she says to her colleague in the front row.

"I tell them they can't have any technology of any kind. Period."

"Really?" says another. "I just tell them it hurts my feelings."

"I can't be the police," says a professor from the back row. "It's their own demise if they have their technology out."

Now back to Mentor Maggie. "Oh yes, I try to keep a cap on it because I don't want anyone shopping on *Victoria's Secret* in class."

I am mortified. I can feel my face morphing into at least ten shades of red. My hands begin to shake, though I'm not sure what exactly is causing me to tremble. The rage? The embarrassment? The shame?

She turns and looks at me, "Oh yes," she says pointing at me, "*you* can have your laptop out." The entire group turns and looks at me.

I can't think about this. Don't cry. Don't cry. Don't cry. I repeat this mantra. Mentor Maggie becomes distracted in another conversation as she distributes the first of what I understand to be many handouts. I turn my attention to Protégé Polly.

"Do you have what you need?" she genuinely asks.

"Do you have this in an electronic format?" She is in the front of the room, and I am in the back, but the room is small enough for her to hear me clearly. The problem is our conversation passes the ears of three other professors in my row.

"Uh, well … I. Um … let's see." I knew it. I *knew* she wouldn't have it. "No Dana. Sorry." I really do want to hide my disappointment, but I have no energy for that now. That energy was (and still is) spent on not crying.

"I don't understand why not. I sent you that e-mail specifically telling you that I use a screen reader, and I'd need these documents in an accessible format."

"I guess I didn't understand what that entails." She is young and apologetic. "I can e-mail this to you, will that work?"

"Well I need them now in order to follow along."

"Why don't we just put this up on the projector?!" One of the professors in my row has invited herself to the conversation. She is well meaning and wants to help, but this only multiplies my discomfort.

"She needs it on her laptop," Protégé Polly announces to the room.

The room breaks up into spontaneous discussion as she opens her computer to send me the e-mail. She has the presence of mind to ask if I'd like a PDF or a Word doc.

"Word, please," I say with only a shadow of sincerity in my voice. Mentor Maggie comes over to see what the delay is. They whisper at the front of the room to one another and gesture to me in the back of the room. There are no words for my embarrassment.

***

Mentor Maggie comes over to me and says, "If you were to get this in an e-mail, would that work?" She wants a simple *yes* or *no*. But there is no simple answer. The truth is, it depends on how much work she has done to make these documents accessible for screen readers. The room is still in discussion, and there are three other professors who are voyeurs in this conversation. I can't explain to her all the details of what makes a document accessible, but the presidential directive issued four years ago does. I decide for the sake of saving face to go for the simpler of the answers.

"Well, yes, if you e-mail me the handouts, I can pull them up on my laptop." But I never say that I can *read* them. Mentor Maggie leaves the room to send electronic versions of the handouts. On the way out, she mouths *"I'm sorry,"* and pats me on the shoulder. I glance up to see the three other professors looking at me and stifle a shudder.

***

I had to tell her to re-start the workshop. She wanted to wait for me to pull up the document and copy/paste it into my screen reader, and read the damn thing. No thanks. I've been enough of a spectacle for one morning.

Protégé Polly spends the next 35 minutes going over the handout she e-mailed to me. I spend the next 35 minutes contemplating the general fucked-up-ness of the situation and occasionally try to keep myself from imploding or bursting into tears.

She moves on to the next handout. I go to my e-mail to find the e-mails from Mentor Maggie, who is still not back in the room. I open the documents, and they are not accessible. I'm looking at a picture of text, and not actual text, rendering my screen reader useless. Now, my computer really is only a machine good for games of solitaire and status updates, all the evils that Mentor Maggie suggests.

"Alrighty, I'm going to break you up into pairs, with one group of three, since we have an odd number in the room." When she gets to me she indicates that I'm in the one group of three. "Maybe someone can read the handout to you?" she gently offers.

That's it! This is the statement in a series of statements serving as double-dog-dares to get me to storm out and slam the door.

My group mates, all tenured professors, smile empathetically at me. They are silently and calmly urging me to stick it out. I appreciate their kindness, but I cannot eat this pile of crap handed to me with the good silver flatware the proctors have laid out.

"Can I see you in the hall please?" I say to Protégé Polly with the same disdain I would reserve for a spoiled child.

I have spent my morning walking a tightrope, trying to strike a balance between what is right (self-advocacy) and what is expected (compliant silence).

"Was there a problem with the documents?"

"Yes. Yes, there is a big problem with the documents. I can't believe this! I tried to get this all worked out with you two before this workshop, so I could avoid this very situation. The documents are not accessible, and the thing is, there is a presidential directive from 2008 that requires all documents for all uses on this campus to be compatible with screen readers and accessible under the Americans with Disabilities Act. Not only are the documents not accessible, but you weren't prepared to deliver them to me. We could have worked this out days ago! But here's the thing: I could have dealt with all of this, it would all have been less than ideal, but manageable if you hadn't set me up for failure. Maggie not only stated, out loud, that laptops were strictly prohibited, but engaged the whole group in a conversation about how people with laptops in settings like this only use them to buy lingerie! Then the very next thing I have to do is pull out my laptop in front of the group! You made me look like a jackass to these people! I've been outed and set up, and that is inexcusable. I'd never do this to any faculty or any student, and for some reason, it's acceptable to treat me like this …"

I halt myself. I could say more, but I realize I'm panting. I managed to get all these words out without taking a breath. Protégé Polly is staring at me, her mouth slack, her eyes wide and, if I'm not mistaken, misty.

"I'm so sorry," she whispers.

"No, I'm sorry." I draw a long sharp breath and wipe away my own tears that have streamed down my face. "I'm upset, it's true, but I should not take it out on you."

"Would you like to wait out here for Maggie?"

"No, there is nothing she can do. It will take days to get the documents accessible, and she can't unsay those words from the beginning of the workshop."

"Okay, is there anything I can do?" she says earnestly.

"No." I catch my breath. "I think it's best if I leave. I'm not leaving out of anger, or because I'm upset. I'm leaving because I really want to get the most out of this workshop, and I can't do that without proper access."

Polly nods, and we both head back inside. I collect my things without looking anyone in the eye, but I can feel them all on me despite the cacophony of the room. I shuffle down the hall and scurry to my office a few buildings away on campus, swallowing every sob that tries to surface itself. I have done nothing wrong, so why do I feel so shameful and embarrassed?

I make it to my office, shut the door, and dial my partner, Joe. When he answers, he doesn't say hello.

"They didn't understand, did they, honey?"

***

The workshop proctors brought their own socially constructed ideas of non-visible disability to the workshop. They knew they would have to interact with someone who has a non-visible disability, yet they did not stop to check their own perceptions and compare their expectations with the reality of the situation. Even the other people in the room, the witnesses to this moment of oppression, reacted according to their misinformed views. A few of them watched in silence, for reasons I cannot know, but some of them spoke. Those who spoke only reacted on an interpersonal level. They wanted to make me feel better, or perhaps they wanted to make Maggie and Polly feel better. No one acknowledged the power discrepancies, inequities, prejudices, or insults that were present. No one even acknowledged that this could happen again or how many times it has happened before.

Culture of Disbelief

Fraser (2007) describes a culture of disbelief, referring to the skepticism those without disabilities have towards those individuals with disabilities, specifically non-visible disabilities. There is something about not being able to see the issue marked on the body of a person that makes others suspicious, particularly if you require exceptions from the normal standards (accommodations). What follows is a discussion of how this culture of suspicion affects interpersonal and intercultural communication.

***

The sobs come hard and deep after Joe's all-knowing salutation.

"They outed me in front of the entire class!" I cough out.

"I'm sorry that happened to you, honey. You don't deserve this." His voice is steady and sure and masking a sense of outrage on my behalf.

"I'm just so tired of feeling like a child. Why am I crying?! I'm an adult, a bona fide grown-up. Why is it that I can't get anyone to treat me like that? I'm either an adult without a disability, or disabled and, therefore, a child." I skip over the details of the situation. He doesn't need them, and they are irrelevant at this point. Between his disability and mine, we've witnessed more kinds of mistreatment than I care to recall. We have both been labeled stupid by the very educators who should have recognized our disabilities. We were both told we are lazy. For a while, he was literally labeled as retarded while attending a private school. Despite the fact that he is a man and I am not, our disabilities are both non-visible and our experiences so similar, it is eerie. What's important now is how to recover and move on.

"You know you could have laughed out loud at them; you could have turned it back around."

I'm sobbing, and incapable of laughter. "I don't know if I could have done that."

"Sure you can. Dana, you are the future. You are the future students, the future faculty, and the future of education. Paper and pencil are already obsolete; soon they will be ghosts of classrooms past. These people are holding on to what little control they have left in the classroom." His words are a soothing balm to my soul, which feels like it has a nice case of road-rash.

"She actually said to the group that students in her class are probably shopping on *Victoria's Secret*. Like that's the only thing I could possibly think to use my computer for! Updating my status and shopping for lingerie." I choke out the words between sobs.

"Goofing off in classes has been around since, well … the beginning of classes, long before computers. In high school, I used to put my comic books inside my history book, because I just didn't care about that class, but you're not one of those people. You really care about education, both your education and the education you give your students. I guess it's hard for them to understand anyone who wants to learn so bad that they jump through all the hoops that you have to with your disability."

"I can't believe they are holding on, so tightly, to this illusion of power and control."

"You're reality sitting right in front of them, right there in the classroom."

"I can't believe the way they treated me! What have I done to them? I'm just me, and that's a terrible, terrible thing."

Then Joe repeats the analogy we use most often to comfort ourselves in these situations. "Would you take a wheelchair away from a handicapped person just because some able-bodied people might use it for a joyride?"

***

The differences between those with visible disabilities, or disabilities marked on the body, and those of us with non-visible disabilities are salient, but we are allies. The context of oppression and accommodations that we deserve and that the law eventually acknowledged are considerably different. But the feeling of oppression is not. The falling away of your stomach, the rising blood pressure, and resulting tension in your veins is the same. The depression, anxiety, and paranoia that hang on the words of others stays with us and bonds all of us with disabilities. Just because my disability is not marked on the outside of my body (it is visible if you are looking at a brain scan) does not mean it is *invisible*. This is a term coined by people without disabilities, but with good intentions. There is never a moment in my life where my disabilities are invisible to me. Just because they may be hard for others to see does not make them invisible; at best this makes them camouflaged.

Terrible Dichotomy

The battle of legitimacy/illegitimacy is at the center of much of the oppression the world has known (Freire, 1970/2003). The notion of legitimacy and illegitimacy creates a terrible dichotomy. I am both legitimate and illegitimate at the same time. I have rights as a student, but my disability sometimes negates those rights on some level. The same phenomena can be seen in the struggles I face as a faculty member. Though my role is different in both of these scenarios (student versus faculty), the struggles I face are consistent. The active and sometimes unintentional ignorance of the people in the academy regarding issues of ableism and inclusion creates conflict with my identity. The same can be said in many situations where a person's identity is threatened because of an inextricable part of their identity, including ethnicity, sexual identity, religion, or age. In other words, if someone challenges something that defines you, the result is conflict, specifically a struggle for legitimacy.

Freire (1970/2003) tells us that we are oppressors at the same time that we are oppressed. We suffer from and participate in our oppression. The same is true with the dichotomy of legitimacy. The terrible dichotomy is this struggle for recognition, acknowledgment, and acceptance. It is the act of being legitimate and illegitimate all at once. Because of my insecurity of my legitimacy and validity, I often find myself unable to take back power when I really need to. Several interactions I discuss here reinforce a feeling that I am in some way wrong just for being myself. Sometimes having a disability can be seen as an inconvenience for others, because they have to bend the rules. Despite the laws, directives, and policies that guarantee my rights as a person with a disability, sometimes voices of disapproval and angst at my requests for accommodation (which in my mind is also disapproval and angst of my identity and my culture) ignite anxiety. I have seen these exchanges as threats to the justice of my identity. Threats are harmless; they are only threats unless, of course, they are *perceived* as credible.

Perception is reality. We are calm if we perceive our environments as being calm. If we perceive our environment as being hostile, threatening, or containing some degree of risk, then we are likely to be anxious and react. Normally this reaction requires just enough energy to neutralize the threat or to help us gain control of our immediate situations. These reactions vary given the contexts of our situations.

The terrible dichotomy can result in a variety of situations and perceptions. For me, it resulted in my determination to secure the acknowledgment and recognition for my identity as an individual who struggles every day with disability, and the other 650 million people worldwide who are members of the disability culture. The problem is that, at some point, we all face challenges to the legitimacy of our identities and cultures. The difference from one individual to another and from one culture to another is how we will rise to meet that challenge.

Note

1. Normal is subjective, and problematic. The status quo is to specifically mark anything outside the norm as different, such as accommodations for disabilities. But society does this without consensus and arbitrarily.

References

Fraser, M. L. (2007). A literate dyslexic (LD). *Hastings Women's Law Journal 18*(2), 223–228.

Freire, P. (1970/2003). *Pedagogy of the oppressed: 30th anniversary edition.* New York: Continuum.

Lakoff, G., & Johnson, M. (2003). *Metaphors we live by.* Chicago, IL: University of Chicago Press.

Section IV

Creating Pathways to Authentic Selves

*T*HE FOURTH, AND FINAL, SECTION OF THE BOOK INCLUDES THREE chapters that demonstrate how cultural-critical autoethnography requires constant self-reflexivity that provides different paths toward greater understanding of self, other, and society. Some of the chapters articulate pathways that are situated along historical, present, and future points of departure/arrival. Other chapters highlight how mass-mediated technologies via the Internet serve as salient avenues in the ongoing process of self-discovery. *Sensemaking, coordinated management of meaning,* and *cultural dialectics* will be introduced as organizing structures in terms of uniting autoethnography and communicative processes.

Sensemaking

Since the 1970s, sensemaking has represented a theoretical framework used by communication scholars interested in applying more humanistic ways of understanding human behavior in various contexts (Dervin & Naumer, 2009). Several theories of sensemaking exist, with a focus on intrapersonal, interpersonal, and computer-mediated communication (other conceptualizations also exist in other fields). Within this description, we focus particularly on Weick's (1995) conceptualization of sensemaking. Accordingly, we draw from the work of Weick, Sutcliffe, and Obstfeld (2005) who define *sensemaking* as the process of "turning circumstances into a situation that is comprehended explicitly in words and that serves as a springboard into action" (p. 409).

According to Weick (1995), sensemaking is a reflexive process that urges people to make sense of the world and how their individual selves work to help in its creation. As such, his theory focuses on sensemaking as a process whereby individuals draw from their personal, social, and cultural lives in the pursuit of understanding. It is not a linear process that has clear and logical structures. Instead, it is conceptualized as a cyclical process that involves both external and internal activity manifested through communicative behaviors. Specific to autoethnography, sensemaking encourages scholars, as "self-conscious sensemaker[s]" to create their own stories and use them as a text ripe for examination (Weick, 1995, p. 22). The focus of the theory is not on decision-making processes, but on the complex ways in which individuals develop an understanding of life events that inform current and future actions.

The cyclical, ongoing process of sensemaking involves a constant evolution of experience, observations, interpretation, evaluation, and action. Different aspects of sensemaking are always in motion. However, Weick et al. (2005) describe how ecological change can occur through a process of various stages: Enactment, selection, and retention. While sensemaking is an ongoing experience, the process is intensified when an individual or set of individuals experience dissonance in the normal flow of their everyday lives. According to the theory, this is *enactment.* Enactment occurs when individual expectations of social life are violated; the result of which is confrontation of the activities within a particular environment. Through the next two stages, individuals attempt to enact sense back in to the world in which they live. *Selection* represents the second stage of sensemaking. Within this part of the process, an individual will generate an interpretation—often times represented in the form of a narrative—of the violation. This process involves intrapersonal cognitive processing, separate from and related to extracted cues from the environment. The final stage, *retention,* is directly related to attempts to reduce uncertainty and create acceptable meaning of the event that triggered the enactment stage. The goal is the creation of plausible interpretations that become part of one's identity. In short, people try to make sense out of equivocal experiences in light of the dissonance that accompanies uncertainty. As summarized by Weick et al. (2005), "sensemaking can be treated as reciprocal exchanges between actors (Enactment) and their environments (Ecological Change) that are made meaningful (Selection) and preserved (Retention)" (p. 414).

Coordinated Management of Meaning (CMM)

Introduced in the mid-1970s as a scholarly response to the social, cultural, and political upheavals of the time (Pearce, 2005), CMM is grounded in a basic premise: Communication is the process by which people "co-create, maintain, and alter social order, personal relationships, and individual identities" (Cronen, Pearce, & Harris, 1982, p. 64). CMM theory contends that people coordinate their lives by managing the ways in which messages have meaning for, and through, larger patterns of meaning. Pearce and Cronen

(1980) describe communication as "a process in which each person interprets and responds to the acts of another, monitors the sequence, and compares it to his or her desires and expectations" (p. 68). Consequently, a coordinated management of meaning depends on particular interaction rules, the content of messages, and the ways in which various kinds of interaction are structured. Within this approach, several models have been developed (e.g., serpentine, daisy, LUUUTT) to assist scholars and practitioners in their attempts to understand human interactions (Pearce, 2005).

According to CMM, people learn behaviors that are appropriate for specific contexts. Specifically, they rely on an interpretative process that includes six levels of understanding that create particular meanings (Pearce & Cronen, 1980). The idea that meaning is situated within multiple levels of embedded contexts is represented in CMM's hierarchy model. The model contains six levels: (1) *content* (the words used to communicate), (2) *speech acts* (how we perform the content), (3) *contracts* (a system of formal and/or informal rules that guide two or more individuals' communication), (4) *episodes* (communication routines that consist of a describable sequence of speech acts), (5) *life scripts* (individual's self-perception that shapes, and is shaped by, communication), and (6) *archetypes* (understandings of speech acts, contracts, episodes, and life scripts that are shared by a particular social group). CMM theory situates archetypes—also described by some CMM scholars as cultural patterns (e.g., Camara & Orbe, 2010)—as the fundamental logic that people use to frame, or define, experience.

Depending on the particular interaction, each of the six levels may function as the highest, or most dominant, form of meaning-making. Because of this, meanings existing on lower levels in the model are situated within—and therefore derive their meaning from—meanings that exist higher in the model. For instance, Pearce (2005) uses CMM to analyze two different cases where the roles of culture, episode, self, and relationship intersected divergently, resulting in various meanings for participants. More recent conceptualizations of CMM (e.g., Camara & Orbe, 2010; Pearce, 2005) argue that contradictory meanings often are created when different levels are positioned in varying places in the hierarchy.

Cultural Dialectics

Drawing from the relational dialectical theory, Martin and Nakayama (1999) offer a productive framework to understand and promote high-quality interactions between diverse people. This approach has been used productively to understand the complexities of intercultural communication (e.g., Semlak, Pearson, Amundson, & Kudak, 2008). *Dialectics* represent competing forces that are important, desirable, and necessary for human existence. As opposed to traditional approaches that understand human existence through binary categories (e.g., male or female, straight or gay, Black or White), a dialectical approach is based on the understanding that life is best understood as a "both/and," not an "either/or" phenomenon. Martin and Nakayama (1999) describe six specific dialectics that must be recognized and negotiated during everyday interactions involving people from diverse backgrounds.

The first cultural dialectic is *cultural* ↔ *individual*. Communication scholars recognize that when individuals interact with one another, their behaviors are reflecting both individual and cultural influences. In other words, some of the communication is unique to their individual personalities and others reflective of a common cultural group. For example, seeing a Chinese American woman as *both* an individual and member of a larger cultural group (and not one *or* the other) is one way to successfully negotiate this cultural dialectic. The second cultural dialectic is *personal/ social* ↔ *contextual*. This particular tension emphasizes how some aspects of communication are relatively constant across situations (reflective of personal/social qualities) while others are specific to particular contexts. This tension helps us understand that seemingly inconsistent behaviors may be more about a particular situational context than a person's individual characteristics (Semlak et al., 2008)

The third cultural dialectic relates to *differences* ↔ *similarities*. In order to maximize your interactions with others, you must recognize how you are similar to, and simultaneously different from, others. Historically, the tendency has been to overemphasize differences between different cultural groups. More recently, efforts exist where people want to focus solely on similarities (e.g., insisting that there is only one human race). The most effective communicators see others as both similar and different in multiple ways (DeTurk, 2011). The fourth cultural dialectic focuses on understanding culture as *static* ↔ *dynamic*. This particular tension highlights the ever-changing nature of culture while simultaneously recognizing how culture is constant and consistent over time. Certainly, cultural patterns remain consistent over time. However, individuals must also recognize how cultural patterns change from generation to generation.

Present/future ↔ *history/past* is the fifth cultural dialectic. Effective communicators balance the recognition that the history informs our present, and that our present is situated within our past. Too often people want to ignore past cultural transgressions and only understand current realities in isolation from any historical events. In a similar vein, others will describe past atrocities without any acknowledgment of significant advances that have been made. Both approaches violate the present/future ↔ history/past dialectic, because they fail to legitimize the important role that both play in everyday interactions. The sixth, and final, cultural dialectic identified by Martin and Nakayama (1999) is *privilege* ↔ *disadvantage*. This particular dialectic is based on the idea that every individual's social location includes areas of identity that are steeped in privilege and others reflective of disadvantage. Because we are all multicultural, one's existence is completely privileged *or* disadvantaged. Instead, we have to recognize how we are all privileged in certain aspects of who we are *and* disadvantaged in others.

Theories as Lenses

In this final section, we have described three theoretical frameworks to help structure your reading of each chapter. Like earlier introductions, we provide these descriptions as a means to structure your critical consumption of each autoethnography. As you read through each chapter, think critically about the following questions:

- How would you describe triggering events that prompted intense sensemaking processes for each author?
- If (when) your life experiences involved similar events, would (did) you engage in the sensemaking process in similar or different ways? How might you explain the similarities and differences that exist? How can the various concepts highlighted throughout the book— intersectionality, privilege, interpersonal ↔ intercultural dynamics— help in your explanation?
- What critical incidents are described in each chapter that help to create meaning for the authors? How do their life experiences reflect archetypes or cultural patterns that help situate their autoethnography?
- What representations of cultural dialectics do you notice in each chapter? How does each author describe their negotiation of these dialectics in their understanding of self and others?
- How might you apply cultural dialectics to different interactions that you have had? How do they help you understand your own and others' communication?
- In addition to the theories highlighted throughout this book, what other theories might also function as a great lens to understanding the autoethnographies in the book?

References

Camara, S. K., & Orbe, M. (2010). Analyzing strategic responses to discriminatory acts: A co-cultural communicative investigation. *Journal of International and Intercultural Communication, 3*(2), 83–113.

Cronen, V. E., Pearce, W. B., & Harris, L. M. (1982). The coordinated management of meaning: A theory of communication. In F. E. X. Dance (Ed.), *Human communication theory: Comparative essays* (pp. 61–89). New York: Harper & Row.

Dervin, B., & Naumer, C. M. (2009). Sensemaking. In S. W. Littlejohn & K. A. Foss (Eds.), *Encyclopedia of communication theory* (pp. 876–880). Thousand Oaks, CA: Sage.

DeTurk, S. (2011). Allies in action: The communicative experiences of people who challenge social injustice on behalf of others. *Communication Quarterly, 59*(5), 569–590.

Martin, J. N., & Nakayama, T. K. (1999). Thinking dialectically about culture and communication. *Communication Theory, 9*(1), 1–25.

Pearce, W. B. (2005). The coordinated management of meaning (CMM). In W. B. Gudykunst (Ed.), *Theorizing about intercultural communication* (pp. 35–54). Thousand Oaks, CA: Sage.

Pearce, W. B., & Cronen, V. (1980). *Communication, action, and meaning.* New York: Praeger.

Semlak, J. L., Pearson, J. C., Amundson, N. G., & Kudak, A. D. H. (2008). Navigating dialectic contradictions experienced by female African refugees during cross-cultural adaptation. *Journal of Intercultural Communication Research, 37*(1), 43–64.

Weick, K. (1995). *Sensemaking in organizations.* Thousand Oaks, CA: Sage Publications.

Weick, K., Sutcliffe, K. M., & Obstfeld, D. (2005). Organizing and the process of sensemaking. *Organizational Science, 16,* 409–421.

CHAPTER ELEVEN

Socioeconomic (Im)mobility

Resisting Classifications Within a "Post-Projects" Identity

Mark P. Orbe

Socioeconomic status is a way of life, and does not necessarily change with your personal or family income. Thus, while my salary today is significantly higher than that of my parents, my life perspective in terms of class remains largely the same.... For example, I rarely buy anything not on clearance—even sale prices are too expensive for me! I continually struggle with my three children (2 teenagers!) who seem to have very expensive tastes and always want to buy things on the spot without checking prices or waiting to buy it off-season. I keep telling them that my shopping is smart, but they are convinced it's because I'm cheap. My middle daughter has, in fact, started calling me "chmart" (a combination of the two!). Because of my early experiences growing up—something I wouldn't trade for the world!—socioeconomic status remains an important issue in most of my interactions with others. (Orbe & Harris, 2008, pp. 100–101)

COMMUNICATION SCHOLARS GENERALLY, AND INTERCULTURAL COMMunication scholars more specifically, have been slow to examine socioeconomic status as a salient cultural issue. Growing up in subsidized low-income housing, I have increasingly become aware of how class is inextricably linked to communication. This recognition was heightened as I traversed the cultural spaces of higher education as an undergraduate and graduate student, and ultimately as assistant/associate/full professor. Over the course of my life, my family's income has grown from being in the lowest to the highest 10 percent (Yen, 2012). Yet, this economic turnaround has not necessarily transformed my sense of self. Instead, it has resulted in a mindfulness of socioeconomic status that presents a constant

Critical Autoethnography: Intersecting Cultural Identities in Everyday Life, edited by Robin M. Boylorn and Mark P. Orbe, 195–208. © 2014 Left Coast Press, Inc. All rights reserved.

psychological and communicative challenge. Several years ago, I penned the opening excerpt as part of a series of "Author Reflections" that were included in an interracial communication textbook. What I wrote then continues to be true in my current life experiences, something that up until this point I have never engaged in any in-depth scholarly process.

In its most basic form, class refers to the relative status according to income, wealth, power, and/or position. Class is a communicative entity (Moon & Rolison, 1998), something that is "always articulated in histori- cally specific circumstances and always incorporates ideological or imaginary components: a sense of community, status symbols, territories, rituals, and gender and racial inflections" (MacLeod, 2009, p. 251). Many often mistake socioeconomic status solely with income. However, as Langston (1992) reminds us, class identity is more than just the amount of money you earn; it's also the presence of economic security. She goes on to clarify: "Class is your understanding of the world and where you fit in; it's composed of ideas, behaviors, attitudes, values, and language; class is how you think, feel, act, look, dress, talk, move, walk" (Langston, 1992, p. 112).

The social class into which one is born has a massive influence on where one will end up (MacLeod, 2009). Although mobility between classes is possible, the overall structure of class relations from one generation to the next remains largely unchanged. As a country—the land of unlimited op- portunity—US Americans embrace the myth of a classless society where ambition, hard work, and intelligence are responsible for individual success. This myth works to keep the working class and poor locked into a system based on the false hope of social mobility (Langston, 1992). Some estimates note that as many as two-thirds of US Americans are working class, low in- come, or lower middle class. In comparison, only 3 percent of US Americans are part of the owning class. Research has designated that, because of the desire to identify with the American Dream—which includes social mobil- ity—most individuals, regardless of their financial circumstances, identify as "middle class" (Moss, 2003). Similar to cultural issues such as race, gender, and sexuality, socioeconomic status is a slippery concept to get hold of.

***

Confession #1: This project has raised a series of nagging questions that continue to cause much reflectivity: What would my racial identity be if my family of origin was middle class? How different would my life be personally, culturally, and pro- fessionally if I were raised with class privilege? I'm convinced that race/ethnicity, class, and regionality are inextricably woven within my current identity. If I was raised in a middle-class, predominately white suburban neighborhood, I suspect that I would self-identify as white and not as biracial (which in the US means "not white"). Environmental context is an important consideration in identity development; middle-class privilege would have resulted in a communicative existence that would have tilted my race more heavily (and conveniently) white than nonwhite.

***

One often-cited (and best-selling) framework for understanding poverty (Payne, 2003) has been diligently criticized for the ways in which it negatively portrays socioeconomic groups in essentializing ways (e.g., Ng & Rury, 2006). However, as I reviewed this work, I couldn't help but see some value in the demonstration of differences in social class. While certainly not true for all individuals across all socioeconomic classifications, some general truths do seem to hold accurate. For instance, I found the comments on "money" to be right on: those in poverty see money as something to be used/spent (out of necessity), while those in the middle class see money as something to be managed. In contrast, the wealthy regard money as a commodity to be conserved and/or invested. Education is also viewed differently based on class. According to Payne, higher education can be seen as valued in the abstract but unrealistic (lower class), crucial for making money and climbing the ladder of success (middle class), or necessary for making and maintaining important social connections (upper class). In my estimate, these insights—as well as others related to social emphasis, food, clothing, time, and language—provide some insights to understanding social class as a communicative entity.

This chapter offers autoethnographic reflections on how my hybrid socioeconomic status is negotiated through a double-consciousness that exists within a larger context of race, ethnicity, gender, and regionality. Through a layered account (Ronai, 1995), I offer confessions, scholarship, and moments of class clarity to situate my shifting identity as a working-class (-minded) academic whose income reflects a middle/upper-class existence. I explicate how my lower-working-class identity was formulated, maintained throughout significant gains in income, and negotiated as a constant challenge in my current everyday interactions. The explicit goal of this scholarly work is to produce a personal-cultural autoethnograpy (e.g., Denzin, 1997) that speaks to my lived experiences. Unlike Payne (2003), my goal is not to document class-based insights for the purposes of generalization. Yet like existing autoethnographies (e.g., Fassett & Warren, 2007), I expect the "collage of moments" (p. 89) featured in the chapter to resonate with others who negotiate working-class poor identities in the academy.

Earlier Lessons Regarding Classifications

Like so many other working-class poor identified individuals, my early years reflected a seemingly classless existence. While I certainly was exposed to middle-class and upper-class lifestyles via media, these realities were

197

consumed as foreign against the backdrop of my everyday life. I was not aware that my life represented a lower working-class poor standing, one that society deemed as disadvantaged, impoverished, and "at-risk" (Fasset & Warren, 2007). My parents worked tirelessly to provide for our family, doing whatever was necessary to make sure that our basic necessities were covered (including using government assistance when needed), and from time to time, certain luxuries were available (e.g., going on a no-frills vacation to Atlantic City). Our reality was as good, if not better, than that of others living around us. It was not until I entered the citywide junior high school that I discovered divisions based on class.

***

Fall 1977: "What elementary school did you attend?" First day in junior high school, my seventh grade art teacher asks each student this question as she takes roll. I recall how she seemed to treat students differently based on their response. She smiled at students from the schools on the other side of the tracks—our town was literally divided by railroad tracks that largely separated the haves and have-nots—but just looked at me and my friends. The look on this woman's face was one of disgust, superiority, and presumed interpersonal negativity. While definitely not ideal, I think that I might have felt better if it had been a look of pity. What a memorable experience from the first day of my educational journey out of my racially diverse, but economically homogeneous, elementary school. What I didn't know then, but I do know now, is that this would be a message—one of negativity, disenfranchisement, and differential treatment—that would become more and more intense over time.

***

This is one of my first memories of learning the stigma that was associated with living in low-income public housing (Moss, 2003), a condition emblematic of "failure, shame, and humiliation" (MacLeod, 2009, p. 6). "The projects" were viewed by outsiders as dangerous, impoverished, and full of despair (Moon & Rolison, 1998). Ironically, my memories of growing up are filled with a sense of security (in the familiar), the richness of a tight-knit community, and countless episodes of joy and laughter. What I remember most vividly is the close proximity of multiple barrack-style units of homes occupied by people of all racial and ethnic backgrounds and the indescribable synergy that was generated through everyday life events. While it is difficult to describe specifics of this early lived reality, what remains most memorable are the sounds of the projects. Music—disco, r&b, salsa, gospel, rap, pop, and the chiming bells that alerted everyone that the ice cream truck was coming. Diverse voices—different languages, boisterous adult interactions, vivacious children's laughter, and comfort of street noise that never ceased. Whatever hardships we endured were couched within a larger frame that did not carry the negative connotations of living in the projects. What I have learned about class, however, is how it's used to predict one's educational, employment, and professional success (Langston, 1992). Supposedly, "ghetto life" puts in motion a lifetime of economic struggle and marginalized existence. I felt the weight of these societal expectations in my junior high college prep classes, which were attended by mostly white, wealthy students from "nice" homes.

***

Fall 1982: There's a sequence from the movie Stand by Me *that permeates with the core of my being. It's a scene where two best friends talk about going off to another school where they will be tracked into different pathways: college prep and trade school. The character played by River Phoenix is smart and ambitious but stigmatized at school because of his working-class poor family. Watching these best friends brought me to tears, because it closely parallels my own life. In the movie, Phoenix's character manages to get re-tracked and ultimately becomes a lawyer. My experiences were different. None of my close friends from the projects were in my junior high college prep classes. I earned good grades, but then sabotaged my academic performance so that I could take lower-level classes with my friends. My strategy to prioritize my peer relationships over my academic success continued until I took a job in high school as a dishwasher and came to the realization that a college education—despite what my friends were doing—was part of my destiny.*

***

The stigma of low-income living has followed me throughout my life and remains a constant in my identity negotiation. My parents moved out of the projects when I was in college, which helped to encourage different class identities for my younger siblings. For a short time after college graduation, I moved back to the same housing projects where I was raised and lived with my older sister and her family. Although I haven't lived in low-income housing since that time (late 1980s), *Bates Woods* remains an important reference point in terms of how I see myself. Whenever I'm back home, I make sure to visit my old neighborhood and show my family where I was raised; this typically includes getting out of the car and walking around to the different spaces where I lived, played, and got into mischief. Interestingly, my wife discourages these excursions and usually stays in the car with the doors locked.

***

Summer 2001: My brother and sister-in-law graciously come to Michigan to help us move into our new house (527 Lodge Lane), one that is double the size of our previous one. As a teenager, I lived with my older sister and her family (three adults and three children in a two-bedroom apartment (73 Ledge Road) in the same housing projects that I had always called home. Noting the extreme contrast in housing accommodations, my sister-in-law comments on how far I've come. She quickly adds on a reminder, "but don't forget, you're only one letter away from Ledge Road."

***

My sister-in-law could not have imagined how accurate her comments were: Despite locations that are hundreds of miles apart geographically (and even more socioeconomically), my identity remains closely aligned with my earlier residence. It is something that manifests itself unexpectedly in my everyday interactions.

***

Spring 1998: My wife and I chose our first house in Kalamazoo based, in part, on the neighborhood elementary school. Martin Luther King Elementary School in Westwood (King-Westwood) is an inner-city public school that has a diverse student body in terms of race, ethnicity, religion, language, and class. One year I was invited to participate in an all-day Strategic Planning Retreat with others from the school. During the day, I became increasingly aware that students and their families from certain neighborhoods (two low-income housing projects) were being criticized as the source of several school problems. I sat and listened as staff described how they "had attempted to do everything possible to get those parents involved, but they just don't care about the education of their children." As I focused in on the white, middle-class, female vice principal who made the comment, I came to a disturbing realization: She could very well be talking about my parents. Immediately, I imagined my elementary school teachers participating in similar conversations. At this point, I shared how uncomfortable I was with how some of the school's parents were being characterized. I disclosed how the comments were especially hurtful because they could describe my own parents. As I spoke, I could not hold back the tears that began to fill my eyes and stream down my face. I shared how my parents knew the value of education but were intimidated by college-educated teachers and administrators who, they knew, looked down on them. I ended my comments by cautioning them about using references to "those people," "them," and "they." Instead, I encouraged them to try and understand particular behaviors from a different set of circumstances than their own and to recognize that some of "them" might be sitting in the room listening to comments. As I finished, a deafening silence followed. The vibe of the room was so awkward that the outside facilitator called for an impromptu break.

"Higher" Education: Expanded Identities

According to Payne (2003) people leave poverty for four different reasons: "It's too painful to stay, a vision or goal, a key relationship, or a special talent or skill" (p. 11). However overly simplistic her typology is, it got me thinking: What was my reason? I didn't have any particular special talent or skill, at least nothing that was any more special than others around me. No key relationship existed. Living in poverty is extremely painful for many folks, so that focus on relationships seems like Payne was overemphasizing individual agency in social mobility. I did have big-time aspirations, but they didn't necessarily come with any realistic goal or vision. Laub and Sampson (2003) suggest that any upward mobility out of poverty is connected with relocation out of the low-income housing environment. For me, going away to college provided me with an opportunity to reinvent myself, understand my identity in a larger contextual frame, and understand the socializing power of class. I guess I should thank all of the local colleges and universities that denied my applications. After applying to several schools, only one—seven hundred miles away—accepted me. Physical relocation placed in motion a series of life changing events for me.

***

Spring 1982: Financial Aid Form. $71. The expected family contribution toward my college expenses, as determined by my family income, was $71. While I was awarded a few small scholarships—most needs-based—the vast majority of my college funding came in the form of federal and state grants and loans. Over the years, I've proudly proclaimed that, "I put myself through college, paying for the application fee, graduation audit, and everything in between." As our oldest daughter began to plan for her first year of college (Spring 2010), I came to a shocking realization: I didn't put myself through college as much as the government paid for my education. Sure, I held down two jobs while in college, but seriously, what a reality check: I wasn't as independent and self-reliant as I oftentimes like to think. I had lots of financial help.

***

While the stigma of living in the projects psychologically stayed with me through my undergraduate and graduate careers, I was able to use the physical distance to downplay my class identity while negotiating university study as a first-generation high school graduate and college student. Part of this strategy was to maintain a public persona that did not reflect any form of lower-class disadvantage. Yet, in more intimate settings (with close friends), I found myself creating powerful support systems with others who also embraced a lower working-class identity as a source of pride, inspiration, and responsibility. Psychologically, my lower class identity was highly salient throughout my student years. However, traveling from the upper northeast to rural southern Ohio meant that my regional identity was most noted by others. My way of dress, language, accent, and "attitude" were the most immediate source of difference. Consequently, being born and raised in Connecticut (one of the richest states in the union) allowed my class background to be overshadowed by my communicative identity as someone from the "East Coast." It wasn't until graduate school that I also understood how male privilege allowed me to ignore how gender was also an important aspect of my identity.

***

Confession #2: My younger brother and I graduated from high school and went to college; none of our sisters did. As I learned to interrogate issues of culture and power in graduate school, I came to a problematic reality: Our parents pressured my brother and me to do more academically because the assumption was that we would be providing for our families. My sisters didn't receive that message; instead they were socialized into domestic roles.

***

In my family, working-class masculinity (Moss, 2003) was in full effect. Manual labor was equated with masculinity, a highly valued trait for men that was juxtaposed against the social inferiority of femininity (Willis, 1977). It was my working class father—a pipefitter for most of his adult life—who would make me feel his calloused hands as he told me: "I want you to have a job where you work with your mind and not your hands." His vision for me was to have the type of job where I would sit behind a desk and wear a shirt and tie every day. I imagine that, in his mind, that was the image of a person in charge (a boss). Ironically, on the occasional visit with my father as an adult, he would—without exception—shake my hand and question if I ever worked a day in my life. At first I wouldn't know how to respond since his perception of men's work was physical labor. But over time, I created a comeback that seemed to suffice: I would tell him that my hands might be soft, but the calluses on my brain were rough as hell!

***

Confession #3: I think about money every single day. Early in my adult life, I would constantly worry about not having enough to pay the bills; living paycheck to paycheck became a developed skill that stays with me today. [My brother and I always say that we aren't afraid of losing what we currently have because, un- like others, "we know how to do poor"—meaning that we know how to survive with little money.] I no longer live paycheck to paycheck, but I constantly think about how much things cost, how much we have saved, and how carelessly reckless people (including some family members) are with money. I am hyperconscious of socioeconomic status in every aspect of my life.

***

Professional Success in the Academy: Conversion, Passing, or Covering?

Universities are a place "where everyone is assumed to be, at minimum, middle class" (Moon, 1998, p. 328). I see this in multiple ways: Ordering food in for lunch, expensive dinners with faculty candidates, ample credit card limits for crazy-high conference costs, office expenses (birthday/bereavement collections and other gifts), and so on. For those of us who were raised in low–income, working-class families, this can create great tension. According to Payne (2003), "An individual brings with him/her the hidden rules of the class in which he/she was raised. Even though the income of the individual may rise significantly, many of the patterns of thought, social interaction, cognitive strategies, etc., remain with the individual" (p. 5). So, what are our options?

Yoshino (2006) offers us a critical framework for understanding assimilation in the US, focusing on gay covering. In particular, he differentiates between conversion (a shift in identity), passing (communicating in ways that hide or deny your identity), and covering (toning down a stigmatized identity to fit in more easily). Despite decades of distance from my working-class upbringing, conversion has never materialized. Over the years, I may have passed in certain settings, but in comparison, I spent more time covering. As Yoshino explains, covering isn't about being invisible. In fact, he asserts that having an underrepresented identity marker can come with certain advantages on the surface level. However, refusing to cover the cultural aspect of that identity is viewed as problematic when in dominant cultural spaces. In terms of class, I see this all the time. I am applauded, praised, and admired for my huge advances up the social ladder; however, when I communicate in ways that are consistent with that aspect of my identity, I am criticized, silenced, questioned, and ultimately alienated. Interestingly, Yoshino's book completely ignores class covering.

***

In a collective autoethnography (Allen, Orbe, & Olivas, 1999), I reflected on my need to reject the general expectation that I would convert, pass, or cover my social class in my research. Ultimately, my commitment to embracing these lived experiences resulted in greater professional success as I worked to uncover aspects of communication that were previously silenced. Ironically, being more "authentic" in my research and writing was rewarded; however, when I make decisions not to cover in my interpersonal interactions, the results aren't as positive. On several different occasions, communicating with honesty, transparency, and without cultural censorship, I have been reprimanded both formally (e.g., letter in my file) and informally (e.g., social isolation). There's a great Dave Chapelle skit where he shows what happens when people "keep it real" in professional contexts. They end up losing their jobs and working at McDonalds. No thanks. So, now I find myself embracing my low working-class identity with no hesitation, but selectively covering with middle-class colleagues, students, and others in order to keep what most would describe as a "good job." I am loyal to who I am and where I came from, but I ain't no fool.

Resisting Classifications: A "Post-Projects Identity"

September 2012: As I work on this writing project—the first focusing on socioeconomic status in my 20+ years of scholarship—I am struck by the power of reflecting on my past and present class-based identity. Most recent epiphany: I'm the only person in my immediate family that doesn't identify as middle class. *My wife of 21 years was raised in a solidly middle-class family and, despite my attempts to "ground" their experiences through my own hyperawareness of class issues, so were our children. So, I find myself living in a household surrounded by middle class-ness, something that situates me as an alien/outsider in my own home. How crazy is that?!?!?*

***

According to an achievement ideology, "success is based on merit, and economic inequality is due to differences in ambition and ability. Individuals do not inherit their social status; they attain it on their own" (MacLeod, 2009, p. 3). Yet, Langston (1992) reminds us that "If hard work were the sole determinant of your ability to support yourself and your family, surely we'd have a different outcome for many in our society" (p. 112). Langston challenges the role of luck, questioning the coincidence that the "unlucky" in the US tend to come from certain race, gender, and class backgrounds. I was one of the "lucky" few that was able to use educational achievements to make my way out of poverty. However, this project has intensified the problematic implications that come with that success.

***

January 2009: I continue to negotiate my communication with individuals from back home, especially those who continue to struggle financially. My childhood best friend recently lost his job, got divorced, had open heart surgery, and continues to struggle with addiction. Communicating via Facebook, and the occasional phone call, is strained. Recently, I found out that another friend, who I considered a little brother, is in prison (again) for selling drugs. Not having spoken to him for several years, I struggled with a desire to reach out to him but not have him feel defensive, judged, or looked down upon. It took me several months to craft a letter and was pleased that he responded quickly. We've been writing back and forth regularly for the past few years. Currently, he is optimistic that President Obama's new policy to revisit differential sentences for crack vs. cocaine violations will mean a 2013 release from prison.

***

Langston (1992) describes a "rags-to-riches myth" that is "perpetuated by creating enough visible tokens so that oppressed persons believe they, too, can get ahead.... Hope through tokenism keeps a hierarchical structure in place and lays the blame for not succeeding on those who don't" (p. 111). She goes on to critique how this "keeps us from resisting and changing the class-based system. Instead we accept it as inevitable, something we just have to live with" (p. 111). This type of understanding, especially in an individualistic society like the US, creates a relentless tendency to blame self (and others) and not the larger system (MacLeod, 2009).

***

Can you imagine how it feels to discover that your success is being used as a means to promote a system of structural oppression that requires token representations of social mobility in order to remain intact? Once this realization is made, some increased feelings of dissonance are unavoidable. Despite currently being financially secure, my socialization to always maintain multiple streams of income—something that my father, who always had multiple jobs, instilled in me—has not faltered. In addition to my university salary, I work diligently to seek out opportunities to "get my hustle on," including writing books, lecturing, always teaching optional summer classes, and running a thriving communication consulting company. This work has allowed my family to experience certain luxuries, including a lake house. I don't fully understand it, but I become very hesitant when telling others about our lake house. Part of it is that I don't want people to see us as snobby, elitist, or uppity (all perceptions that I had when I was younger, and to some extent, still have today). Another part, I imagine, is akin to "survivor's guilt," the fact that our ability to purchase a second home comes at a time when family members and friends are struggling to keep their own homes from foreclosure. Part of my identity as a working-class person in the academy is negotiating aspects of my life that are clearly NOT part of a working-class existence.

***

Borrowing from Touré's (2011) conceptualizations of new racialized identities, I'm trying to embrace a "post-projects identity." This manifestation of communicative identity means that I'm not trying to advance beyond my poor, working-class background. Instead I embrace it for who I am, but simultaneously work to resist narrow understandings of what it means to be "classed" in US society. Like Touré, "post" doesn't reflect a desire to move

205

beyond class or strive for social mobility; it looks to a more nuanced framework that can recognize socioeconomic status in inclusive, non-stereotypical ways. "Post" identities resist essentialism through recognizing that any one person is more than just their social class. By extension, it can also mean that we do not disvalue those things that are deemed "lower class" while promoting middle-class values as more respectable. Interestingly, recent discussions concerning the middle class have helped me understand why so many people may seek a middle-class label (Yen, 2012). Doing so allows an avoidance of the (not so equally condemning) stigmas that come with being lower class or upper class. Maybe that is what is going on with my hesitancy in sharing that we have a summer home—I love the privileges that come with it, but want to avoid the negative stigmas (especially among the working poor) that accompany such a luxurious asset.

Concluding Thoughts: Shifting Metaphors of Understanding

November 1998: Following a research presentation at an HBCU (historically Black college/university) a faculty member describes me as a "cultural enigma" and then proceeds to ask her question about my research. In this context, my assumption was that she was referring to what many perceive as my racially ambiguous appearance. This is why I fully embrace the concept of intersectionality and use it within my own research, teaching, and consulting. My communicative identity does not make sense when people try to understand it through a unidimensional cultural lens. Just focusing on race or gender or class or age or regionality raises lots of unanswered issues about why I communicate—talk, dress, act, react, confront, and so on—the ways that I do. However, when people assume an intersectional approach to understanding my communicative identity (as a 40-something Spanish Filipino/White man raised in a predominately Black and Puerto Rican low-income housing projects) it makes more sense.

***

Over the years, I have discovered several metaphors to help me understand my communicative identity as a "blue-collar scholar" in the academy. A previous pastor helped me contemplate how I respond to life stressors by comparing it to how different objects react to being placed in boiling water. In his sermon, he described how a carrot and an egg both had unproductive reactions (getting soft/mushy and a hardened shell, respectively). He suggested that, under life stressors, we should be like a tea bag—we should exist in boiling water by impacting the water around us in positive ways. Reflectively, I worked hard to function like a tea bag, but immediately realized that over time the tea bag would get weaker and weaker. This realization intensified as my tenure in the academy increased. Years later, I learned of the "boiled frog syndrome" through a research project on international students (Urban & Orbe, 2007). The idea here is that if you place a frog in boiling water, it will immediately get out. However, if you place the frog in water and heat it until it boils, it will stay put and eventually become soup. In a previous publication (Orbe, 2007), I questioned if I had unknowingly let academic socialization kill an important part of who I was—was I a boiled frog in the academy?

Recently, another metaphor—that of a ceremonial turkey—triggered a realization that is at the heart of this autoethnography on social (im)mobility. Arundhati Roy (as described by Touré, 2011) highlights how much ado is made each year when the US president pardons a turkey before Thanksgiving. One particular bird is spared in a highly public affair and able to live out its natural life in a Virginian park. What is not readily acknowledged, however, is how fifty million other turkeys raised for the holiday are slaughtered and eaten. Roy argues that this is how new racism works, something that I immediately connected to achievement ideology and classism in the US. A few poor working-class individuals, like myself, are publicly celebrated, while millions continue to struggle without any fanfare whatsoever. In fact, they are criticized publically and privately for not doing enough to warrant selection as a "ceremonial turkey."

It is probably my class background that loves metaphors using everyday objects to shed light on complex issues such as socioeconomic status. Over the years, each of these has prompted great—albeit somewhat painful— reflectivity in terms of my identity. Yet, this chapter has allowed me the opportunity to engage these issues in ways that have led to an important epiphany: I am not an inanimate object (carrot, egg, or tea bag) or an animal (frog or turkey). I have a voice that can be used to challenge existing conceptualizations of class, especially those that essentialize diverse, complex human existences into binary categories of "haves" and "have-nots." Personally striving for a "post-projects identity" means that I embrace that aspect of who I am, but do not confine myself to social stigmas that situate it as inherently negative. I am much more than my class identity can signify independent of other salient cultural identity markers. Professionally, I can use the relative privilege that comes with advanced degrees and what I would define as a middle-class salary to share my story with others who otherwise would continue eating turkey every Thanksgiving without any critical recognition of what it symbolizes for self, others, and the larger society. This chapter is my part in using personal-cultural autoethnography to enhance greater understanding of the saliency of social class in the US.

References

Allen, B. J., Orbe, M., & Olivas, M. R. (1999). The complexity of our tears: Dis/enchantment and (in)difference in the academy. *Communication Theory, 9*(4), 402–429.

Denzin, N. K. (1997). *Interpretive ethnography: Ethnographic practices for the 21st century.* Thousand Oaks, CA: Sage.

Fassett, D., & Warren, J. T. (2007). *Critical communication pedagogy.* Thousand Oaks, CA: Sage.

Langston, D. (1992). Tired of playing monopoly? In M. L. Anderson & P. H. Collins (Eds.), *Race, class, and gender: An anthology* (pp. 110–120). Belmont, CA: Wadsworth.

Laub, J. H., & Sampson, R. J. (2003). *Shared beginnings, divergent lives: Delinquent boys to age 70.* Cambridge, MA: Harvard University Press.

MacLeod, J. (2009). *Ain't no makin' it: Aspirations & attainment in a low-income neighborhood* (3d ed.). Philadelphia, PA: Westview Press.

Moon, D. G. (1998). Performed identities: "Passing" as an inter/cultural discourse. In J. N. Martin, T. K. Nakayama, L. A. Flores (Eds.), *Readings in cultural contexts* (pp. 322–330). Mountain View, CA: Mayfield.

Moon, D. G., & Rolison, G. L. (1998). Communication of classism. In M. L. Hecht (Ed.), *Communicating prejudice* (pp. 122–135). Thousand Oaks, CA: Sage.

Moss, K. (2003). *The color of class: Poor whites and the paradox of privilege.* Philadelphia: University of Pennsylvania Press.

Ng, J. C., & Rury, J. C. (2006). Poverty and education: A critical analysis of the Ruby Payne phenomenon. Teachers College Record. Retrieved October 10, 2012, from http://www.tcrecord.org/12596

Orbe, M. (2007). Critical reflections from a resistant boiled frog: Striving toward a critical communication pedagogy as articulated by Deanna Fassett and John Warren. *The Review of Communication, 7*(3), 298–302.

Orbe, M., & Harris, T. M. (2008). *Interracial communication: Theory into practice.* Thousand Oaks, CA: Sage.

Payne, R. K. (2003). *A framework for understanding poverty* (3d ed.). Highlands, TX: Aha Process, Inc.

Ronai, C. R. (1995). Multiple reflections of child sex abuse: An argument for a layered account. *Journal of Contemporary Ethnography, 23*(4), 395–426.

Touré. (2011). *Who's afraid of post-blackness?: What it means to be black now.* New York: Free Press.

Urban, E., & Orbe, M. (2007). The "syndrome of the boiled frog": Exploring international students on US campuses as co-cultural group members. *Journal of Intercultural Communication Research, 36*(3), 117–138.

Willis, P. E. (1977). *Learning to labor.* Aldershot, UK: Gower Press.

Yen, H. (2012, July 18). "Middle class" fuzzy in politics. *Kalamazoo (MI) Gazette*, p. A8.

Yoshino, K. (2006). *Covering: The hidden assault on our civil rights.* New York: Random House.

∾

CHAPTER TWELVE

Mindful Heresy, Holo-expression, and Poiesis
An Autoethnographic Response to the Orthodoxies
of Interpersonal & Cultural Life

Sarah Amira de la Garza

*I*RELAND ALWAYS HAS SURPRISES FOR ME WHEN I VISIT. THIS TIME, I have some time to myself. My students have all gone to discover the delights of the music scene in downtown Galway. I walk away from the city center and head towards some of the streets on the west end of town, near the coast. The lights reflect off the clouds, giving the end of day a little more brightness than usual.

It's an Irish summer, and it's cool, the kind of cool that is warm to folks who don't live in the desert infernos I have called home most of my adult life. I love the feel of the air on my cheeks; it keeps me awake, alert. The heat in Arizona closes the mind, like a fire, burning fuel. I breathe deeply and wonder where I am walking. That is my approach to my autoethnographic method. No matter where I am, the world around me is full of messages, if I can only recognize them and really have the courage to travel into them, rather than jump to a favored or familiar, defensive, or fearful interpretation. Sometimes rapid sensemaking is really the avoidance of sense. Dissonance is about music that one hasn't learned to hear. Over time, I've come to know that those discordant notes of unfamiliar or triggering realities are often the introductory movements to some of the most beautiful and mysterious ballads I had no idea my life was ready to compose. And so, I set out, walking, and sensing, releasing those clutching impulses to plan or retreat into something predictable. It's quiet. It's Saturday night, and most of the activity is elsewhere. I turn the corner off the main street I'd been walking.

There are cars moving on the streets. Not lots of traffic, but a slow appearance of automobiles, all turning into a small lot up ahead to my right. I notice a few cyclists going the same way, and a woman walks out of her house, proceeding across the street, headed in the same direction. I decide to join the flow and come to realize as I take in more of the signs around me, that I'm headed to a Saturday vigil Mass at a local Catholic parish. I walk by the open front doors of the church building and see bright lights emitting golden warmth off of walnut-colored pews and a red carpet. The colors are a brilliant contrast to the gray tones on the street and in the sky. The altar is dressed in green. No, not because this is Ireland, I tell my hyperactive, ridiculous mind chatter. I can't remember what the green means for the church calendar. I note, with interest, that not remembering feels sad to me. I want to shake it off, but I work to stay with it.

"You're a Jew now, *Amira*," my chastising inner voice tells me, and I feel a discomfort at hearing the sound of my new name "inside myself" in an unfamiliar way. "You can't go in there." Who said anything about going in there? Is that what I really want to do? I feel incredibly uncomfortable, bound. I walk past the church to the sidewalk along its side, and find a bench inside an area fenced off by wrought iron, and there is a statue of some sort there. I can see the little grotto built around it. Good. Let's go take a look. I'll take pictures. I am aware I'm pretending to myself that this is what I want to do. I try to feel at ease, but I am not. I want to go inside the church. I want to go to Mass. I am struggling with the price of attempting to constrain myself.

I used to blame Catholic school catechism for this kind of guilt. But this time I was hearing Jewish voices in my head. Echoes of something I called Jewish voices. I remember my friend Chuck, a scholar of kabbalah and literature, asking me, "When you convert, Christina, what will you do about your indigenous spiritual practices?" I shot back at him quickly, "I'll always be who I am ancestrally, Chuck. Just because I convert to being a Jew doesn't change that I am ancestrally Indian,[1] any more than having been Catholic could erase that I'm of Sephardic ancestry." He nodded, thinking, and we didn't pursue the topic anymore. But it had triggered me. Now, in Galway, four years later, I was perhaps feeling something I'd avoided. But *why?*

Remembering Chuck's question and admitting that I'd left something unresolved, that I had not been completely honest with myself, seemed to relieve some of the discomfort I'd been feeling. It was fear, really, and for the moment, it abated. During this moment, I decided that I would go into the church, armed with a double-barreled rationalization to continue my denial of whatever it was that was able to stir up so much distress in me. I am an ethnographer, I said to myself. I am in Ireland. Why *wouldn't* I want to attend a mass here and see what they're like? And, drawing on the same distorted reasoning that I'd used with Chuck years earlier, "I can honor my

Catholic ancestors; I can't just write them off, too!" My steps took me into the church. It takes a long time to release old scripts.

* * *

No matter what I have studied, I have always been led back to issues of silenced truths, repressed expression, and hegemonic mimicry. When I was just learning to write, I took a pencil and wrote the word *NO* on photographs in the family photo album, on walls, and on pages of the "baby book" of mementos my mother had collected about my life. My mother didn't stop me, and I sense this would help my voice to survive, years later.

* * *

"*¿Garza?*" Pati's eyes opened widely. I nodded. Pati was one of the five other women who lived in the boarding house where I would be living for the first six months of 1999, for the remainder of my Fulbright stay in Chihuahua, Mexico. We were introducing ourselves to each other, and as is common in Mexico, that involves sharing the family names, so I had shared mine. González, (a nod); Martínez (two nods); Urueta (a raised head and discussion of my family's historical roots in Chihuahua, where there is a Parque Urueta); Gutiérrez (still more talk of my family in Chihuahua); and then I said, "Garza."

"*Ese es un nombre judío,*" Pati stated with an indefinite tone, as if questioning with her statement. I had not known it was so readily known as a Jewish name. I didn't say much, but I recalled my aunts Celestina and Hortencia joking about how we were more comfortable with Jews, about how we were probably Jews, about how Tía Cande (short for Candelaria) had "looked" Jewish, as had Uncle John and even Papa Cosme. I didn't know. But in my gut, I knew?

I used to sit in the small chapel by the cathedral in Chihuahua to pray—at least I called it prayer; truly, I was thinking more about how my great-grandmother Cristina and grandmother Carmen might have sat in the same chapel sixty years earlier when they lived in Chihuahua, waiting to leave Mexico for Texas. I didn't think about how they were fleeing Mexico because they wanted so badly to be free to attend Mass, during *La Cristiada,* or the *Cristero* war, when the postrevolutionary Mexican government had instituted anticlerical rules and begun persecuting Catholics. On one side of my family, people had struggled to continue practicing outlawed Judaism, and on the other, to practice outlawed Catholicism. Now they both live in me.

* * *

Like a machine on automatic pilot, the power of my hand worked to override the mental chatter as I walked in the door of the church in Galway, the Church of St. Mary, Claddagh, or also called, Our Lady of Galway. I felt a "voice" inside me chime into the reflective conference that was now, obviously, in full session inside me. It's interesting really, how that which we call knowing is hardly a systematically organized body of knowledge, but one that is subjectively framed and understood. Can we ever really decide so surely that we know something, except that the world around us is somehow supporting us? Or is it possible that these tensions and inner conflicts are actually the knowing? Maybe we would all know more if would voice our tensions and uncertainties more often, and our "certainties" less often.

My hand moved to the holy water font as I entered the church, my body so well rehearsed in this ritual that I was startled by it. It had been about eight years since I'd been to Mass. As I touched the water, a debate ensued inside me about the legitimacy of the water's power, its uses to dispel the devil in exorcisms, questions about possible bacteria and disease-bearing organisms living in it, and whether, as a Jew, I was supposed to be doing this. Of course I wasn't. But I did. I made a note to reflect on this neurotic chatter. If I "knew" less, I could be certain far more easily.

As I pulled my wet fingers from the holy water font, I felt incredibly awkward. Do it. No, don't do it. You've got to do it. Wipe your fingers off. No, I can't do that. Wait—did I just hear an "I" in that chatter? Who said that? I could feel a wave of anxiety, my body beginning to feel like a chamber of echoes for the voices of all the persons I've ever been. Just then, I could hear a sort of whispering secret conspirator, attempting to help me in a game of "hot-cold." You're getting warmer ... but do you want to go there? Might I be able to privilege, or even recognize, the sound of *my own voice*?

I did it anyway—I made the sign of the cross on my forehead, and like thousands of times before, brought my moist fingers to my lips and heart, repeating the sign. I felt my breath release. There, I did it, but had I? When I made the "sign of the cross," I consciously refused to say the words, and instead, recalled that the ancient form of the Hebrew letter "tav" was a cross-shaped letter, used as a mark on the forehead, for truth. This is thought by some to have been the practice redefined by the Christian Church (Masvie, 2012).

As the Mass began, I began to cry when my body automatically recited prayers I'd not said in over nine years. Something inside me felt at home, but when the priest spoke, and it was time to recite the "profession of faith," derived from the Nicene Creed, it was absolutely clear to me that I did not, in fact, believe this prayer. In fact, I was clearly aware of too much history about it, and about the early church, to even give it credibility as rooted in a prayer the apostles prayed. The motions of my body—kneeling, praying, even blessing myself, soothed me. Thinking about the Church's efforts to retroject Christian meaning to ancient Hebrew practices causes me to feel a familiar ambivalence. Fully present, but "not there," I work to return. The warm, fuzzy feeling had left, but the mindful heresy had begun.

* * *

Constanza and Alonso de la Garza were burned at the stake in 1526, in Las Palmas, Gran Canaria, as heretics during the Spanish Inquisition. They had been accused of Judaizing, of practicing Judaism. I traveled there in 2008, after having learned of the executions in a book by Jewish historian, David Raphael. I contacted him, and he encouraged me to travel there and to find the records for their autos-da-fé, which he said were located in the historical archives of Las Palmas.

It was about a two-mile walk through the streets of Las Palmas from my hotel to the archives at the Museo de las Canarias, where Dr. Raphael had told me the records were kept. I had been foolish to assume I'd get access by just showing up, but I'd trusted online references, and hadn't pursued it strongly. You'd think maybe I didn't really want to see them. In fact, the archives were closed to researchers that day. It was a relief.

I knew that what I was hiding from myself, if not from others, was that I didn't want to tell anyone who might ask about my interest, why I was looking for these particular records. "You see," I might have said, I imagined myself speaking to the imaginary inquisitors, "I am interested because my family is of the de la Garza name, and I converted to Judaism, *but I'm not a heretic?*" No one asked me why I wanted to look at the records; they simply told me they were closed. So, I feigned disappointment and muttered a question about whether the rest of the museum was open to viewing (I already knew it was). The level of my discomfort made me more uncomfortable. I felt like I was playing a game of hide-and-seek, but one where I hoped never to be found, and I was both the hider and the seeker. Imagine, if this is what I felt *here,* in 2008, what it was like in 1526!

The museum was full of evidence of the anthropological practice of collecting and studying the human remains of past civilizations. Skulls were displayed with pride, as were the artifacts of the indigenous Canarians who created statuettes and icons of the female vulva. Context was sadly missing, and I felt caught in a bad joke of some sort: What happens to the woman who's afraid to admit she is a Jew but doesn't want to claim Catholicism, and feels more comfortable praying in a church than many synagogues?—She is sent into a purgatory of colonialist representation and narratives. I felt conspicuous as I looked through the gift shop, as if every eye was upon me, *knowing.* It's interesting; we are most self-conscious when we think we are somehow not fitting in with some norm. Self-consciousness is a good guide to an awareness of established, authorized, and often enforced lifeways, otherwise known as orthodoxies.

While I was busy buying postcards and miniature clay replicas of indigenous abstractions of the vulva as mementos, I ran across a section of books on Canary Island history. Right there, in between several other books, I found a book of transcriptions from the inquisition records of the sixteenth century in Las Palmas. Among the few records included in the book, were those of Alonso and Constanza de la Garza.

* * *

"You know," Reb Ayla began, "you don't need to change your name to become Jewish." In 1998, I had begun studying with the intention of deciding whether I would convert to Judaism. By the year 2001, I had decided to convert. Coincidentally (or not), "2001 was the year David Raphael published his book on crypto-Jews in Monterrey and Texas, and the following year I decided to change my name legally before my conversion. I had a reason for doing so, and following some rule was not it.

"My birth name is **Maria Christina**," I told Ayla, "and **no** name could be more obviously Christian! If I had ancestors who had to hide their Judaism behind a Christian facade, why would I want to have a name that would hide my Judaism?" For me, it felt like justice of some sort—it was almost five hundred years later, but it felt like a way to honor the de la Garzas who had been burned at the stake. One of my maternal great-grandmothers was Honorata de la Garza, and I chose to take the family name linked to our Sephardic ancestry, *de la Garza*. In Inquisitional Spain, choosing this name upon conversion could have functioned as an encoded public thumbing of the nose to the Catholic Church. Other fifteenth and sixteenth century Jews would have known that "garza," (today the blue heron) was the vulture, an unclean bird. By converting, they had become unclean. This is what I had learned from David Raphael's book. I also learned that their heirs had worked to prove their Christianity to gain back the rights (to own property, leave the country, among others) denied them by virtue of the Inquisition trials.

* * *

"Are you going to?" Nick whispered to me. I tried to ask him to repeat his question by squinting my face. We were seated at the memorial funeral mass for his cousin, Pat, and were surrounded by his family members on the pews around us. "Communion," he clarified, gesturing as if putting a host in his mouth. We held back laughter.

"I don't know," I shrugged. I felt the growingly familiar tightness in the chest that accompanies the anxiety I feel when I am faced with questions about my religion. I wanted to be able to answer either YES or NO with a sense of clarity, but I couldn't. Both responses were heavily laden with terribly uncomfortable ambiguity. Religion is the one area where I fully feel the embodiment of orthodoxy struggling to control me.

I honestly can't remember if we rose to receive communion or not. I can actively visualize both remaining seated while family members walked up the aisle, and returning to my seat after having taken the host into my mouth. But I can't, or don't want to, or am afraid to, remember. It is important for me to note just how strongly these things affect the mind and behavior; it is just as important to note how much work it is to notice.

* * *

My years studying Torah, Hebrew, and Jewish history and religion, were very beautiful years of deep, personal spiritual practice. I was a "lapsed Catholic," but so was most of my immediate family—everyone except my mother—so I didn't give that much thought. Even as I was studying my legacy of silencing as a woman of Mexican Catholic heritage, actively de/constructing prayers and iconographic ways of knowing how Mary and other archetypal feminine figures prominent to Mexican women, and how they influenced me (de la Garza, 2004), even then, I did not stop to think much about how the forms of prayer and embodied cultural spirituality would fare if I converted to Judaism. My mind is Jewish, but my body is Mexican, and Catholic?

* * *

"Next Sunday is time for Peter's Pence," Father Chuck shared with us while we ate. I was a lector at my local parish, and five of us were out for lunch with the pastor. Two years earlier, in 1995, I'd suffered a miscarriage about three and a half months into a pregnancy, then struggled with a highly dysfunctional marriage and a spouse who no longer lived with me, but who refused to talk about getting a divorce. I was in a shambles emotionally, and through the grief over the miscarriage, I had turned to a private practice of going to daily masses on the Arizona State University campus. It soothed me. It didn't matter if I didn't believe all the prayers or disagreed with some teachings; something about the ritual, the kneeling, the collective recitation, and taking communion, was helping to heal me. So I felt comfortable when Father Chuck asked us what we thought about the annual contribution for funds to support the Vatican.

"I never give to Peter's Pence," I blurted.

Father Chuck looked at me, and asked why. The others were silent.

"Because I believe that if the Vatican needs money to run the house of Peter, they should sell the gold and items that they took from the Americas," I said, thinking of the codices and items of lost history for indigenous peoples that were locked up in Rome. Surely the artwork stored away alone would bring a pretty "pence."

"But it was all collected for the glory of God," Father Chuck, replied. It seemed so incredibly and simplistically ludicrous to me all of a sudden, and I responded.

"I hardly believe that God's glory is affected by anything we do, and certainly not by the torture and oppression and forced conversions of innocent people," I replied. The conversation ended with Father stating that there were, indeed, many opinions. And I remembered the familiar silencing phrase, "The Church is not a democracy." My words that day were the beginning of my public journey out of silence. I hadn't kept quiet.

* * *

Mama Fina's house was a little bit of heaven to me. It was the one place in the world where I always felt safe. Even when Papa Cosme would come home drunk and have a tantrum, I was never afraid, because Mama Fina, my grandmother, and Lula, my aunt who lived with them, were there. Nothing could happen to me as long as I was with them. The smell of the candles burning on her altar atop her chest of drawers in the room she shared with my grandfather gave the house an aroma that to this day causes my whole body to release tension. The house was quiet, austere, and womblike to my childhood soul.

One day, she called me into her bedroom so I could see something. I must have been about four years old. Above her bed, on the wall, she had images of the saints hanging, and she had something up there that had a little compartment. The room was shadowy, and although I know it was a tiny house, my memory of the room is of a place with ceilings so high I don't remember seeing them, and walls as expansive as a horizon. She reached up where she had a statute of the Santo Niño de Atocha, the one with little sandals and a basket and a water gourd, and she brought something down in her hand, telling me to be very careful as she moved to show it to me.

She opened her hand to show me a white wafer. I had not made my first communion yet, so I didn't know what it was. She told me it was the *cuerpo de cristo*. I knew that meant it was holy. She told me she had taken it from church and that she kept it in her room so she could pray there without having to go to the church. She let me hold it, and I held it very, very carefully, not wanting to break it. I looked up at her, and she took it slowly back from me and chuckled and smiled like she did whenever she watched me do anything. I was too young to realize that my grandmother had just told me she had stolen the holy Eucharist from church, that she had her own rules for where and how to pray, and that she was sharing them with me. She was teaching me a way to be.

* * *

I am not searching for God. I never have. I have never felt the need to be "saved," but I have certainly had times when I felt lost in my life. From the time I was a very young child, I felt wonder when I looked at the rays of sun beaming from behind a cloud, and when I walked down a path in the woods, I felt protected. The major fears in my life have all come from experiences I have internalized, or which somehow caused an unconscious, involuntary response to certain conditions. I witnessed fights between my parents that frightened me, saw that punishment from teachers and authority figures could often be unjust or unmerited, and over the years watched how group influence could turn an ally into someone who would betray my trust. Prejudice and bigotry and religious zeal can convert a family member or friend into an enemy. The confidence and trust that I know to be my natural state became something that I learned to keep secret. Slowly, the habits of doubt and suspicion became more familiar in my everyday life. The world required a different me, it seemed. I needed to learn to be a person, not merely a human.

"We come into the world as individuals, achieve character, and become persons," (Goffman, 1959, p. 30). Erving Goffman quoted this line from Ezra Park in his book *Presentation of Self in Everyday Life,* and it was immediately etched upon my mind the first time I read it during my master's program. I felt I had read the explanation for the mysteries that were at the core of my life's most powerful motivating force: staying true to my personal truth, no matter what I found myself saying or doing "out there." I learned very early, as the eldest child, and a girl, that there were things I was supposed to do, things I was not supposed to do. I listened to my father's dinner table conversations about politics from before I could understand them, and he narrated a life of strategy and resistance to a world of discrimination, injustice, and more importantly, hope. I watched how stress and an insistence on telling the truth could unravel my mother's ability to deal with reality. I was taught that there was a devil hiding behind a rock to tempt me and that only by the grace of God and perhaps the presence of a guardian angel could I be spared from this. I learned to be a person from an early age, and so when I had learned to write, I knew that what I wanted to write was, "NO."

Matthew Fox (1980; 1981;1995) tells us that the voice of the prophet in society is the voice that says "No!" to that which cannot be taken for granted. When the world around us is going insane, do we join it? The prophet is not just an archetypal figure or a vestige of the past, but one who actively interferes with that which is unjust. The anger of the prophet is not personal, but collective. And when I read the words of Matthew Fox in 1992, I sat down and wrote, by hand, what I felt was a personal calling. I called it "A Cry for Heresy." I put the draft away, never showing it to anyone, but knowing it was work I needed to do. Twenty years would go by before I could begin writing about it again. Over those years, I came to see how anyone wishing to be a change agent had to be capable of withstanding the pressures to conform. She had to be capable of choosing, actively and intentionally, to be a heretic to the orthodoxies of the world—because so many of the "Nos" in everyday life are the responses to taken for granted customs or practices.

As an infant, the first request I ever made using a word, was for water, reaching and asking for *agua.* I was thirsty. As a child, the first word I ever wrote to express a message to the world was *NO.* As an adult, the thirst I work to sate has been for the freedom to choose, in a world in which those choices are made for us by systems and cultures, traditions and sacred orthodoxies that choke the beauty out of human spirits. There is nothing that causes my whole being to revolt, like the evidence of constrained and hegemonic "freedom." I know it well, because I have lived it. I have embodied it. It is the ritual of interaction that we believe to be **natural**, when in fact it is **normal**. And that which seems normal, or traditional, or powerful, begs for the critical, "right questions," (Browne & Keeley, 2011) so that while we are persons, we don't lose our individuality. In my life, it has become my own personal way of life to be a mindful heretic when that is what is called for.

* * *

In her creative nonfiction book chronicling the letters between Galileo and his daughter, Dava Sobel (2000) informs us that after the Inquisition began to try scientists for their works that contradicted official Church teachings, they ceased the practice of writing their scientific reports in contextually rich narrative—which would incriminate anyone mentioned in them. There, was born the passive voice with the absent subject as "necessary" for scientific, and eventually, academic, writing. They wrote empty narrative reports of science and made themselves seem puppets whose agents were never seen—out of fear, not method.

* * *

It's ironic that in the fifteenth century, a public Jew would face expulsion from Spain, but under the rules of the Inquisition, the Inquisition could not try a Jew. Only a converted Jew could be tried. It was the narration of a false Christian self that was the heresy. When called before one's auto-da-fé, the accused were required to provide a *narrativa*, a narrative rendering of one's life. It did not matter to tell exactly what one had done, but that what was told would function to convince and portray a life of a faithful, or innocent Christian soul, to be spared additional torture, imprisonment, or death (Kagan & Dyer, 2011). It could be argued that all colonialist discourse has such a dynamic.

The days of auto-da-fé trials and burnings at the hands of the Inquisition are long gone, but the mind of a continent and the colonies formed by its agents keeps alive the awareness of the power of one's narrative, the *narrativa*, to determine the social, political, and economic outcomes in one's life. We live in a world that is full of evidence that demonstrates that, whether or not the practice is rooted in the Inquisition, human beings continue to know that the way in which one "spins" their narrative can make a great difference in the way others will treat them, in the way others will perceive them—in whether they will be deemed acceptable.

This cultural mind-set is similar to that which some have come to call the "inquisitorial mind" (Alcalá, 1987). This process of narrating one's life to avoid negative repercussions is at the foundation of orthodox communication. Because of this, we become committed to our narrative, but indifferent to the person we create through it. Lacan (2007) would likely call this ambivalence. This inquisitorial "mind" is one of narrative ambivalence, of an internalized awareness of the social call for mimicry (Bhabha, 1984), a reflection of the human tendency to avoid the negative repercussions of dissent.

* * *

The mindful heretic is not ambivalent, but multivalent. Uncertainty is the seed of potential. Having multiple narratives is not identity; it is game. Mindful heresy is not game or strategy, but poiesis, creative expression. There is no binary of game or poiesis; they are organically tied together. Without poiesis, one can get caught in the game. Game helps us share our creativity. The mindful heretic creates a narrative path out of the brambles of embodied awareness of coercion, constraint, and habituation, violating norms in order to live with them. The mindful heretic revels in paradox and does not seek monosemic representation as evidence of correctness.

Correctness is evasive, not static. To be a mindful heretic is not to be incorrect, but to deny the notion that correctness is static. Mindful heresy is not an attempt to find stability. But neither is it a knee-jerk response of rebellion. It is, rather, a public acknowledgment of tension and contradictions in one's being. My spiritual and cultural lives have shown me that I will never reach a sense of what is true, as if the truth is a final destination, a place to rest. The truth to me is like a butterfly. It flits and flies, vanishes and dies, comes to life after sleeping in a cocoon. To seek truth is to feel exhilaration at a butterfly landing on my hand as well as loss and yearning when it chooses to up and fly away.

To be a mindful heretic, I must admit to myself how important are the very ties I transgress with my life and voice. While I acknowledge my ability to connect and unite intimately and in powerful solidarity with others, I privilege the acknowledgment that none of these unions are, on their own, stable foundations for my existence. Real stability is tension, I've learned. It is balance. I've discovered this by being a crypto-Catholic, crypto-Jewish, oft-times postmodern Buddhist yogi with a Chicana aesthetic. If I try to tell a story as if it is my definitive story, I cannot. In the inner chatter of learned responses is the evidence of the need for the heresy. I need not be socially correct to be of value. My experiences with religion have taught me how to be a human being apart from it. I have learned to know G-d when violating the orthodoxies claiming to know **the** way to G-d. I have become myself by defying what I "am."

Identity is a myth that gives us comforting pleasure and stability, but it is not who we are. Our stories are evidence of our incredible capacity to create ourselves as persons, and to wield power over all who can be drawn into the spell of imagination. As I learn more about my history, the ethics of my shared memory (Margalit, 2003) evolve, and I cannot be faithful to identity or orthodoxy. I am not of one history. None of us are. As a mindful heretic, I recognize this, and have come to realize how absolutely vital and, yes, sacred, is every decision I make about what I will hold as real. What appears as *contra*diction, is in fact, not a "counter" to one's expression (*contra-dicere*) but a form of *holo-expression*, of complete and dynamic expression of one's being—not incompatibility of one's being, but a wholeness of being.

Despite the continuous metamorphosis and elusive nature of truth, without temporary snapshots of tentative certainty (de la Garza, 2007), we humans cannot do much. We must, at some level, believe in something—even if only that the ground is solid—in order to act and be. And so we narrate ourselves, as a way to better see the whole, to not escape it. I have chosen to narrate a certain tentativity.

* * *

By choosing to be what I have called a mindful heretic—a person who consciously and intentionally violates the normative beliefs, behaviors, and/or expectations of a group or association she deeply reveres in order to *maintain* reverence for its value—I am choosing to *risk* who I am in order that I may *be* who I am. I have come to know that each time I narrate in order to be proper, or orthodox, I numb myself to an ethics grounded in my embodied life experience, in favor of ideological identity. I distance myself from the very life that I live and the knowledge gained from the paths I have traveled. To be a fully cultural, social human being, I have found that mindful heresy is vital. It is mindful, because I am aware of the price one can pay, when those persons heavily identified with norms and propriety wield their inquisitorial swords. As a mindful heretic, I know that the only vow I have made in my life is to consciously revolt (Kristeva, 2001, 2002) and willingly present myself and my experience without the masks and veils of colonialist, hegemonic, and socially preferred orthodoxies. My vow is to return, to renew, to reflect, and to construct and claim that which enables me to give to the world that has given me so much with which to work. Mindful heresy allows for a life of sincere gratitude, rather than perfunctory acknowledgments of fear or submission.

Note

1. Native American.

References

Alcalá, A. (1987). *The Spanish Inquisition and the inquisitorial mind.* New York: Columbia University (distributor for East European Monographs).

Bhabha, H. (1984). Of mimicry and man: The ambivalence of colonial discourse, *October, 28,* 125–133.

Browne, M. N. & Keeley, S. M. (Eds.). (2011). *Asking the right questions: A guide to critical thinking,* (10th ed.).Upper Saddle River, NJ: Pearson.

de la Garza, S. A. (2004). *María speaks: Journeys through the mysteries of the mother in my life as a Chicana.* New York: Peter Lang.

_____. (2007). The four seasons of ethnography: A creation-centered ontology for ethnography. In M. K. Asante, Y. Miike, & J. Yin, (Eds.), *Global intercultural communication reader* (pp. 143–164). New York: Routledge.

Fox, M. (1980). *Breakthrough: Meister Eckhart's creation spirituality in new translation.* New York: Knopf Doubleday/Image.

Fox, M. (1981). *Whee! We, wee all the way home: A guide to sensual, prophetic spirituality.* Santa Fe, NM: Bear and Company.

Fox, M. (1995). *Wrestling with the prophets.* San Francisco, CA: Harper.

Goffman, E. (1959). *Presentation of self in everyday life.* New York: Doubleday Anchor.

Kagan, R. L. & Dyer, A. (2011). *Inquisitorial inquiries: Brief lives of secret Jews and other heretics.* Baltimore, MD: Johns Hopkins University Press.

Kristeva, J. (2001). *The sense and non-sense of revolt.* (Herman, J., translator). New York: Columbia University Press.

Kristeva, J. (2002). *Revolt, she said.* Los Angeles, CA: Semiotext(e).

Lacan, J. (2007). *Ecrits.* New York: Norton.

Margalit, A. (2003). *The ethics of memory.* Cambridge, MA: Harvard University Press.

Masvie, T. (2012). Was the cross mark a Jewish symbol? Caspari Center for Jewish and Biblical Studies. http://caspari.com/new/en/resources/article-archive/683-was-the-cross-mark-a-jewish-symbol-

Raphael, D. T. (2001). *The conquistadores and crypto-Jews of Monterrey.* Valley Village, CA: Carmi House.

Sobel, D. (2000). *Galileo's daughter: A historical memoir of science, faith, and love.* New York: Penguin.

CHAPTER THIRTEEN

⌐✺⌐

Favor
An Autoethnography of Survival
Rex L. Crawley

I APPROACH CRITICAL AUTOETHNOGRAPHY AS A METHODOLOGICAL opportunity "to produce analytical, accessible texts that change us and the world we live in for the better" (Holman Jones, 2005, p. 764). As an act of emancipation, autoethnography gives voice to the culturally muted in ways that scientifically challenge the boundaries of our notions of understanding. Simultaneously it contributes to our emancipation from the creative limitations of validity, reliability, and generalization. Critical autoethnography pushes the envelope by freeing us to examine cultural phenomena from a perspective rooted in our own lived experiences and allows us to lay claim to the "scientific-ness" of our innate inner-selves. Of most importance to me is the methodological emancipation of autoethnography, which allows researchers to embrace intersubjectivity, emotionality, and lived experience, rather than trying to bury, deny, or defend it.

A self-proclaimed "Denzinite," my approach to thick description has its ultimate roots in participant observation as conceived by Geertz (1973), but is more heavily influenced by Denzin's (2001) concept of interpretive interactionism. Situated in autoethnography, this work fits nicely in the critical exploration of the cultural synergy that is created through cultural interaction. Defined generally, interpretive interactionism is the "point of view that confers meaning on problematic symbolic interaction" (Denzin, 2001, p. 32) and seeks to produce, perform, and interpret cultural phenomenon. Interpretive interactionism connects to critical autoethnography, because the two approaches intersect at the point of essence seeking, by attempting to locate epiphanies (themes/accounts) in interactional situations where

Critical Autoethnography: Intersecting Cultural Identities in Everyday Life, edited by Robin M. Boylorn and Mark P. Orbe, 222–233. © 2014 Left Coast Press, Inc. All rights reserved.

personal troubles become public/cultural issues (Crawley, 2011). In this work I use blog posts to reflect on and chronicle my experience as a cancer survivor. My cancer experience(s), my deep commitment to my Christian faith, and the family and friends who supported me situates this account for autoethnographic exploration.

There are two themes from the blog posts that are particularly significant. One focuses on what I refer to as "Black Masculinity" and the extent to which African American men are uncomfortable dealing with the nurturing aspects of interpersonal relationships and the vulnerability of illness. The other theme focuses on what I refer to as "favor" and how Christianity and faith coalesce to help me deal with and survive a horrific and oftentimes debilitating life circumstance. For the purpose of clarity I will explicate my post-blog observations about these two themes as a prelude to the blog accounts.

Black Masculinity and Its Impact on Unmet Nurturing Needs

Historically Black men have been characterized as un-nurturing, uncaring, and oftentimes uneducated (Blankenhorn, 1995; Jackson & Hopson, 2011). These negative stereotypes have been reinforced by images in the media that continually depict Black men as savage-like and irresponsible. Other stereotypes are based on reality and the lived experiences of Black men, but have been misconstrued, thus contributing to misperceptions. Reflexively, I must admit that this potential for misinterpretation is a concern for me as I present my blog accounts associated with my experiences with Black men. In the blog account titled "Managing conversations about having cancer—other Black men," I share my thoughts and encounters with the Black men in my life while I was going through chemotherapy. My experiences coupled with my understanding of these Black male behaviors allow for insight into the Black male experience while simultaneously leaving us (Black men) vulnerable to, intentional or unintentional misinterpretation.

Black masculinity research in communication, education, and sociology has begun to respond to these negative depictions by advancing research that focuses on some of the positive attributes of Black males (Wallace, 2002, Mutua, 2006). Understanding the psychological history associated with Black male pain and suffering is critical to the accurate interpretations associated with autoethnographic projects. This research is in direct response to the stereotypical depictions of Black males and attempts to contribute to a deep insider understanding of the impact of cancer on a Black male, the spiritual relationships associated with healing, and a brief glimpse at how one Black man understands and rationalizes relationships with other Black men.

The "Favor" Experiences of a Christian African American Male Cancer Survivor

A popular notion of favor is rooted in traditional Christianity. Contemporary interpretations suggest that when one has God's favor, one is endowed with a sense of protection and reaps spiritual and material benefits. I am particularly drawn to the definitions of favor that include the distinction that it is oftentimes unfair, bestowed upon one as a reward of spiritual faithfulness, obedience, and/or grace. In the context of this essay, favor is inspected as an essential and recurring theme or epiphany that helps contextualize my lived experiences as an African American male cancer survivor. The work attempts to amplify, indirectly, some of the Christian practices that enhance faith, acting as both a coping mechanism and a way to rationalize how and why bad things happen to good people. The work is designed to situate, within Christianity, how survivorship and faith are inextricably connected, especially in a Christian faith–based relationship. Finally, the work opens up for inspection the role of practices such as the laying on of hands, speaking in tongues, intercessory prayer, and deep faith.

This autoethnography evokes thick description and produces text as a means of making personal experience meaningful and scientific. As an intercultural endeavor, the work positions personal narrative against the general backdrop of religion, interpersonal relationships, and health communication. Methodologically, the data and subsequent thematic accounts are derived from experiences that were chronicled and posted via a real-time blog. In the following blog accounts[1] I voyeuristically detail the thoughts and experiences associated with a chemotherapy experience. In particular, I highlight the ways in which fighting cancer has illuminated how the religious concept of God's favor impacts my personal and professional relationships.

Here We Go (Again)!

They say timing is everything, and in this case it is very true. Three weeks ago I was diagnosed with Lymphoma Non-Hodgkin's disease, a form of cancer that impacts the lymph-nodes in your body. They say it is one of the "better" cancers to have since the survival rate is so high. Interestingly, it is found more often in older people (over 55).

This is not my first experience with Lymphoma. I was diagnosed in 1991 while I was a graduate student at Ohio University. It was a ten-year ordeal that ultimately led to a bone marrow transplant and open heart surgery. The good news is that from 1999 until 3 weeks ago, about 13 years, I was cancer free and confident that this chapter of my life would not be revisited. But here we go again!

This time I decided to be public with my experiences so that others can learn and gain from it. I also feel that sharing my journey with others will be therapeutic for me. So I am starting a blog to chronicle my experience. I will share the details of the experience and my reactions to them to help readers understand the issues associated with managing a traumatic and unexpected life event. I feel that I am offering a perspective into the field of medicine from a Black male perspective that is important and somewhat unique.[2]

Posted 23rd October 2011 by *Dr. Rex*

***

A Wild Day

Yesterday was a wild day. I was at work and received a call from my oncologist Dr. Rahman. He informed me that the results from my CT-scans were back and that he was able to detect a growth around my right kidney that was obstructing the function of the kidney. He said I would need to have a urologist insert a stint to resume proper functioning and then we would need to do a biopsy of the mass to determine if the lymphoma was back.

This happened around 10 o'clock in the morning. My initial assignment was to contact my urologist to schedule the stint procedure, then I had the task of sharing the frightening news with my family, specifically my wife. Because of my previous experiences with cancer, I felt my siblings would be fine but I wasn't sure how Daria (my wife) would take it. She is a trooper and has dealt with my illnesses pretty well over the last 7 years of our marriage but she lost her dad and sister this year, and her mom and brother in the recent past. I worried about how she would respond to my news.

I knew I had to tell her in person. The drive home gave me some time to put things in perspective. I called her and told her that I was headed back home to talk. The 7-minute drive home felt like an eternity!

When I got home Daria was outside. We entered the house together and I wanted to clear the air and break the tension. I grabbed her and said, "I'm pregnant and you are the mother," we both laughed hysterically. I shared the diagnosis with her matter-of-factly. I was careful not to imply that I thought the growth in my abdomen was cancerous. I focused on the immediate issue which was the impaired kidney function.

She was her normal loving and optimistic self. She held me and told me that we would get through it together as a family. It was a beautiful moment. We talked medical strategy then decided we would only share the information with our immediate family and best friends. We thought about the implications of sharing my diagnosis at work and decided that we would share limited information as needed. I was planning to apply for a promotion and we decided that it would be best not to cloud the process with health issues.

I told Daria that I didn't intend to let my illness impact my effectiveness at home or work. As I prepared to leave she asked me to join her in prayer. She prayed a healing prayer for me, her, and our family. On my way out the door she thanked me for trusting her enough to share the situation with her immediately. She said "us Kirby girls are tough," (referring to her family name) and she was right. She is one of the strongest people I know.

Posted 24th October 2011 by *Dr. Rex*

***

Oh My GOD!

Today is Sunday and I am surprisingly still at Trinity Medical Center after having had a large mass biopsy on Friday. I thought the procedure would be easy. In fact, I thought it might be outpatient surgery. I didn't know that extracting a large mass from my stomach would be so traumatic. My surgeon told me the procedure would require a 4-inch incision and that he would then assess whether or not he would remove the entire mass or extract just a portion of it. The PT scan revealed three significant masses and only one of them was accessible.

When I returned from surgery it was hard to assess the extent of the pain. I was sedated and slept most of the day on Friday. When I woke up I was in extreme pain. I felt like I had been stabbed in my stomach. I never realized how critical abdomen muscles are to performing simple tasks. I could not roll over, sit up or walk. I was supposed to be released on Saturday, but I was in so much pain that Dr. Knob thought I should stay another day. My stomach was bloated and I was on a lot of pain medication.

On Saturday I had a lot of company. My sister, Sylvia, came to town to be with me, and my dad, mom, Aunt Grace, and Joziah visited. Later that evening Daria and Xavier (our son) came, and our pastors Bishop and Sister Dawkins stopped by.

I feel better today (Sunday). Dr. Knob stopped by early and examined me. He said that I may go home today. I have to get up and walk to get the air out of my stomach. He told me one of the signs of bowel recovery is gas, which explains why he asks me if I have farted every time he comes to my room. I have been farting up a storm so I guess that means I get to go home.

Posted 25th October 2011 by *Dr. Rex*

***

R-ICE

Today is my first day of chemotherapy. It was scheduled for 8:00am, it is 10:20am and I am still waiting. The first stage of the cycle is pre-chemo treatment consisting of Tylenol, Benadryl, and saline fluids. The main drug is Rituxin. It isolates the lymphoma cells for destruction. We hope the drug will help reduce the size of the tumors in my stomach. That way we can remove the damn things. Did I mention how much I hate this kidney stint? Luckily I have not had any bleeding since the biopsy.

My dad arrived at 8:30am and announced that my mom had a dentist appointment and would be here later. At 9 o'clock my mother walked into the room saying she canceled her appointment. She wanted to be here for me since Daria had to drop Xavier off at school, pick up some work, and run some errands.

At around 11:00am Daria arrived. We all sat in the room nervous about what was going to happen, and silent because we didn't know what to say to each other.

My mom broke the ice, "Are you ready?"

"Ready as I can be, I guess." That was code for I really didn't want to talk about it. My wife suggested we pray. We joined hands and the two most important

*women in my life, my wife and my mother, begged God for his protection
and mercy. They were careful to ask for courage and strength. They prayed
for my family, the doctors, the technology, the nurses, the people who make the
medicine, and the architect who built the hospital; it was a thorough prayer.*

*Nurse Connie arrived at 11:22am with the drug cart. It was R-ICE time.
RICE is the name of the combination of drugs developed for this type of cancer.
The R is for the Rituxin that destroys lymphoma cells, and is administered
over a four hour period during the first treatment. It is the most toxic drug
and requires constant monitoring for dangerous side effects. Typically if a
person makes it through the first round, the rest is smooth sailing.*

Posted 28th October 2011 by *Dr. Rex*

***

So What Happens after All These Drugs Are in You ... You Ask?

*It is wonderful to be home. Xavier is screaming. Daria is scurrying about the
house. Neighbors are stopping by. These are all signs of recovery, normalcy.
But it is only a temporary normal. I was released from the hospital to recover
from the first round of treatment. The next treatment is scheduled three weeks
from today. The reality is chemo is just the beginning, and what it feels like
to get chemotherapy is a very different experience from what it feels like when
the chemo does its work, which is to seek and destroy fast growing cells.*

*At first I thought it would be a breeze. I was equipped with all the drugs a
person could imagine, I had Percocet and Oxycodone for pain, I had sleeping
pills, and about 10 other prescriptions for anything else that could go wrong.*

*I spent the first days at home sleeping off the nausea; I thought it was smooth
sailing until I realized something destructive was happening inside my body. It
felt like my insides were being crushed. A slow ache combined with nausea makes
you want to sleep forever. Other times, all of a sudden, I am burning up. Hot then
cold, hot then cold, mostly cold though. I spend most of my day curled up under
blankets, trying to escape the sickening smell of the chemicals that are everywhere
in my body. Every time I urinate I smell it all over again. The chemicals are so
strong that we are advised to flush the toilet multiple times after extractions.
Interestingly my family does not seem to notice the smell, but it is extreme for me. I
asked Daria to buy those plug in air fresheners to mask the smell. It does not work.*

***

*Today a new sensation began. All of a sudden my lymph nodes get
irritated whenever I get ready to eat food. It is a stingy, burning
sensation behind my ears. It is like I am about to suck on a lemon.*

*The final sensation associated with the burning of fast growing cells is skin
sensitivity. The best way to describe it is by saying that my skin feels sore. There
are times when my skin aches, not a burning or a wound kind of hurt, but an ache.
Typically you associate aching with an organ or a part of the body, but this feeling
is when your skin is so sensitive to touch that you want to live suspended in space
to avoid touching anything. It hurts! Sometimes I can use lotion or oil to soothe
the ache, but most of the time I have to suck it up and wait for the pain to pass.*

227

***

The next journey will be WBCs or white blood cells. I went to the doctor for an injection that is supposed to stimulate white cell production because of the intended destruction of white blood cells from the chemo. Your white blood cells (WBCs) support your immune system. Some of the side effects of low WBCs are fever, painful urination (check), rash, and low energy. In a nut shell you become vulnerable to any and all infections. Did I mention I think I may try a half day back to work on Wednesday?

Posted 31st October 2011 by *Dr. Rex*

***

Managing Conversations About Having Cancer—Other Black Men

I made it through my first week back to work as a "cancer survivor/patient." It is interesting how all-consuming cancer can be, even at work. Most folks were glad to see me back and surprised at my decision to manage this crisis so publicly. Most people are used to dancing around the "C" word, so it catches them off guard to know I am willing to share my experience, and that I am interested in their perspectives and experiences dealing with cancer.

For the most part my Black male counterparts have difficulty talking about illness, especially cancer. I have a lot of Black male friends via my participation in men's groups such as Kappa Alpha Psi and the Boule. In each group I have held leadership positions so I literally know thousands of brothers.

With few exceptions, I can on one hand count the number of Black men I know who are able to deal with the psychological issues associated with participating in the wellness nurturing of another Black man. Please do not get me wrong I am not suggesting that my brothers do not love and respect me, I know they do, but I also know that they do not know how to show nurturing love. This experience has taught me a lot about how to show man-to-man love.

I get text messages and email messages from fraternity brothers (bruhs) affirming their prayers and thoughts, I received fruit baskets from my local Boule and Province Kappa chapter, and I have gotten cards from individual brothers, so I know they are thinking about me and they care. The process stops there though. Very few bruhs are comfortable calling and asking me how I am doing. I believe they want to respect my space, and establish our boundaries. Culturally, in America, we are conditioned to believe that sick people want to heal and die in private. Sometimes that is the case, but more often sick people die feeling unloved, betrayed and abandoned by their friends.

As a healthy Black man I was guilty of saying I was going to visit someone in the hospital, or send a card, or make a call that never happened. In hindsight I realize that my lack of follow through wasn't because I didn't care, it was because I was scared to face the reality of seeing a strong Black man become defenseless and vulnerable. I was also scared of awkward moments of silence, and being confronted about what took so long to get t/ here. The fear is paralyzing and oftentimes leads to broken relationships.

The exceptions are extraordinary. Some friends call my wife to check in when I don't feel like talking, or leave a message to see how I am doing. To date I do not recall one Black man ever calling and saying, "Hey man, how are you handling this emotionally?," "How is your son dealing with you being sick?," or, "What does it feel like to go through chemo?," which are questions I have been asked by non-Black male, caring friends and family.

Typically Black men ask, "How are you doing?" and hope that you say "Fine" (the Black male catchall phrase for all things emotional). Their brevity is not out of a lack of concern, but in response to a socialization process that gives them an easy out in difficult encounters. We are not, for the most part, nurturers. We are providers (and protectors). I am able to rationalize the behavior of Black male friends based on my own lived experiences; but there are others whose behavior in illness is inexplicable. Some friends are "ghost" during difficult times: no phone calls, no visits, no emails, no cards, just complete denial that anything is wrong. When the difficult time passes they reappear as though nothing ever happened.

Posted 4th November 2011 by *Dr. Rex*

***

Fear and Faith Are Incompatible

Psalms 118:17—I shall not die, but live, and declare the works of the Lord

There is an interesting relationship between faith and fear. I have come to learn that faith and fear are incompatible. If you are a Christian and you believe in God's ability to do all things, including heal cancer, then you can't be afraid. According to my faith, I choose to believe the report of the Lord in Psalm 118:17, that I will not die.

When I find myself operating in fear, it usually means that my faith is under attack. I have learned to fortify my faith by surrounding myself with faith(full) people. For example, I have a team of prayer warriors.

My thinking about faith and my attitude about overcoming cancer was inspired by a conversation I had with my sands (a term used to refer to a fraternity Brother who I pledged with) who drove down from Maryland to visit me. Todd asked me if my diagnosis was terminal. It struck me as surprising that death had not been a concern for me. I never believed that I was going to die. Todd was relieved that all of this "blogging" was not a morbid, last moments in life, type thing. I assured him that I was confident that I would survive and be a living testimony.

For those of less or different faith, there is, in fact, even empirical evidence that suggests Non-Hodgkin's Lymphoma is a treatable cancer, especially for patients under 50. Further my faith in God extends to oncologists. I am confident in His ability to use modern medical science to usher in His will through healing. I was in remission for 12 years when I was diagnosed.

I hope tonight's blog helps assure you that while this wilderness experience is far from convenient, death is not and has never been a consideration or option. My medical team and I are confident that this 4-cycle regiment of R-ICE will render my cancer into remission and I will bring in the new year cancer-free.

Posted 7th November 2011 by *Dr. Rex*

***

Spirituality Meets Modern Medicine

Days 3 & 4 of chemo have been pretty uneventful. It is 10:00am on Sunday and I am scheduled to be released after this 4th day of chemo has run its course. Day four usually takes about 5 hours so I suspect that I will be headed home by 7pm.

As devastating as this experience has been there are bright spots. While having cancer is one of the most horrible things that could ever happen to a person, I am confident that God is with me and has orchestrated this for my good. I have learned not to question God or try to figure things out. It will all become plain in the end.

For example, some years ago a good friend contacted me about becoming a board member of an organization called the National Marrow Donors Program (NMDP). The NMDP board is composed of the best and brightest transplantation surgeons, nurses, survivors and administrators in the country. I initially passed on the invitation to apply, but years later she contacted me again and I agreed to interview for a board seat. I was appointed to the board and have been a member ever since. This board has a multi-million dollar budget and a mission to facilitate bone marrow transplants through its administration of the only bone marrow registry in the country.

Fast-forward 5 years, I am diagnosed again, the week before a NMDP meeting in Phoenix, Arizona. At that meeting I shared my diagnosis with a few board members who immediately suggested I talk to Dr. Sergio Giralt, a transplant surgeon and Chief of Transplantation at Sloan Kettering Memorial Hospital in New York City (the number one Lymphoma Center in the world). I met with Sergio and he listened to my story and agreed with the plan of my medical team. He gave me his card, with his cell phone number, and asked me to call him because he felt I would need another transplant, and that he would do it at Sloan. I was still emotionally raw from the recent diagnosis, but elated that I had been connected with the best surgeon and the best hospital in the country. Must be God right? When I shared the news with one of my board friends she told me she had a Manhattan apartment walking distance to Sloan Kettering and offered it to my family when we were in New York City for appointments and ultimately the transplant, if necessary. God?

A non-Christian might call this coincidence, luck, or networking, but my faith tells me that "all things work together for the good of them that love the Lord and are called according to His purpose" (Romans 8:28). I feel that my cancer experience is an opportunity to build my faith and the faith of those around me. Every day I wake up with a smile on my face, despite the pain in my body, because I know my life is a testament to God's love, protection, and favor.

Posted 20th November 2011 by *Dr. Rex*

***

Dear God . . .

Like the Psalmist wrote "thou hast turned my mourning into dancing; thou hast put off my sackcloth, and girded me with gladness" (Psalms 30:11). Because of the assurance I have in Your power and grace I am able to stand in confidence of Your ability to not only bring me out of the wilderness but bring me out with joy. Father,

I thank you for favor and praise you for your uncanny ability to supply me with the very desires of my heart in the face of what would appear to be darkness.

Only in relationship with You could strength be rationalized in this cancer situation. Because Your word reminds me that "no weapon formed against me shall prosper" I am able to glean hope, trusting that while it may not be clear what you are doing, it will all work together for my good.

In the times that I struggle to understand you, I have Your Word to lean upon. I thank you God for the years of fortification that you provided through the teachings of great men and women of the Gospel throughout my life. I could never live this life and manage these circumstances without relationship with You.

You are my fear manager and have demonstrated to me the revelation that fear and faith are incompatible, how could I be afraid if I have true faith in Your ability to bring me out? There are some people who believe my faith is misplaced and is but a coping mechanism for dealing with this health crisis, but I agree. You are the only way I can cope with poison running through my veins; You are the only mechanism I have to cope with the regular separation from my family. You and You alone are the center of my contentment, it is in You that I find joy in pain, laughter in sorrow, and hope in despair.

I make no apologies for the confidence and trust I place in you Lord. Blessed assurance is knowing that you are the King of Kings and Lord of Lords. The realization that I am in relationship with you, my Father, makes this wilderness experience less bleak, knowing that I am in relationship with the Creator of the universe and that my Father owns the cattle on a thousand hills, I operate in wealth, prosperity and divine health. Son-ship in you means that my inheritance is great. Your Kingship makes me a prince.

As I approach the end of this journey, I am reminded of Ecclesiastes 3:3 that lets me know that there is a time for everything, a time to kill; and a time to heal; a time to breakdown; and a time to build up; a time to weep, and a time to laugh; a time to mourn and a time to dance. I praise You for this season in my life that has drawn me closer to You. I remain confident in your ability to do super-abundantly above all that I might expect or even desire.

I am in search of Your essence and lessons in this experience, I know that anytime You allow pain to enter my life it is because You are preparing me for a major blessing. My heart and mind is open to receive whatever it is that You have for me in this next phase of my life. I stand ready to receive it and praise you in advance. You are an awesome God and relationship with You has proven to be the best inheritance that my parents and forefathers could have ever gifted me. Selah!

Posted 14th February 2012 by *Dr. Rex*

Conclusion

Having laid claim to the "scientific-ness" of my innate inner-self through this autoethnographic exploration, it seems appropriate to recontextualize this data by providing some concluding and reflexive (self) analysis. This personal narrative lacks the generalizabilty of traditional research and is posited as a personal articulation of the intersectionality inherent to cancer survivorship. Cancer has added to my identity another level of consciousness, here again described as intersectionality, and what W. E. B. Dubois (1903) refers to as double consciousness. This postmodern version expands it to suggest that it is not double consciousness, but multiple consciousnesses intersecting to form the whole of me. Furthermore this work, as an interpretive project, situates for inspection, faith and favor, as religiously universal. The project is not designed to denigrate other personal experiences with faith and/or favor but instead demonstrates how a belief system in general can be used to both rationalize and empower a person in times of trouble.

Methodologically it is interesting to watch the communicative weaving of cultural patterns into the fabric of the autoethnographic project. The notion of intersectionality presents itself in ways that allows the cancer incident to navigate its way through the interpersonal dimensions of my life. The varied parts of myself as an African American man, patient, husband, father, son, brother, friend, academic, and Christian all collide within the boundaries of this project. To suggest that this data could, in Denzian fashion, be reduced to an essential and recurring theme would have a negative impact on the ultimate goal of essence seeking. The power of this autoethnographic journey is its ability to empower me as cancer patient, but to also bring light to some of the issues associated with survivorship especially from the often muted Black masculinist perspective.

Sharing these intimate and detailed accounts proved empowering to others as expressed by the blog commenters. One friend shared that her African American father was so traumatized by his cancer experience that he could never find words adequate enough to describe it. She shared that even after his death she remained disconnected from the true impact of cancer on his life, and she did not have any sense of what he might have gone through, psychologically and emotionally, until she read the detailed accounts of my experience. Her response to my blog forced me to realize the power of autoethnography, intersectionality, and intercultural communication research.

Note

1. This chapter includes selected excerpts from the author's blog, A Healthy Disregard for the Impossible, which can be accessed in its entirety at http://dr-rex.blogspot.com/

2. H. L. Goodall offered auto/ethnographic accounts of his post-diagnosis of pancreatic cancer on his blog, available at www.hlgoodall.com. He used his blog to chronicle his experience and feelings and to keep his readers informed about his condition. In addition to age and race differences between us, and different diagnoses and prognoses, Goodall was an active blogger before his diagnosis, while my diagnosis inspired me to create a blog.

References

Blankenhorn, D. (1995). *Fatherless America: Confronting our most urgent social problem.* New York: Basic Books.

Crawley, R. L. (2011). Black man, Black boy: An autoethnographic exploration of the issues associated with Black men raising Black boys. In R. Jackson & M. Hopson (Eds.), *Masculinity in the Black imagination* (pp. 187–196). New York: Peter Lang.

Denzin, N. (2001). *Interpretive interactionism.* Thousand Oaks, CA: Sage.

DuBois, W. E. B. (1903). *The souls of Black folk: Essays and sketches.* Chicago, IL: A. C. McClurg & Co.

Geertz, C. (1973). *The interpretation of cultures: Selected essays.* New York: Basic Books.

Holman Jones, S. (2005). Autoethnography: Making the personal political. In N. Denzin & Y. Lincoln (Eds.), *Handbook of qualitative research* (pp.763–791). Thousand Oaks, CA: Sage.

Jackson, R. L., & Hopson, M. C. (2011). *Masculinity in the Black imagination: Politics of communicating race and manhood.* New York: Peter Lang.

Mutua, A. D. (Ed.). (2006). *Progressive Black masculinities.* New York: Routledge.

Wallace, M. O. (2002). *Constructing the Black masculine: Identity and ideality in African American men's literature and culture, 1775–1995.* Durham, NC: Duke UP.

Conclusion

Critical Autoethnography: Implications & Future Directions

*A*S EDITORS OF THIS VOLUME WE SOUGHT TO EXAMINE THE ways that social identities and relationships, in addition to cultural identities and interactions, factor into our everyday lived experiences. While other books have focused on situated experiences of difference (Bardhan & Orbe, 2012; Muhs, et al., 2012; González, et al., 2012) or the need to acknowledge and appreciate diversity (Allen, 2010; Moraga & Anzaldúa, 1983), our book offers both personal narratives and cultural critiques.

We sought to expand intersectional representations through autoethnography in order to interrogate cultural experiences from the inside out. Given the overlap of themes and the universality of some lived experiences, the autoethnographies in this collection are in conversation with each other. For example, how do race, gender, and spirituality influence one's experience of cancer diagnosis (see chapters by Crawley; Mingé & Sterner)? In what ways do both temporary and permanent disabilities influence our interpersonal relationships and interactions (see chapters by Crawley; Mingé & Sterner; Morella-Pozzi)? Why do our impersonal interactions, with coworkers, caregivers, doctors, and strangers matter (see chapters by Crawley; Mingé & Sterner; Morella-Pozzi)? How is sexual orientation and fluidity influenced by societal and cultural expectations of normality (see chapters by Adams; Alexander; Johnson; Santoro)? How does social class intersect with our identity negotiation of race, ethnicity, and gender/sex (see chapters by Alexander; Boylorn; Orbe; Roberts)? What role does ethnicity and experience play in our spiritual practices (see chapters by Crawley; de la Garza)? How do stereotypes and expectations sometimes dictate our social performances of self (see chapters by Boylorn; Hao; Johnson; Yomtoob)? How can we teach and learn from our everyday lived experiences of culture and discrimination?

The critical-cultural autoethnographies in this book look at simultaneous and infrequent roles of privilege and marginalization that occur at the intersections of socially ascribed and constructed identities. By looking at individual co-cultures (within and beyond the US), we were able to isolate examples of the fluidity of social identities and how they are oftentimes negotiated within our interactions and relationships with others. The inextricable ties between intercultural and interpersonal communication are made explicit through this volume.

Our intersectional analysis looks at self-identifications, social identifications, and cultural signifiers. We hope that this interdisciplinary collection serves as an opportunity for intercultural and interpersonal scholars, as well as interdisciplinary scholars and autoethnographers, to interrogate how overlapping and seemingly opposing identity affiliations influence our personal lives, relationships, and narratives. We encourage those who write autoethnography and those who are interested in autoethnography to consider how a critical lens can assist in telling individual stories in the context of broader culture. We feel that this book confirms the importance of acknowledging and evaluating our differing worldviews through the stories we tell.

Intercultural communication challenges us to consider how cultural factors influence social interactions, while interpersonal communication requires us to pay attention to our relational and interactive exchanges with known others. We see a connection between intercultural communication, interpersonal communication, and autoethnography and the ways they interact within sociocultural and sociopolitical contexts. Successful autoethnography that offers critical cultural analysis can engage both genres simultaneously and help us approach difference with open eyes and open hearts. Critical autoethnography that involves our multiple affiliations with co-cultures and communities is both ethical and representative, with the ability to speak to and speak with more traditional texts.

Connections and Theories

Critics of autoethnography have described the methodology as a form of "soft research" or "me-search" that is atheoretical, ungeneralizable, and self-absorbed (e.g., Atkinson, 2006). Much of the criticism appears situated within traditional assumptions about what counts as scientific scholarship and the production of knowledge (Ellis & Bochner, 1996). The approach we assume within this edited volume is that theorizing takes a variety of forms and can be engaged through multiple points of contact and streams of processing. Theorizing, as opposed to theory, "captures the essence of something alive, fluid, and current" (Orbe, 2005, p. 66) and cannot be regulated to rigid conceptualizations of what should or should not be counted as scholarship. In their own way, each of the chapters reflects various efforts—both explicitly and implicitly—at theorizing intersections of personal, social, and cultural identities. The motivations for theorizing may vary, but for many autoethnographers, theorizing one's own lived experiences can be, as articulated by hooks (1991), liberatory—reflecting a search for healing.

> I came to theory because I was hurting—the pain within me was so intense ... I came to theory desperate, wanting to comprehend—to grasp what was happening around and within me ... I saw in theory then a location for healing. (p. 1)

In this context, everyday theorizing is a natural human process that has great significance in its own right. Yet, as we demonstrated throughout the book, it can be contextualized within other theoretical conceptualizations as well.

Given this, we advocate for theorizing as a means to interpret our own, as well as others' stories (Madison, 2012). Within this volume, we have identified twelve established theories that we believe are applicable to the chapters in this book: *narratology, symbolic interactionism, relational dialectics theory, self-presentation theory, communication theory of identity, complicity theory, standpoint theory, co-cultural theory, cultural contracts theory, sensemaking, coordinated management of meaning,* and *cultural dialectics.* We realize that this list is not exhaustive and that most if not all of the chapters can be read through any of these theories that offer interpersonal and intercultural frameworks for understanding self-generated narratives.

While contributors were not asked to incorporate theoretical links within their chapters we feel that the bridge sections serve as a way of situating each autoethnographic essay as worthy of critique and critical interpretation. By looking at the chapters through a theoretical lens it is more apparent how and why communication is a central component in our interpersonal and intercultural lives. Extending the metaphor of theory as lens, we encourage readers to expand the theoretical frameworks that can be used to explain, understand, and provide insight into the autoethnographies featured in this edited volume. This can be accomplished through two different means. First, we can explore how additional theories—in and outside of the field of communication—might be added to our repertoire of theoretical lenses. Second, we can foster more comprehensive understanding by advocating for and simultaneously drawing from two or more theoretical lenses as we engage each autoethnography. This second strategy is akin to the image of bi- or trifocals, and if done correctly, can provide a seamlessly vivid means to understand the lived experiences of self and others.

Contributions & Future Implications

We strongly encourage intercultural scholars to use autoethnographic methods as a way of talking about and explaining global and domestic cultural similarity↔difference. Critical praxis autoethnography can be beneficial because it legitimates first-person accounts of discrimination and difference and can therefore aid in the critique of colonialism, racism, sexism, nationalism, regionalism, and ethnocentrism. However, it can also simultaneously reveal commonality within the human experience, something that encourages connection as a means toward greater appreciation of how all individuals have fundamental needs for respect, dignity, and self-expression. In this regard, autoethnography can help challenge assumptions with "truths" that are situated within assumptions of difference or similarity.

A limitation of autoethnography, however, is that its focus on independent experiences can in some cases jeopardize larger cultural issues. Therefore while we champion autoethnography as an opportunity and way of sharing important realities about intercultural experiences, we do not endorse it at the expense of other methodologies such as phenomenology, cultural interviews, focus groups, and traditional ethnography that effectively represent and implicate larger or more muted groups (for example African women who may face similar discriminations due to gender/sex and class but have distinct experiences of discrimination from African American women due to their nationality, language, religion, and so on, or disabled working-class lesbian women whose experiences are similar but largely different from those who may not share their ability, class, or orientation status). Multiple methods and stories are necessary in order to have a wide representation of difference and displacement, especially in the context of intersectionality.

This book contributes to ongoing conversations about how autoethnography enhances our understanding of particular experiences and difference (Bochner & Ellis, 2002; Ellis & Bochner, 1996; Holman Jones, Adams, & Ellis, 2013). Because this volume focuses exclusively on interpersonal↔intercultural experiences of similarity↔difference, we believe it is unique. *Critical Autoethnography: Intersecting Cultural Identities in Everyday Life* offers a critical-cultural and intersectional focus of autoethnography. Another unique feature of this book is the inclusion and consideration of communication theory, intersectionality, and cultural-relational components at the same time.

We believe the chapters in this book are in conversation with each other while also standing alone to instigate further research and interest in cultural representation. We hope that this book inspires writers to consciously consider how their various standpoints influence their perceptions, experiences, and insights. We believe that the future of autoethnographic research is connected to encouraging research from people who live their lives on the margins and who are members of nondominant groups. We believe that the next wave of autoethnographic research will include co-cultural members telling stories that offer multiple points of view of similar experiences (see Ellis & Rawicki, 2013). We think that these critical-cultural autoethnographies will interrogate stereotypes and canonical narratives of normativity, create spaces for expansive, not limited, views of identity, and seek intersectional analyses of our experiences. Autoethnographies by and about underrepresented populations have the capacity to hone in on our constant negotiation of multiple identity positions at once (as both privileged and disadvantaged in myriad ways). Autoethnography has the capacity to break down walls of difference and help outsiders access insider perspectives and insiders feel heard. The narratives included in this book are only the beginning.

References

Allen, B. J. (2010). *Difference matters: Communicating social identity* (2d ed.). Long Grove, IL: Waveland Press.

Atkinson, P. (2006). Rescuing autoethnography. *Journal of Contemporary Ethnography, 35,* 400–404.

Bardhan, N., & Orbe, M. P. (Eds.). (2012). *Identity research and communication: Intercultural reflections and future directions.* Lanham, MD: Lexington Books.

Bochner, A. P., & Ellis, C. (Eds.). (2002). *Ethnographically speaking: Autoethnography, literature, and aesthetics.* Walnut Creek, CA: Alta Mira Press.

Ellis, C., & Bochner, A. P. (Eds.). (1996). *Composing ethnography: Alternative forms of qualitative writing.* Walnut Creek, CA: Altamira Press.

Ellis, C., & Rawicki, J. (2013). Collaborative witnessing of survival during the holocaust: An exemplar of relational autoethnography. *Qualitative Inquiry, 19*(5), 366–380.

González, A., Houston, M., & Chen, V. (Eds.). (2012). *Our voices: Essays in culture, ethnicity, and communication.* New York: Oxford University.

Holman Jones, S., Adams, T. E., & Ellis, C. (Eds.). (2013). *The handbook of autoethnography.* Walnut Creek, CA: Left Coast Press, Inc.

hooks, b. (1991). Theory as liberatory practice. *Yale Journal of Law and Feminism, 4,* 1–12.

Madison, D. S. (2012). *Critical ethnography: Method, ethics, and performance* (2d ed.). Los Angeles, CA: Sage.

Moraga, C., & Anzaldúa, G. (Eds.). (1983). *This bridge called my back: Writings by radical women of color.* New York: Kitchen Table.

Muhs, G. G., Niemann, Y. F., González, C. G., & Harris, A. P. (Eds.). (2012). *Presumed incompetent: The intersections of race and class for women in academia.* Boulder, CO: University Press of Colorado.

Orbe, M. (2005). Continuing the legacy of theorizing from the margins: Conceptualizations of co-cultural theory. *Women & Language, 28*(2), 65–66.

Index

Hao, Richie N, 22, 24, 102, 108, 234
Harris, Angela P., 234, 238
Harris, Linda M., 190, 193
Harris, Tina M., 19, 25, 195, 208
Harris, Trudier, 129, 130, 142
Harris-Perry, Melissa V., 129, 133, 136, 137, 139, 140, 141, 143
Harter, Lynn M., 45, 46
Harvey, Steve, 98, 108
Hausman, Bernice, 93, 95
Health, 23, 34, 40, 44, 45, 69, 225, 228, 231
Health care, 44–45
Health communication, 224
Healthy Disregard for the Impossible, A (blog), 224–230
Hecht, Michael L., 15, 24, 29, 31, 76, 77, 79, 80, 125, 126, 127
Hegemonic norms, 16, 23, 133, 157, 218, 220
Hennen, Peter, 172, 174
Heteronormative discourse, 67
Heteronormativity, 22, 93
Heterosexual/heterosexuality, 63, 65, 71, 90–94, 113, 142, 167
Heterosexism, 79, 91
Hicks, Terence, 57, 60
Hierarchy, 54, 163, 173, 191
High school, 48, 49, 50, 51, 52, 54, 55, 57, 59, 102, 104, 106, 164, 186, 199, 201, 202
Higher education (*see also* "Education"), 48, 50, 57, 180, 195, 197, 200–201
High risk students, 55
Hispanic identity (*see* "Latina/o identity")
History, 84, 119; family history, 65, 66, 88
Historicity, 107
HIV/AIDS, 62, 113
Holder, Aisha, 136, 142, 143
Holman Jones, Stacy, 15, 18, 24, 25, 45, 46, 84, 88, 94, 95, 173, 174, 222, 233, 237, 238
Holo-expression, 220
Home, 33, 34, 45, 69, 84–86, 88, 101–102, 117, 165, 199, 204, 212; in the body, 82, 89, 172
Homophobia, 64
Homosexual/homosexuality (*see* "Nonheterosexual")
hooks, bell, 133, 136, 143, 236, 238
Hope, 58, 114–116, 162, 170, 173, 205, 217, 231, 235; false hope, 196
Hoppe-Nagao, Angela, 30, 32

Hopson, Mark C., 223, 233
"horizon of possibility," 121
Houston, Marsha, 19, 25, 234, 238
Hunt, Stephen K., 55, 60
Hybrid/hybridity, 22, 24, 82, 97, 100–101, 102, 106–108, 197
Hyde, Michael J., 69, 72

Ideology, 114, 121, 163, 173, 204, 207
Identity, 14–16, 18–24, 28–29, 33, 45, 48, 50, 54, 57, 59, 62, 72, 75, 76–79, 83–84, 88, 93, 94, 97, 100, 102–108, 110–111, 113–114, 119, 120, 123, 124, 126, 130–133, 145, 156, 157, 159, 166, 170–173, 176, 177, 179, 180–181, 187–188, 190, 193, 196–197, 199, 200–207, 219–220, 231, 234–238
Identity gaps, 77, 79
Identity politics, 45, 111, 113
Il/legitimacy, 23, 178, 180, 187
Illness narrative, 23, 34, 45, 33–46, 224–232
Illocutionary act, 91
Images, 29, 45, 75, 79, 93, 130, 134, 136, 137, 138, 140, 141, 144, 156, 159, 161, 163, 166, 170, 171, 223
Image management, 75–76
Implicature, 78
In-between(ness), 102, 106
Indian identity, 81, 210
Ingratiation, 76
Innate inner-self, 222, 231
Injustice, 15, 132, 134, 135, 136, 217
Intercultural communication (research), 16, 19–20, 124, 186, 191, 235; (defined), 20
Interlocking oppressions, 18
Interpenetration, 77
Interpersonal ↔ intercultural continuum, 19
Interpersonal communication, 15, 20, 235
Interpretive interactionism, 222
Intersectionality, 16–18, 23, 48, 75, 82–83, 91, 97, 111, 113, 131–132, 145, 176, 206; critical intersectionality, 114, 119, 120; of being and becoming, 119; of identity, sexuality, geography, and ability, 33–59; of race, gender, class, and education, 47–59; of race, sexuality, culture and gender, 62–72; of race, sexuality, culture, and gender, 110–122, 159–172; of race/ethnicity, class, nation, 97–108; of race, gender/sex, and class, 129–142; of race, nationality, class, and sexuality, 144–157;

About the Authors

Tony E. Adams, PhD, is an Assistant Professor in the Department of Communication, Media and Theatre at Northeastern Illinois University. His book, *Narrating the Closet: An Autoethnography of Same Sex Desire* (2011), received the 2012 National Communication Association (NCA) Ethnography Division Best Book Award, the 2013 "Book of the Year" award from NCA's GLBTQ Division and the Caucus on LGBTQ Concerns, and the 2012 Organization for the Study of Communication, Language, and Gender Outstanding Book Award. He also coedited, with Stacy Holman Jones and Carolyn Ellis, the *Handbook of Autoethnography* (2013).

Bryant Keith Alexander, PhD, is Professor and Dean, College of Communication and Fine Arts at Loyola Marymount University. He is an active scholar and lecturer with publications in leading journals and book volumes. He is the coeditor of *Performance Theories in Education: Power, Pedagogy, and the Politics of Identity* (Erlbaum), the author of *Performing Black Masculinity: Race, Culture, and Queer Identity* (AltaMira), and *The Performative Sustainability of Race: Reflections on Black Culture and the Politics of Identity* (Peter Lang).

Robin M. Boylorn, PhD, is Assistant Professor of Interpersonal and Intercultural Communication in the Department of Communication Studies at the University of Alabama. Her teaching and research focuses on issues of diversity and social identity centering on the intersectionality of race, gender/sex, and class. Her publications include articles in *Qualitative Inquiry, Liminalities, Cultural Studies ↔ Critical Methodologies, Critical Studies in Media Communication, International Review of Qualitative Research,* and *The Handbook of Autoethnography.* She is the author of *Sweetwater: Black Women and Narratives of Resilience* (Peter Lang, 2013), which received the inaugural H. L. "Bud" Goodall Jr. and Nicholas Lee Trujillo "It's a Way of Life" Award in Narrative Ethnography (2013). She is also a member of the scholar-activist group, The Crunk Feminist Collective.

Rex L. Crawley, PhD, is Assistant Dean and Professor of Communication in the School of Communications and Information Systems at Robert Morris University. In addition, he serves as the endowed chair of the Uzuri Think

Tank, a research center focused on exploring issues centering on African American male academic achievement. His research interests are primarily focused on issues of race and higher education administration.

Sarah Amira de la Garza, PhD, (formerly María Christina González, PhD, Texas) is a Southwest Borderlands Scholar at Arizona State University (Tempe), where she also directs the Innovative Inquiry Initiative in the Hugh Downs School of Human Communication. A performance ethnographer and postcolonial methodologist, her work routinely interrogates culture, spirituality, and gender as realms of habituated practice and sites for de/reconstruction. She has held two Fulbright scholarships to Mexico, developing a Four Seasons ontology and methodology as a postcolonial-indigenous response to conventionally received ideals for inquiry. She is the author of *María Speaks: Journeys into the Mysteries of the Mother in My Life as a Chicana* (Peter Lang, 2004) and is presently completing an ethnographic novel dealing with immigration, modernity, and relationships in the Mexico of NAFTA and preparing to debut her one-woman performance, "Las Cuatro Ánimas," exploring trauma, ethnicity, and polyphrenia in the purgatory of academia.

Richie Neil Hao, PhD, is an Assistant Professor in the Department of Communication Studies at the University of Denver. His research interests are at the intersections of intercultural, pedagogical, and performance studies. More specifically, he is interested in the performances, constructions, and (re)presentations of Asian Pacific Americans, transnational diasporic hybrid identities, whiteness in popular culture, pedagogy, and other everyday contexts. He has recently published articles in *Cultural Studies ↔ Critical Methodologies, Review of Communication,* and *Text and Performance Quarterly.*

Amber L. Johnson, PhD, is an Assistant Professor of Languages and Communication at Prairie View A&M University. Her research trajectory merges qualitative and rhetorical research design in the areas of identity, intersectionality, sexuality, and new media. Her focus is on narratives of sexuality and intersections of race, class, geography, education, and beauty. Dr. Johnson earned her PhD from the Pennsylvania State University, and her MA and BA from Saint Louis University.

Jeanine M. Mingé, PhD, is interested in performance studies, feminist theory, queer theory, community art, and arts-based inquiry. All of her work is dedicated to cultivating social justice. She is equally enthralled by and creates the communicative presence of visual imagery, poetry, installation art, narrative, and performance. Her book, coauthored with Amber Lynn Zimmerman, is entitled *Concrete and Dust: Mapping the Sexual Terrain of Los Angeles* (Routledge Publishing Company in the series *Innovative Ethnographies*). She has also published work in *Qualitative Inquiry, Studies in Symbolic Interactionism* and *The Handbook of Autoethnography.*

Dana L. Morella-Pozzi is a Lecturer at San José State University in California. She received her master's degree in 2008 in Communication Studies and is currently pursuing her PhD in post-secondary education. She has struggled with learning disabilities all her life, but was not diagnosed until she was in community college. During her studies as a master's candidate, she decided to start helping other students with disabilities and instructors with disabilities. She has published autoethnographies and letters about disability since 2008.

Mark P. Orbe, PhD, is Professor of Communication and Diversity in the School of Communication at Western Michigan University where he has a joint appointment in Gender & Women's Studies. His teaching and research explore the inextricable relationship between culture and communication in a variety of contexts. He has published more than 100 books, journal articles, and book chapters on issues related to culture, power, and communication. He is also the immediate past secretary-general of the World Communication Association.

Tabatha L. Roberts is a PhD student at Southern Illinois University where her academic interests are in critical communication pedagogy and intercultural communication. Her first scholarly article on co-cultural theorizing was published in *Howard Journal of Communications*.

Patrick Santoro, PhD, is an Assistant Professor of Theatre and Performance Studies at Governors State University where he teaches courses in acting, directing, solo performance, performance art, performance auto/ethnography, and writing as performance. His research explores issues of loss, identity, and gender and sexuality.

John Burton Sterner has lived in the Malibu, California, and Topanga Canyon, California, areas for more than 28 years. He is a loving father, an avid surfer, a plumber by trade, and all-around loving and open person. He gives and has given his time and energy to everyone he meets. And he does it all with an open heart and a smile.

Desiree Yomtoob, PhD, completed her doctoral studies at the Institute of Communications Research at the University of Illinois, Urbana/Champaign. Her areas of interest are performance, autoethnography, and Third World feminism. She is currently writing about post-911 US racial politics.